SPANISH
AT YOUR FINGERTIPS

SPANISH
AT YOUR FINGERTIPS

Clark M. Zlotchew, Ph.D.

ALPHA
A member of Penguin Group (USA) Inc.

ALPHA BOOKS

Published by the Penguin Group

Penguin Group (USA) Inc., 375 Hudson Street, New York, New York 10014, USA

Penguin Group (Canada), 90 Eglinton Avenue East, Suite 700, Toronto, Ontario M4P 2Y3, Canada (a division of Pearson Penguin Canada Inc.)

Penguin Books Ltd., 80 Strand, London WC2R 0RL, England

Penguin Ireland, 25 St. Stephen's Green, Dublin 2, Ireland (a division of Penguin Books Ltd.)

Penguin Group (Australia), 250 Camberwell Road, Camberwell, Victoria 3124, Australia (a division of Pearson Australia Group Pty. Ltd.)

Penguin Books India Pvt. Ltd., 11 Community Centre, Panchsheel Park, New Delhi[md]110 017, India

Penguin Group (NZ), 67 Apollo Drive, Rosedale, North Shore, Auckland 1311, New Zealand (a division of Pearson New Zealand Ltd.)

Penguin Books (South Africa) (Pty.) Ltd., 24 Sturdee Avenue, Rosebank, Johannesburg 2196, South Africa

Penguin Books Ltd., Registered Offices: 80 Strand, London WC2R 0RL, England

International Standard Book Number: 978-1-59257-638-8
Library of Congress Catalog Card Number: 2006920577

09 08 07   8   7   6   5   4   3   2   1

Interpretation of the printing code: The rightmost number of the first series of numbers is the year of the book's printing; the rightmost number of the second series of numbers is the number of the book's printing. For example, a printing code of 07-1 shows that the first printing occurred in 2007.

Printed in the United States of America

Note: This publication contains the opinions and ideas of its author. It is intended to provide helpful and informative material on the subject matter covered. It is sold with the understanding that the author and publisher are not engaged in rendering professional services in the book. If the reader requires personal assistance or advice, a competent professional should be consulted.

The author and publisher specifically disclaim any responsibility for any liability, loss, or risk, personal or otherwise, which is incurred as a consequence, directly or indirectly, of the use and application of any of the contents of this book.

Trademarks: All terms mentioned in this book that are known to be or are suspected of being trademarks or service marks have been appropriately capitalized. Alpha Books and Penguin Group (USA) Inc. cannot attest to the accuracy of this information. Use of a term in this book should not be regarded as affecting the validity of any trademark or service mark.

Most Alpha books are available at special quantity discounts for bulk purchases for sales promotions, premiums, fund-raising, or educational use. Special books, or book excerpts, can also be created to fit specific needs.

For details, write: Special Markets, Alpha Books, 375 Hudson Street, New York, NY 10014.

Publisher: **Marie Butler-Knight**

Editorial Director: **Mike Sanders**

Managing Editor: **Billy Fields**

Acquisitions Editor: **Michele Wells**

Senior Development Editor: **Phil Kitchel**

Senior Production Editor: **Janette Lynn**

Copy Editor: **Krista Hansing**

Cover/Book Designer: **Kurt Owens**

Indexer: **Heather McNeill**

Layout: **Ayanna Lacey**

I dedicate this book to my good friend of more than three decades: the Argentine writer Fernando Sorrentino; his wife, Alicia; and his children, María Angélica, María Victoria, and Juan Manuel.

CONTENTS

INTRODUCTION

You're a busy person. You don't have the time to wade through volumes of explanation or reams of verbiage to get the specific information you need. You've had some experience with the Spanish language, but you're a little hazy on some of the grammatical points.

You know how important the Spanish language is today, whether you travel—for business or pleasure—to Latin America or Spain, or have contacts with people from those parts of the world. You are aware that approximately 350,000 people speak Spanish as their native language. You realize that today the Spanish language is extremely important right here in the United States, where it is practically an unofficial second language. For any of these reasons, you want to sharpen your skills in this important language.

You don't need a full course in Spanish. You already have a reasonably sufficient command of the vocabulary, so you don't need long word lists. Besides, you know that you never finish learning the vocabulary of any language, including your own. In addition, you know that once you have a basic vocabulary, the words you learn from there on depend on what you intend to do with the language. A full-length course in Spanish will not provide the kind of specialized vocabulary you need.

Well, then, what exactly do you need? You need a well-organized reference book that deals with the grammatical structure and syntax of the Spanish language. You want to be able to look up precisely the grammatical point that you need. You need to find this information when you need it. You don't want to have to go searching through a beginner's textbook—with all the unnecessary vocabulary lists and exercises—to find what you want. Neither do you want to have to struggle with an index of a beginner's textbook, hoping to find exactly the grammatical point you need, if you're lucky, when you need it.

What you need is *Spanish at Your Fingertips*. You want to find the specific point of grammar that you need, right when you need it. Most important: on your way to finding what you're searching for, you won't have to read anything that's not directly related to the information you want.

The author of this book is an expert in his field. He has taught Spanish for many years and knows what kind of questions students ask about the grammar of the language. In explaining the grammatical points to you, he anticipates the kind of questions you will have. His explanations are concise, uncomplicated, and down-to-earth. They are practical. There's no wandering off on tangents, because he knows you are not interested in tangents. You want the correct answer to a very precise question. This is what you will get in this book.

This book is structured in a clear, well-organized style that uses just enough explanation to satisfy your needs. So as not to waste your time, the language is concise and to the point. This book takes what could seem like a very complicated subject and delivers it to you in clear, simple, precise terms. You will find only the most useful information about the grammatical subject you look up.

In addition to the information about the specific point you are investigating, each chapter has sidebars of two types that will help you: one type of sidebar, "Words to Go," defines terms used in explaining the point of grammar.

WORDS TO GO . . .*WORDS TO GO* . . .*WORDS TO GO*

Defined words that appear in the main text of a chapter for the first time in that chapter appear in bold so you know to look for them in the sidebar. They also appear in bold at the beginning of the definition in the sidebar.

◄ *SEE ALSO* ►

The other type, called "See Also," tells you what chapter and section to look in to find related information. You have the choice, of course, of looking up that related information or ignoring it. It all depends on your needs at the moment.

For your convenience, this book includes a glossary, with all the grammatical terms defined throughout the book. If you need to be reminded of a particular term without finding a chapter and page on which it is defined, you can simply look up the term in Appendix A, "Glossary."

Appendix B, "Resources," is a list of other resources that can help you improve your knowledge of Spanish. You will find a section listing dictionaries.

1
PRONUNCIATION

1.1 VOWELS AND VOWEL COMBINATIONS

Vowels

Vowel Combinations

Vowels

The best way to learn how to pronounce a foreign language is to listen to speakers of that language, whether in person, on tape, on TV, or in films. If your television receives Spanish-language programs, you might want to listen to an hour per day of news reports or follow a soap opera. Don't be discouraged if at first you don't understand a single word! After a few weeks, as you study the language and listen to the programs, you will be able to pick out words here and there, and then more and more, until finally you understand whole sentences.

If you don't have a way to hear native speakers actually speaking Spanish, studying this chapter will help you pronounce Spanish so you'll be easily understood. One factor that makes Spanish pronunciation easier to learn than English is the vowel system. Spanish has only 5 vowels, each represented by one letter of the alphabet. This differs from English, which has 9 to 13 vowels (depending on the dialect) represented by 5 letters.

In this section, you learn to pronounce the five Spanish vowels correctly.

A—The vowel represented by this letter is pronounced like the A of *Ah!*

E—This vowel is pronounced something like our exclamation *Eh!*

I—This vowel is pronounced like the *EE* of *see*.

O—This vowel is pronounced like the O of *Oh!*

U—This vowel is pronounced like the *OO* of *tool*.

The following table provides the letter of the alphabet, the vowel sound, a Spanish word containing this vowel, and the pronunciation of that word. The word stress is shown by uppercase letters used for the stressed syllable.

SPANISH VOWEL PRONUNCIATION

Vowel	Sound	Spanish	Pronunciation
a	*ah*	mano	*MAH-noh*
e	*eh*	pena	*PEH-nah*
i	*ee*	mirar	*mee-RAHR*
o	*oh*	goloso	*goh-LOH-soh*
u	*oo*	cuna	*KOO-nah*

Try not to make the Spanish vowel *E* end with a *Y* sound, as in the English word *say*. Also avoid making the Spanish vowel *O* end with a *W* sound, as in the English word *go*.

Vowel Combinations

When two vowels come together in Spanish, one right after the other, the two vowels either combine into a **diphthong** as one syllable or create two different sounds. Whether two vowels combine into a diphthong depends on the identity (strong or weak) of the vowels involved. In this section, you learn about **strong** and **weak vowels** and how they interact.

WORDS TO GO . . . WORDS TO GO . . . WORDS TO GO

A **diphthong** is the combination of two vowels in a single syllable.
Strong vowel refers to the vowels *A, E,* and *O.*
Weak vowel refers to the vowels *I* and *U.*

Strong Vowel with Weak Vowel

When a strong vowel (*A, E, O*) comes either before or after a weak vowel (*I, U*), the two vowels combine to form a diphthong, which is one syllable. The strong vowel retains its full value and dominates the diphthong. In other words, the strong vowel is heard completely, whereas the weak vowel is heard only partially.

If the vowel *A* occurs before the vowel *I,* the *A* is heard longer than the *I.* In other words, the combination *AI* (a diphthong) is *not* pronounced *AH-EE,* but instead is pronounced *AHY,* which is one syllable or part of one syllable, not two. It doesn't matter which vowel comes first; the strong vowel is always strong and the weak vowel is always weak. If we reverse the previous combination, we have *IA.* This is *not* pronounced *EE-AH,* but is pronounced *YAH.*

The following table shows you how to pronounce Spanish diphthongs by giving an English word with the closest sound, a Spanish word that contains the diphthong, and the pronunciation of the Spanish word.

SPANISH DIPHTHONGS

Diphthong	Sound	English	Spanish	Pronunciation
ai	*ahy*	tie	baile	*BAHY-leh*
ia	*yah*	yacht	liana	*LYAH-nah*
ei	*ehy*	day	seis	*SEHYS*
ie	*yeh*	yes	siete	*SYEH-teh*
oi	*ohy*	toy	boina	*BOHY-nah*
io	*yoh*	yoke	lección	*lek-SYOHN*
au	*ow*	how	sauce	*SOW-seh*
ua	*wah*	wasp	cuatro	*KWAH-troh*
eu	*ehw*	—	Europa	*ehw-ROH-pah*
ue	*weh*	way	bueno	*BWEH-noh*
ui	*wee*	tweet	cuidado	*kwee-DAH-doh*
iu	*yoo*	beauty	ciudad	*syoo-DAD*

The last two entries in the table are diphthongs produced with the two weak vowels and no strong vowel; I discuss this in the following section.

The Spanish diphthong *EU* has no close equivalent in English; this is why the space is left blank in the English column. If you have trouble reproducing this sound, use the two-syllable *EH-oo* at first, stressing the *EH* element. Say it several times, each time giving more time to the *EH* and less to the *OO*. It should finally come out as the one-syllable *EHW*.

Two of a Kind

Two weak vowels form a diphthong dominated by the first vowel. The diphthong produced by the combination *UI* has the sound of *WEE*. When reversed, the sound produced is *YOO*. (See last two entries in the previous table.)

Two strong vowels do not form a diphthong. Instead, each vowel maintains its full value and creates a separate syllable. For example, the word *caer* has two syllables: *kah-EHR*. The following table shows words with contiguous strong vowels.

WORDS WITH TWO CONTIGUOUS STRONG VOWELS

Combination	Sound	Spanish	Pronunciation
ae	*ah-eh*	trae	*TRAH-eh*
ea	*eh-ah*	brea	*BREH-ah*
ao	*ah-oh*	bacalao	*bah-kah-LAH-oh*
oa	*oh-ah*	canoa	*kah-NOH-ah*
oe	*oh-eh*	poeta	*poh-EH-tah*
eo	*eh-oh*	creo	*KREH-oh*

Weak Becomes Strong

You already know that the vowels *I* and *U* are weak vowels. However, if either the *I* or the *U*, *in* contact with any other vowel, is stressed, the vowel that is accented (stressed) becomes strong.

The last three letters of the words *miseria* and *librería* are not pronounced in the same way. The last *I* and the *A* of *miseria* form a diphthong because the *I* is a weak vowel next to *A*, a strong vowel. They are part of the syllable *-ria*. The word has three syllables and is pronounced *mee-SEH-ryah*.

Conversely, the *I* and the *A* of *librería* do *not* form a diphthong. The *I* is accentuated and therefore becomes a strong vowel so it makes two distinct syllables: *rí* and *a*. *Librería* is pronounced with four syllables: *lee-breh-REE-ah*.

1.2 CONSONANTS

Sounds Not Found in English
Sounds Similar to English

One great advantage of learning Spanish is that many Spanish consonants are similar (though not *identical*) to English consonants. No problem! Others are pronounced with sounds that are very different or do not exist at all in English. Since these can present some difficulty, we start with them.

Sounds Not Found in English

Below you will learn about the consonant sounds that do not exist in English.

Letters *G* and *J*

In most dialects of Spanish, the letter *J*, and the letter G before *E* or *I*, make sounds that do not exist in American English. Some dialects, however, employ a sound that *is* very much like its English counterpart.

In the Caribbean, Southern Spain (Andalucía), and certain coastal areas of Latin America, the sound is very much like the English sound of the letter *H*. You certainly can use this pronunciation and be absolutely correct, but we'll discuss the other sounds to make sure you will recognize it in Spanish.

In most of Mexico; the Andean region of South America from Colombia through Ecuador, Peru, and Bolivia; and Chile, Argentina, and Uruguay, the sound does not exist in American English, but is similar to the guttural CH in the German word *Ach!* and in the Highland Scottish word *loch*. This guttural quality is even more pronounced and harsh in northern Spain.

The following table shows words pronounced in different dialects of Spanish. The H represents the sound of the same consonant in English. The KH represents the sound of the German *Ach*. The G represents the sound of G in the English word *go*. (Remember, G sounds like this except when it's in front of *E* or *I*.)

Spanish Word	Pronunciation A	Pronunciation B
bajo	*BAH-hoh*	*BAH-khoh*
jardín	*hahr-DEEN*	*khahr-DEEN*
Juan	*HWAHN*	*KHWAHN*
gente	*HEHN-teh*	*KHEHN-teh*
ángel	*AHN-hehl*	*AHN-khehl*

The Double *RR*

The so-called double *RR* represents a sound that does not exist in American English. This sound is very much like the one children produce when imitating the sound of a motor or of a machine gun. Technically, it is called a trill or a multiple vibrant, and it is produced by flapping the tip of the tongue in rapid succession, against the **alveolar ridge** from three to seven times. The result is like the sound of a card in a bike's spokes or a flag flapping in a stiff wind.

WORDS TO GO . . . WORDS TO GO . . . WORDS TO GO

The **alveolar ridge** is the hard ridge of gum right behind and above the upper teeth.

This same sound is represented by a single *R* when it is the first letter in the word.

The double *RR* consonant has dialectal variants. In the Andean region, from Colombia to the northwest corner of Argentina, people tend to pronounce the double *RR* something like a *ZH* sound, like the *S* in the English word *treasure* or the French *J*.

In Puerto Rico, some speakers pronounce the *RR* like *HR*—that is, like a breathy *H* followed closely by a single-tap *R*. Other Puerto Rican speakers pronounce *RR* like the *CH* in the German *Ach!*

Letters *B* and *V*

In almost every dialect of Spanish, there is no difference in pronunciation between the letter *B* and the letter *V*, just like the English word *cat* would be pronounced the same way if incorrectly spelled *kat*. However, two different sounds are involved. This difference depends not on the letter used, but on the consonant's position in relation to other sounds.

If the letter *B* or *V* comes after a pause or comes at the beginning of a phrase, the sound represented by both letters is very much like the sound of *B* in English. If *B* or *V* comes after an *M* or *N*, the same is true; the combination sounds like *MB*.

With the exception of these cases (after a pause or *M* or *N*), *B* and *V* have a sound that doesn't exist in English. The two lips come together, but not as firmly as when producing the English *B*. Instead, the lips are relaxed and leave a very slight opening, resulting in a sound in between the English *B* and the English *V*. I'll show this sound as *BH*. The following table shows the pronunciation of the letters *B* and *V* in various situations.

Spanish Word(s)	Pronunciation
Voy	*BHOY*
No voy	*NOH-BHOY*
El burro	*ehl-BHOO-rroh*
Un burro	*oom-BOO-rroh*
¡Burro!	*BOO-rroh*
Venezuela	*beh-neh-SWEH-lah*
A Venezuela	*ah-bheh-neh-SWEH-lah*
En Venezuela	*em-beh-neh-SWEH-lah*

Sounds Similar to English

The other Spanish consonants are close to the way they sound in English, but some are represented by different letters than in English.

Single *R*

The Spanish single *R* (as opposed to the double *RR*) sounds almost identical to a sound we have in American English, but we don't represent this sound with the letter *R*. The sound is made by tapping the tip of the tongue once against the alveolar ridge. It's the sound made by the double *T* or double *D* in English words like *better* or *ladder*, after the stressed syllable. That's the sound of the letter *R* in Spanish.

The written Spanish *R* at the first letter in a word has the sound of double *RR*. For example, the word *rico* is pronounced *RRI-koh*, rather than *RI-koh*.

Sounds of the Letter *D*

The sound of Spanish letter D is very similar to the sound of English in three cases:

▶ At the beginning of a phrase or after a pause

▶ After the letter *N*

▶ After the letter *L*

However, in all other positions, the letter D sounds very much like *TH* in the English words *the* or *that*—but not a soft *TH* as in *think*. I use *DH* for this sound in the following table.

PRONUNCIATION OF THE LETTER D

Spanish Word(s)	Pronunciation
dónde	*DOHN-deh*
adónde	*ah-DHOHN-deh*
día	*DEE-ah*
el día	*ehl-DEE-ah*
un día	*oon-DEE-ah*
qué día	*KEH-DHEE-ah*

1.3 THE SPELLING SYSTEM

Letters Y and LL

Letters S, C, and Z

Letter C and Combination QU

Letter G and Combination GU

Combination CU Plus Vowel

Combination GU Plus Vowel

Ü (U with Dieresis)

Letter H (Silent)

Letter N vs. Letter Ñ

Spelling in Spanish is infinitely easier to learn than the English spelling system. Such a close fit exists between Spanish spelling and pronunciation that Spanish-speaking countries do not even teach "Spelling"! However, there are a few quirks, which you'll learn about in this section.

Letters Y and LL

In most Spanish dialects, the letter Y and the combination LL are pronounced exactly the same. However, the sound they produce can vary from the sound of the English Y to the sound of the English J. It doesn't matter which sound you use; you will be understood. But you should get used to *hearing* it pronounced as the English J (or close to it) so you won't be thrown off by hearing an English J when you're expecting to hear a Y.

In Argentina and Uruguay, these letters sound more like the S in the English word *treasure* or a French J (symbolized here by ZH). In the Buenos Aires area, college-age and younger speakers make the same consonant sounds more like the soft SH in the English *show*.

Some dialects distinguish between the pronunciation for the letter Y and LL. They pronounce Y like the English Y or J, and LL like the English LY or the LLI in *million*.

As you can see, a Spanish word like *calló* might be pronounced either *kah-LYOH, kah-YOH, kah-JOH, kah-ZHOH*, or even *kah-SHOH*. A word like *cayó* might be pronounced either *kah-YOH, kah-JOH, kah-ZHOH*, or *kah-SHOH*, but never *kah-LYOH*.

The difficulty is not in pronouncing these sounds, but recognizing the words when they're spoken by a native speaker.

To become accustomed to understanding different speakers, practice saying words that contain these consonants in various different ways. This way, the various pronunciations won't sound strange to you.

Letters *S, C,* and *Z*

In all dialects of Latin American Spanish, the *S* and the *Z* sound exactly the same, as does the letter *C* when it precedes the vowels *E* or *I*. The sound is like the *S* in the English *say*.

The Spanish word *cinco* (SEENG-koh) could just as well be misspelled *sinco* or *zinco*, and would be pronounced in exactly the same way. They would be, of course, misspellings, just as the spelling for English *ceiling* could be *seiling*, but would be pronounced the same. The word *zapatos* is pronounced *sah-PAH-tohs*.

In most of Spain, however, when the letter *C* precedes *E* or *I*, it's pronounced like the soft *TH* in the English word *think* or the name *Thelma*. In Spain, the letter *Z*, no matter where it is located, is also pronounced like the *TH* in *think*. In these regions, *cinco* is pronounced *THEENG-koh*, while *zapatos* is pronounced *thah-PAH-tohs*.

Letter *C* and Combination *QU*

Unlike the letter *C* before *E* or *I* (shown in the previous paragraph), the letter *C* before a consonant or before the vowels *A, O,* or *U* has the sound of *K*, so the combinations *CA, CO,* and *CU* (if the *U* is not followed by another vowel) have the sounds *KAH, KOH,* and *KOO*.

Spanish Word(s)	Pronunciation
creer	*kreh-EHR*
clase	*KLAH-seh*
Carlos	*KAHR-lohs*
como	*KOH-moh*
cura	*KOO-rah*

If CE and CI are pronounced *SEH* and *SEE*, how are the sounds *KEH* and *KEE* written in Spanish? The answer is:

▶ The combination QU plus E (as in *que*) gives the pronunciation KEH.

▶ The combination QU plus I (as in *quinto*) gives the pronunciation KEE.

Letter *G* and Combination *GU*

Unlike the letter G before E or I, the letter G before a consonant or before the vowels A, O, or U has a sound as in the English *good*; the combinations GA, GO, and GU (if the U is not followed by another vowel) then have the sounds GAH, GOH, and GOO.

Spanish Word(s)	Pronunciation
grano	GRAH-*noh*
globo	GLOH-*bhoh*
gancho	GAHN-*choh*
gorra	GOH-*rrah*
gula	GOO-*lah*

What about the sounds GEH and GHEE? If CE and CI are pronounced SEH and SEE, how are the sounds GEH and GHEE written in Spanish? (The pronunciation for GHEE rhymes with McGee.) The answer is:

▶ The combination GU plus E (as in *guerra*) gives the pronunciation GHEH.

▶ The combination GU plus I (as in *guitarra*) gives the pronunciation GHEE.

Combination *CU* Plus Vowel

Whenever the letters CU are followed by a vowel, the CU combination is pronounced like a *KW*.

Spanish Word(s)	Pronunciation
cuatro	KWAH-*troh*
cuero	KWEH-*roh*
cuota	KWOH-*tah*

Combination *GU* Plus Vowel

When the letters GU are followed by the vowel A, the GU combination is pronounced like a GW.

Spanish Word(s)	Pronunciation
guardar	*gwahr-DHAHR*
igual	*ee-GWAHL*

Ü (*U* with Dieresis)

You have seen that GE and GI are pronounced HEH and HEE, respectively. You have also seen that GUE and GUI are pronounced GEH and GHEE, respectively. The sounds still not accounted for in Spanish **orthography** are GWEH and GWEE.

WORDS TO GO . . .*WORDS TO GO* . . .*WORDS TO GO*

Orthography refers to the spelling system of a language.

To signify the sounds GWEH and GWEE, the Spanish spelling system uses GÜE and GÜI. The two dots over the letter U are called the *dieresis*, which signals that the U between the G and either the E or I should be pronounced.

Spanish Word(s)	Pronunciation
güero	*GWEH-roh*
agüero	*ah-GWEH-roh*
güiro	*GWEE-roh*
agüilla	*ah-GWEE-yah*

Letter *H* (Silent)

The letter H is always silent. For example, the word *honor* is pronounced *oh-NOHR*. The word *ahora* is pronounced *ah-OH-rah*.

Letter *N* vs. Letter *Ñ*

The letter N is pronounced the same as it is in English. Do not confuse N with Ñ. This letter has a tilde over it and is pronounced like the NI in the English word *onion* or the *NY* in *canyon*. The difference is extremely important. For example, the verb SONAR means "to sound" or "to ring," like a telephone or doorbell. The verb SOÑAR means "to dream."

1.4 ACCENTUATION (STRESS) AND CAPITALIZATION

Accentuation (Stress)

Capitalization

The following subchapter will show you how the accentuation system works and how the system of capitalizing letters differs from English.

Accentuation (Stress)

The Spanish accentuation system is very clear and logical. Give the following rules 10 minutes, and they'll be permanently fixed in your head. You'll know how to accentuate any Spanish word you see in print, even if you have never heard it spoken.

Rule 1. If a word ends with a vowel (or *N* or *S*), the stress is automatically placed on the *next-to-last* syllable.

Rule 2. If a word ends with a consonant other than *N* or *S*, the stress is automatically placed on the *last* syllable.

Rule 3. If a word breaks rules 1 or 2, place an *accent mark* over the stressed vowel to show where the stress is.

See the examples in the following table; the stressed syllable is in uppercase.

RULES OF ACCENTUATION ILLUSTRATED

Spanish Word	Stressed Syllable	Written Accent Mark	Reason
todo	*TOH-dhoh*	No	Ends with vowel
todos	*TOH-dhohs*	No	Ends with S
habla	*AH-blah*	No	Ends with vowel
hablan	*AH-blahn*	No	Ends with N
pared	*pah-REHDH*	No	Ends with consonant
verdad	*behr-DHAHDH*	No	Ends with consonant
hablar	*ah-BLAHR*	No	Ends with consonant
último	*OOL-tee-moh*	Yes	Breaks Rule 1
próximo	*PROHK-see-moh*	Yes	Breaks Rule 1

continues...

(continued)

RULES OF ACCENTUATION ILLUSTRATED

Spanish Word	Stressed Syllable	Written Accent Mark	Reason
ojalá	oh-hah-LAH	Yes	Breaks Rule 1
Hernández	her-NAN-des	Yes	Breaks Rule 2
Gómez	GOH-mes	Yes	Breaks Rule 2
capitán	kah-pee-TAN	Yes	Breaks Rule 1

Singular nouns that have written accent marks on the last syllable, like *capitán*, lose that written accent mark when pluralized: *capitanes*. This is because the pluralized word does not break any rules; it follows Rule 1. It ends with an –S; therefore, the stress is automatically on the next-to-last syllable: *kah-pee-TA-nes*.

◀ SEE ALSO 3.2, *"Singular and Plural Nouns"* ▶

Written accent marks are also used for reasons that have nothing to do with accentuation. To differentiate in writing between two words that are spelled the same but have different meanings, one gets the written accent mark and the other does not. For example, *si* means "if," but *sí* means "yes."

Capitalization

The use of upper- and lowercase letters differs somewhat in Spanish from English. Spanish customarily uses lowercase letters in …

▶ Adjectives and nouns of nationality (but uppercase for names of countries).

▶ Book titles, only in the first letter of the title.

▶ Names of months.

▶ Names of days of the week.

In the case of book titles, uppercase is used only in the first letter of the title and in the first letter of the subtitle, if there is one. It is also used in the first letters of **proper nouns** incorporated into the title. Example: *Interpretaciones a la obra de Carlos Fuentes*.

A **proper noun** is the name of a specific person or place, such as Mary, Robert, Boston, Mexico, and so on.

On the other hand, uppercase letters are used for the first letter of each word except for prepositions, conjunctions, and pronouns, in the titles of journals and magazines, as in English.

After having read and absorbed this entire chapter, you can now pronounce any word in Spanish and be understood by any native speaker. You also understand how the spelling system works and will be able to pronounce any word you see written, even if you have never heard it before.

2

TIME, DATE, AND OTHER NUMBERS

2.1 NUMBERS

Cardinal Numbers

Numbers with Nouns

Ordinal Numbers

Counting is an important feature of any language. Whether you're making a purchase and need to understand the price, or asking how many blocks, miles, or hours it is to your destination, numbers are indispensable. In this section, you learn how to count up through the millions.

Cardinal Numbers

You will use **cardinal numbers** in most situations. These are the numbers we use for counting and calculating: one, two, three, four, five, and so on.

WORDS TO GO . . .WORDS TO GO . . .WORDS TO GO

Cardinal numbers are the numbers we usually use for counting (one, two, three ...).

Numbers 1–100

The list below shows the numeral in the left-hand column with the Spanish word for it spelled out in the right-hand column.

1	uno
2	dos
3	tres
4	cuatro
5	cinco
6	seis
7	siete
8	ocho
9	nueve
10	diez

Forms of *uno* are also used to form the indefinite articles, *un* and *una*.

◀ **SEE ALSO 3.4, *"Indefinite Articles"* ▶**

The numbers 11 through 15 resemble 1 through 5, but they change enough that these numbers are best simply memorized.

11	once
12	doce
13	trece
14	catorce
15	quince

From 16 through 99, most numbers take a consistent form: the decade number (10, 20, 30, and so on) plus *y*, plus the appropriate number 1 through 9. Notice next that there's an alternative form for the numbers 16 through 29. This abbreviated form is the most common form for these numbers.

Numeral	Full Form	Common Form
16	diez y seis	dieciséis
17	diez y siete	diecisiete
18	diez y ocho	dieciocho
19	diez y nueve	diecinueve
20	veinte	
21	veinte y uno	veintiuno
22	veinte y dos	veintidós

Written accents are used in some of the abbreviated forms of numbers from 16 to 22. This applies to 116, 216, 316, and so on, not just 16 to 22. This is in line with the rules of Spanish accentuation.

◀ **SEE ALSO 1.4, *"Accentuation (Stress) and Capitalization"* ▶**

30	treinta
31	treinta y uno
39	treinta y nueve
40	cuarenta
41	cuarenta y uno
49	cuarenta y nueve

50	cincuenta
51	cincuenta y uno
59	cincuenta y nueve
60	sesenta
61	sesenta y uno
69	sesenta y nueve
70	setenta
71	setenta y uno
79	setenta y nueve
80	ochenta
81	ochenta y uno
89	ochenta y nueve
90	noventa
91	noventa y uno
99	noventa y nueve

Numbers 100 and Higher

The numbers from 100 to 999 are formed by adding the century numbers (100, 200, and so on) in front of the appropriate number from 1 to 99, as shown here. Two forms exist for the Spanish number 100; the first form is the most commonly used. This does not occur with any of the other hundreds.

100	ciento; cien
101	ciento uno
102	ciento dos
103	ciento tres
109	ciento nueve
110	ciento diez
111	ciento once
117	ciento diecisiete
155	ciento cincuenta y cinco
199	ciento noventa y nueve
200	doscientos

201	doscientos uno
215	doscientos quince
218	doscientos dieciocho
275	doscientos setenta y cinco
299	doscientos noventa y nueve
300	trescientos
301	trescientos uno
400	cuatrocientos
500	quinientos
600	seiscientos
700	setecientos
800	ochocientos
900	novecientos

Notice that the number 100 in Spanish does not take the indefinite article, even though English uses "one" or "a" before this number. But the hundreds after 100 do take the number of hundreds (*dos*, *tres*, and so on) as well as the plural form (*doscientos*, *novecientos*, and so on).

For the numbers 1,000 and higher, punctuation differs from English. In almost all of Latin America and on the European continent, a period is used instead of a comma to express thousands and millions. Conversely, the comma is used instead of a period to express decimals (for example, 1,5 in Spanish equals 1.5 in English).

1.000	mil
1.001	mil y uno
1.002	mil y dos
1.056	mil y cincuenta y seis
1.999	mil y novecientos y nueve
2.000	dos mil
2.017	dos mil diecisiete
5.000	cinco mil
9.999	nueve mil novecientos noventa y nueve
10.000	diez mil
15.002	quince mil dos

19.998	diecinueve mil novecientos noventa y ocho
20.000	veinte mil
90.000	noventa mil
1.000.000	un millón
2.000.000	dos millones
5.450.832	cinco millones cuatrocientos cincuenta mil ochocientos treinta y dos
90.900.999	noventa millones novecientos mil novecientos noventa y nueve

To keep confusion to a minimum, when discussing conversions later in the chapter, we will adhere to the English use of commas and decimals.

There's a difference in the handling of the thousands and the millions. No plural is used for the thousands: 5.000 is cinco mil. The millions, on the other hand, are handled as nouns, with singular and plural. Note also that the number 1.000.000 (handled as a noun) is *un millón*, while 1.000 is simply *mil*.

Numbers with Nouns

When numbers are used to modify nouns, some numbers must agree in number and gender; others do not agree.

Numbers That Do Not Change

The numbers from 2 to 199 make no adjustments to agree with the number and gender of the nouns they modify. Consider these examples:

dos mesas	2 tables
cinco mesas	5 tables
setenta y cinco mesas	75 tables
ciento cincuenta y cuatro mesas	154 tables
ciento noventa y nueve mesas	199 tables

Numbers That Do Change

To a certain extent, some numbers do make adjustments to agree with the nouns they modify. These numbers involve either the number 1 or the plural of 100.

You already know that the number 1, which also serves as the indefinite article, agrees in number and gender with the noun(s) it modifies. The same is partially true of the number 1 when it is part of a larger number. It agrees in gender—but not number—with the noun modified by the entire number. It behaves like the indefinite article, except that it doesn't pluralize. See the following examples:

veintiún libros	21 books
veintiuna sillas	21 chairs
cuarenta y un cuadernos	41 notebooks
cuarenta y una salas	41 living rooms
noventa y un hombres	91 men
noventa y una mujeres	91 women
ciento noventa y un periódicos	191 newspapers
ciento noventa y una revistas	191 magazines

When simply counting, the number 100 can be either *ciento* or *cien*. As you saw in the list of numbers, when *ciento* comes before a smaller number (as in 120), the full form *ciento* is always used. When it modifies a noun, it is always *cien*—for example, *cien libros, cien sillas, cien hombres, cien mujeres*, and so on. But from 200 on, the ending agrees in number (plural) and gender with the noun it modifies. See the following examples:

doscientos libros	200 books
doscientas sillas	500 chairs
quinientos hombres	500 men
quinientas mujeres	200 women
novecientos cuadernos	900 notebooks
novecientas mesas	900 tables

Ordinal Numbers

The **ordinal numbers** refer to the order or position in which the item is placed: first, second, third, fourth, fifth, and so on. Beyond the tenth, the Spanish ordinal numbers are hardly used at all. Following are the ordinal numbers you will use most often.

Ordinal numbers refer to the order in which an item is placed, such as first, second, third, and so on.

primero/a	first
segundo/a	second
tercero/a	third
cuarto/a	fourth
quinto/a	fifth
sexto/a	sixth
séptimo/a	seventh
octavo/a	eighth
noveno/a	ninth
décimo/a	tenth

For ninth, in addition to *noveno/a*, the variant *nono/a* is also sometimes used.

The word *cuarto*, in addition to meaning fourth in a numbered sequence, also means "quarter," as in one fourth. As a noun it also can mean a room.

Ordinal numbers are used much less in everyday Spanish than in English. You will want to know some of the situations in which they are or are not employed. The two most common differences are in referring to royalty or church hierarchy and in dates.

In English, we refer to a specific king by name and ordinal number, as with Henry the Eighth. If there were 25 Henrys (which there aren't), we would naturally call the last one Henry the Twenty-Fifth. In Spanish, the ordinal number in such cases would be used only up to the tenth Henry. From there on, the *cardinal* number would be used. The same is true in referring to the popes.

Carlos XI ("Once")	Charles XI ("the Eleventh")
Carlos XXV ("Veinticinco")	Charles XXV ("the Twenty-Fifth")
Papa Juan XXIII ("veintitrés")	Pope John XXIII ("the Twenty-Third")
Papa Benito XVI ("dieciséis)	Pope Benedict XVI ("the Sixteenth")

Dealing with dates also differs in Spanish. Whereas English customarily uses ordinal numbers for days of the month, such as July Fourth (or the Fourth of July), the *first* day alone employs the ordinal number in Spanish. "January First," for example, is *el primero de enero*. "May First" is *el primero de mayo*. But from the second onward, the cardinal numbers are always used. See the following examples:

el dos de enero	January 2nd
el dos de mayo	May 2nd
el seis de enero	January 6th
el nueve de mayo	May 9th
el veinticinco de enero	January 25th
el treinta de mayo	May 30th

◄ *SEE ALSO 2.3, "Dates"* ▶

2.2 | WEIGHTS AND MEASURES

Temperature

Distance Measurements

Liquid Measurements

Weights

Excluding the United States, most of the world uses the metric system for weights and measurements, and the Celsius (Centigrade) system for temperatures. This section provides you with the metric and Celsius equivalents. Of course, it also furnishes the Spanish vocabulary for the English terminology.

The Spanish word for "measure" is *medida*. The conversion tables given in this chapter for weights and measurements show only one or two decimal places; they are not meant to provide precise correspondences. From them, you will gain a serviceable idea of the difference between weights and measures in U.S. terms and in the Spanish-speaking world and beyond.

Temperature

Americans use the Fahrenheit system for measuring the temperature. Most of the world uses another scale, called Celsius or Centigrade. In Spanish, the preferred term is *Centígrado*. You need to know three other terms here: The Spanish word for "temperature" is *temperatura*. The Spanish word for a degree of temperature is *grado*. The Spanish word for "under" is *bajo*.

Fahrenheit	Centígrado
–20°F	28.8 grados bajo cero C (–28.8° Celsius)
–10°F	23.3 grados bajo cero C (–23.3°C)
0°F	17.7 grados bajo cero C (–17.7°C)
5°F	15.0 grados bajo cero C (–15°C)
10°F	12.2 grados bajo cero C (–12.2°C)
20°F	6.6 grados bajo cero C (–6.6°C)
30°F	1.3 grados bajo cero C (–1.3°C)
32°F	0 grados C (0°C)
35°F	1.6 grados C (1.6°C)
40°F	4.4 grados C (4.4°C)
45°F	7.2 grados C (7.2°C)

Fahrenheit	Centígrado
50°F	10.0 grados C
55°F	12.7 grados C
60°F	15.5 grados C
65°F	18.3 grados C
70°F	21.1 grados C
75°F	23.8 grados C
80°F	26.6 grados C
85°F	29.4 grados C
90°F	32.1 grados C
95°F	34.8 grados C
100°F	37.6 grados C
125°F	51.6 grados C

There's an easy method for converting from Centigrade to Fahrenheit, but it doesn't provide a precise equivalent. Double the Centigrade figure and add 30. The answer is close to the Fahrenheit equivalent. It works out perfectly for 10°C. Double it to get 20, and add 30; you get 50°F. The further you stray from that temperature in either direction, the further you are from an accurate reading.

Distance Measurements

Excluding the United States, most of the world uses the metric system for measuring distances.

Meters/Feet

The United States uses feet as a basic measure of distance. However, Latin America and most of the world use the metric system, with meters as the basic measure. See the following table for meter-to-feet equivalences. The Spanish for "meter" is *metro*. The Spanish for "foot" is *pie*.

METERS TO FEET (METROS A PIES) AND FEET TO METERS (Y PIES A METROS)

Meters (Metros)	Feet (Pies)	Feet (Pies)	Meters (Metros)
1	3.28	1	0.30
2	6.56	2	0.60
3	0.91	3	9.84

continues...

(continued)

METERS TO FEET (METROS A PIES) AND FEET TO METERS
(Y PIES A METROS)

Meters (Metros)	Feet (Pies)	Feet (Pies)	Meters (Metros)
4	1.21	4	13.12
5	1.52	5	16.40
10	3.04	10	32.80
15	4.57	15	49.21
20	6.09	20	65.61
25	7.62	25	82.02
30	9.14	30	98.42
40	12.19	40	131.23
50	15.24	50	164.04
75	22.86	75	246.06
100	30.48	100	328.08
500	152.40	500	1640.41
1.000	304.80	1.000	3280.82

The meter (*el metro*) is somewhat longer than the English yard (*una yarda*), or 3 feet (*tres pies*). Another way to look at the difference is that 1 foot (*un pie*) is 0.30 of a meter and that 100 feet equal 30.48 meters.

Kilometers/Miles

In measuring greater distances, the United States uses the English mile as a basic unit. In most of the rest of the world, the basic metric unit is the kilometer. The Spanish word for "kilometer" can be spelled two ways: *kilómetro* and *quilómetro*.

The letter *K* is not used in traditional Spanish words; it can be used for words of foreign origin, as in kilómetro. However, Spanish orthography also allows for Hispanization of foreign words, using the regular Spanish spelling rules, as in quilómetro.

See the following conversion table.

Millas	Kilómetros	Kilómetros	Millas
1	1.60	1	0.62
5	8.04	5	3.10

Millas	Kilómetros	Kilómetros	Millas
10	16.09	10	6.21
20	32.18	20	12.42
30	48.27	30	18.64
50	80.46	50	31.07
100	160.93	100	62.14
500	804.65	500	310.70
1000	1609.30	1000	621.40

Another way to look at the conversion is to say that 1 kilometer equals 0.62 of a mile, while 1,000 kilometers are equivalent to 621.40 miles.

Liquid Measurements

The United States uses the *gallon* as a liquid measure, whereas most of the world uses the *liter*. The Spanish term for the English gallon is *galón*. The Spanish term for the metric liter is *litro*. See the gallon-to-liter conversion table.

Galones	Litros	Litros	Galones
1	3.7	1	0.26
5	18.9	5	1.32
10	37.8	10	2.64
25	94.6	25	6.60
30	113.5	30	7.92
40	151.4	40	10.56

Or look at it this way: 1 liter (*un litro*) amounts to 0.26 of a gallon, while 50 liters are equivalent to 13.20 gallons.

Weights

For weights, the United States measures in English pounds; the metric system uses kilograms. A kilogram is 1,000 grams.

▶ The Spanish word for "weight" is *peso*.

▶ The Spanish word for "pound" is *libra*.

▶ The Spanish word for "kilogram" is *kilogramo*. It can also be spelled *quilogramo*. Just as we do in English, Spanish often shortens these terms to *kilo* or *quilo*.

TIME, DATE, AND OTHER NUMBERS

The following table gives common conversions from pounds to kilos and back.

Pounds (Libras)	Kilos	Kilos	Pounds (Libras)
1	.4	1	2.2
2	.9	2	4.4
3	1.3	3	6.6
4	1.8	4	8.8
5	2.2	5	11.0
10	4.5	10	22.0
15	6.8	15	33.0
20	9.0	20	44.0
25	11.3	25	55.1
50	22.6	50	110.2
100	45.3	100	220.4
200	90.7	200	440.8

Another way to look at this is that 1 kilogram roughly equals 2.2 pounds, 10 kilograms equal 22.0 pounds, and 100 kilograms equal 220.4 pounds. To convert kilos to pounds, multiply the number of kilos by 2.2. To convert pounds to kilos, divide the number of pounds by 2.2.

2.3 | DATES

Days of the Week
Months of the Year
Stating the Year
The Complete Date

For both business and social situations, you must know how to express the date. This involves knowing the days of the week, the months, and the years.

Days of the Week

In the following vocabulary, notice that the days of the week are not capitalized in Spanish.

hoy	today
ayer	yesterday
mañana	tomorrow
el día	the day
la semana	the week
los días de la semana	the days of the week
domingo	Sunday
lunes	Monday
martes	Tuesday
miércoles	Wednesday
jueves	Thursday
viernes	Friday
sábado	Saturday

Note: El día is masculine.

To pluralize the five days of the week that end with the letter *s* in the singular, do *not* change the noun itself; simply use *los* instead of *el* with the name of the day. For example:

Trabajo el lunes.	I work on (this) Monday.
Trabajo los lunes.	I work on Mondays.

But if the day ends with a vowel, the usual rule applies:

Trabajo el domingo.	I work on (this) Sunday.
Trabajo los domingos.	I work on Sundays.

◀ SEE ALSO 3.2, *"Singular and Plural Nouns"* ▶

Months of the Year

The months of the year correspond to our 12 months. In the following vocabulary notice that the first letters of Spanish months are not normally capitalized:

el mes	the month
el año	the year
los meses del año	the months of the year
enero	January
febrero	February
marzo	March
abril	April
mayo	May
junio	June
julio	July
agosto	August
se(p)tiembre	September
octubre	October
noviembre	November
diciembre	December

The Spanish word for September can be spelled (and pronounced) with or without the letter -p- in the middle.

◀ SEE ALSO 1.4, *"Accentuation (Stress) and Capitalization"* ▶

Stating the Year

When written as numerals, the years look the same in Spanish as in English, but they're pronounced differently. The years of the twenty-first century are expressed in the same style used in English, using the Spanish words for the number, of course. For example:

2000   dos mil

2001   dos mil uno

2005   dos mil cinco

2010   dos mil diez

However, referring to the twentieth century and earlier, the style is different. Instead of saying the equivalent of "nineteen thirty-two," the Spanish method provides the equivalent of "one thousand nine hundred thirty-two." See the following examples:

1932   mil novecientos treinta y dos

1957   mil novecientos cincuenta y siete

1866   mil ochocientos sesenta y seis

1776   mil setecientos setenta y seis

1492   mil cuatrocientos noventa y dos

◀ SEE ALSO 2.1, "Numbers" ▶

The Complete Date

See the following examples for putting together the day of the week, the day of the month, and the year:

Hoy es martes, el veintiocho de febrero de dos mil ocho.

(Today is Tuesday, February 28, 2005.)

Un día importante en la historia de los Estados Unidos de América es el cuatro de julio de mil setecientos setenta y seis.

(An important day in the history of the United States of America is July 4, 1776.)

2.4 TIME

Different Concepts of Time

Telling Time

Spanish uses three different words for the English *time*. These are *not* synonymous or interchangeable; each has its own meanings and uses.

Different Concepts of Time

El tiempo is the word for time in a general and theoretical sense. It is also the word for time as a commodity, something you can have or not have.

El problema del tiempo y el espacio	The problem of time and space
El tiempo pasa rápidamente.	Time passes swiftly.
No tengo tiempo.	I don't have time.
Tengo mucho tiempo.	I have lots of time.

La hora literally means "the hour" and is the word for time on the clock.

¿Qué hora es?	What time is it?
Es la hora de salir.	It's time to leave.
¡Ya era hora!	It's about time!

This last sentence is actually idiomatic. Literally, it means "It was already hour."

La vez is the word for time in the sense of an occasion, a point in time.

una vez	once
dos veces	twice
esta vez	this time
la última vez	last time
la próxima vez	next time
¿Cuántas veces?	How many times?

The word *vez* is a noun that ends with the letter *-z*. Like all other such nouns and adjectives, the *-z* is changed to a *-c* before adding *-es* to pluralize.

Telling Time

Telling (or asking) the time in Spanish involves using the verb *ser*. When asking the time, you would say, "¿Qué hora es?"

The answer is different for one o'clock than for two o'clock or three o'clock, and so on. See the following sentences:

Es la una.	It's one o'clock.
Son las dos.	It's two o'clock.
Son las tres.	It's three o'clock.

◁ SEE ALSO 15.2, "Two Forms of Being: ser vs. estar" ▷

To speak of minutes after the hour, give the hour and then add y (*and*) plus the number of minutes past the hour:

Son las tres y diez.	It's ten after three.
Es la una y veinte.	It's one twenty.

To express the number of minutes before the hour, give the coming hour and then add *menos* plus the number of minutes before the hour:

Son las cinco menos diez.	It's ten to five.
Es la una menos veinticinco.	It's twenty-five to one.

As in English, special terms exist for *quarter past* and *half past*, although, as in English, you can use the numbers for *fifteen* and *thirty*, respectively:

Son las ocho y cuarto.	It's a quarter past eight.
Son las ocho y quince.	It's eight fifteen.
Son las siete y media.	It's half past seven.
Son las siete y treinta.	It's seven thirty.

To be more specific about the time, you can add:

de la mañana	in the morning; A.M.
de la tarde	in the afternoon; P.M.
de la noche	in the evening; at night; P.M.

For example:

Son las cinco y cuarto de la tarde.	It's a quarter past five P.M.

Just as in English, there are separate terms for noon (*el mediodía*) and midnight (*la medianoche*).

Fue la medianoche.	It was midnight.
Sería el mediodía.	It was probably noon.

The last sentence literally means, "It would be noon."

◀ *SEE ALSO 7.2, "Present Tense: Irregular Verbs"* ▶

◀ *SEE ALSO 8.2, "Preterit Tense: Irregular Verbs"* ▶

3
NOUNS AND ARTICLES

3.1 MASCULINE AND FEMININE NOUNS

Based on Endings

Deceptive Endings

Based on Meaning

Must Be Memorized

Dual-Gender Endings

In Spanish, every single **noun** has a **gender.** Every Spanish noun is either masculine or feminine; there are no neuter nouns. It is essential to know the gender of nouns in Spanish, for many reasons. One reason is that **adjectives** and **articles** must agree with the nouns they modify in both number and gender.

WORDS TO GO . . . *WORDS TO GO . . . WORDS TO GO*

A **noun** is the name of a person, place or thing. A **proper noun** is the name of a specific person or place, such as *Mary* or *England*. A **common noun** is the designation of a group, category, or individual member of that group or category, such as *family, man, woman, city, nation,* and so on.

Gender refers to whether a noun is feminine or masculine.

An **adjective** is a word that modifies or describes a noun.

Articles are a form of adjective that limits a noun. Articles include *the, a,* and *an.*

Based on Endings

One way to tell whether a noun is masculine or feminine is to look at the ending. Nouns that end with …

- ▶ the letter *-o* are almost always masculine: *el libro* (book), *el río* (river).
- ▶ the unaccented letter *-a* are usually feminine: *la mesa* (table), *la silla* (chair).
- ▶ the accented letter *-á* are masculine: for example, *el sofá* (couch), *el papá* (dad).
- ▶ the letter *-d* are always feminine: *la verdad* (truth), *la pared* (wall).
- ▶ the ending *-ión* are always feminine: *la nación* (nation), *la región* (region).

▶ the ending *-umbre* are always feminine: *la certidumbre* (certainty), *la lumbre* (fire, light).

▶ the ending *-ez* are always feminine: *la vejez* (old age), *la estupidez* (stupidity).

Deceptive Endings

There are Spanish words that do not follow the preceding rules. Three words end with the letter *-o* but are feminine:

▶ *La modelo*. This feminine word refers to a female fashion model. Any other kind of model (a model for a ship or structure, or a male model) is masculine: *el modelo*.

▶ *La mano* (hand).

▶ *La radio* (radio).

Some words end with an unaccented *-a* but are masculine:

▶ *El Papa* (the Pope).

▶ *El día* (the day).

▶ A small group of words of Greek origin end with *-ma*, *-pa*, and *-ta* and are masculine: *el mapa* (map), *el planeta* (planet), *el programa* (program), and so on.

That does *not* mean that all Spanish words ending with *-ma*, *-pa*, and *-ta* are masculine; many words with these endings are feminine.

Based on Meaning

A noun might not end with one of the endings listed, but the word itself often gives a clue to the gender. If the noun specifically denotes a female, the noun is grammatically feminine; for example, *la mujer* (woman) is feminine. Likewise, if the noun denotes a male, it is masculine; for example, *el hombre* (man) is masculine.

Must Be Memorized

Many Spanish nouns have no built-in clues to their gender, yet every native speaker of Spanish knows which are feminine and which are masculine. It is important for you to know this as well because articles and adjectives are affected by the gender of the nouns.

◀ *SEE ALSO 5.2, "Adjectives in Agreement"* ▶

Whenever you learn a new noun, your clue to its gender is to memorize the definite article along with the noun. All new vocabulary will be shown from this point on with the definite article.

Dual-Gender Endings

Nouns that end with *-ista* can be either masculine or feminine, depending on the sex of the person mentioned. The article used with such a noun reflects the gender of the person described. Whether masculine or feminine, the following types of nouns always end in *-ista*.

el pianista	the (male) pianist
la pianista	the (female) pianist
el comunista	the (male) Communist
la comunista	the (female) Communist
un sadista	a (male) sadist
una sadista	a (female) sadist

◄ *SEE ALSO 3.3, "Definite Articles"* ►

◄ *SEE ALSO 3.4, "Indefinite Articles"* ►

3.2 SINGULAR AND PLURAL NOUNS

Ending with a Vowel

Ending with a Consonant

Exceptions

All Spanish nouns have number: they are either singular or plural. A noun can be changed from singular to plural in two ways, depending on whether the noun, when singular, ends with a vowel or a consonant.

Ending with a Vowel

If a noun ends with a vowel, simply add the letter -s to make it plural. For example, to pluralize *libro*, add -s. The result is *libros*. See the following examples:

el libro (s)	los libros (pl)
la mesa (s)	las mesas (pl)
el hombre (s)	los hombres (pl)
el espíritu (s)	los espíritus (pl)

Ending with a Consonant

If a noun ends with a consonant, add the letters -es to make it plural. For example, to pluralize *pared*, add -es. The result is *paredes*. See the following examples:

la pared (s)	las paredes (pl)
la nación (s)	las naciones (pl)
la mujer (s)	las mujeres (pl)
la virtud (s)	las virtudes (pl)

If the noun ends with the letter -z, change the -z to -c before adding -es. See the following examples:

la actriz (actress)	las actrices (actresses)
la luz (the light)	las luces (the lights)

When a word has a written accent mark on the last syllable in the singular, such as *nación* in the previous list, it loses that written accent mark in the plural (*naciones*) because it no longer breaks the rules.

◄ *SEE ALSO 1.4, "Accentuation (Stress) and Capitalization"* ▶

Exceptions

Just as in English, there some exceptions to the previous rules for pluralization. The very few words in this category end with -s. *Caution:* This does *not* mean that *all* words that end in -s are exceptions.

la crisis (s)	las crisis (pl)
el paréntesis (s)	los paréntesis (pl)
el martes (s)	los martes (pl)

The five days of the week fit into the category described (words ending with -s).

◄ *SEE ALSO 2.3, "Dates"* ▶

3.3 DEFINITE ARTICLES

Formation of Definite Articles
Use of Definite Articles

Both English and Spanish use the definite article, which indicates reference to a specific object (e.g., *the* man upstairs, not just any man). English has only one definite article, *the*. Spanish uses definite articles similarly to English, but not all the time. In this section, you learn how to use the definite article in Spanish. But first, let's focus on how they are formed.

Formation of Definite Articles

You've already seen Spanish definite articles used with nouns, but we now explain their formation. In Spanish, the definite articles must agree in number and gender with the nouns they modify.

Masculine Singular

The definite article that modifies a masculine singular noun is *el*:

el libro	the book
el cuarto	the room
el hombre	the man
el piso	the floor

Masculine Plural

The definite article that modifies a masculine plural noun is *los*:

los libros	the books
los cuartos	the rooms
los hombres	the men
los pisos	the floors

Feminine Singular

The definite article that modifies a feminine singular noun is *la*:

la mesa	the table
la sala	the living room

la mujer	the woman
la pared	the wall

Feminine Plural

The definite article that modifies a feminine plural noun is *las*:

las mesas	the tables
las salas	the living rooms
las mujeres	the women
las paredes	the walls

Use of Definite Articles

Spanish uses definite articles in much the same way English does. But Spanish makes more use of the definite article than English does.

With Specific Nouns

Both English and Spanish use the definite article with a noun that is both specific and concrete:

el chico	the boy
el cuaderno	the notebook
la lección	the lesson
el curso	the course

In each of these cases, the noun is specific (the listener knows which boy the speaker is referring to) and concrete (it is not an abstraction).

With Unique Nouns

Both English and Spanish also use the definite article with a unique noun: there's only one in the whole world, or so it is commonly understood:

el sol	the sun
la luna	the moon
la Tierra	the Earth
el Presidente	the President (only one in the whole country)

With Generic Nouns

Herein lies a major difference between Spanish and English usage. The definite article in Spanish is not limited to specific nouns, as it is in English. It is also used with **generic** nouns.

> **WORDS TO GO** . . .*WORDS TO GO* . . .*WORDS TO GO*
>
> A **generic** noun is one that refers in general to all the members of a group classified by that noun.

Note these examples of definite article used with generic nouns in Spanish, and see how they differ from the English equivalent:

El hombre es …	Man is … (man in general)
Las mesas son …	Tables are … (tables in general)
Los animales son …	Animals are … (animals in general)
Los libros son …	Books are … (books in general)

With Abstract Nouns

English never uses the definite article to modify **abstract** nouns. Spanish always does.

> **WORDS TO GO** . . .*WORDS TO GO* . . .*WORDS TO GO*
>
> An **abstract** noun is one that cannot be seen, felt, tasted, heard, or otherwise perceived by our five senses. For example, love, hate, freedom, and intelligence are abstractions.

Note the contrasts between Spanish and English in the following examples:

el amor	love
la libertad	liberty, freedom
el odio	hate, hatred
la inteligencia	intelligence

With Titles

In English, the definite article is not used with titles such as Mr., Mrs., Miss, Ms., Dr., Prof., Captain, Admiral, and so on. In Spanish, the definite article is used with all titles *when speaking about a specific person.* See the following examples:

el señor Gómez	Mr. Gomez
la señorita Smith	Miss Smith
la doctora Hernández	Dr. (feminine) Hernandez
el profesor Sarmiento	Prof. Sarmiento

You do *not* use the definite article when *addressing* the person in question—for example:

¿Cómo está usted, profesor Sarmiento?	How are you, Prof. Sarmiento?
¿Adónde va usted, Srta. Smith?	Where are you going, Miss Smith?

3.4 INDEFINITE ARTICLES

Formation of Indefinite Articles
Use of Indefinite Articles

English and Spanish also employ indefinite articles, which indicate reference to any of a group of like objects (e.g., *a* house in Los Angeles, meaning any house in Los Angeles). There are differences, however, in the way English and Spanish use indefinite articles.

Formation of the Indefinite Articles

English uses two forms of the indefinite article: *a* and *an* (a book, an apple). Spanish has four forms of the indefinite article based on the number one, which in Spanish is *uno*. But the exact form *uno* is never used in front of a noun.

Masculine Singular

The number *uno* is shortened to *un* when used in front of a masculine singular noun:

un libro	a book, one book
un hombre	a man, one man
un cuaderno	a notebook, one notebook
un chico	a boy, one boy

Masculine Plural

The indefinite article used with a masculine plural noun is *unos*:

unos libros	some books, a few books
unos hombres	some men, a few men
unos cuadernos	some notebooks, a few notebooks
unos chicos	some boys, a few boys

Feminine Singular

The form of the indefinite article used with a feminine singular noun is *una*:

una silla	a chair, one chair
una mesa	a table, one table

una mujer	a woman, one woman
una chica	a girl, one girl

Feminine Plural

The form of the indefinite article used with a feminine plural noun is *unas*:

unas sillas	some chairs, a few chairs
unas mesas	some tables, a few tables
unas mujeres	some women, a few women
unas chicas	some girls, a few girls

Use of Indefinite Articles

Some Spanish uses of the indefinite article are similar to English, but this article is used much less in Spanish.

As in English

The indefinite article is used in English to modify a nonspecific noun, one that has not been mentioned previously. When we use the definite article, as in "the boy," the implication is that we know which specific boy is being referred to. But if we use the indefinite article, as in "a boy," the implication is that we don't know exactly who the boy in question is.

One use of the indefinite article in Spanish corresponds to this English usage. The expression *un chico* refers to some nonspecific boy. The Spanish indefinite article can also be taken for its numerical meaning: *un chico* can be translated as "one boy."

English Uses, Spanish Does Not

The plural indefinite article is equivalent to the English "some" or "a few," as shown in earlier examples.

In English, the verb *to be*, plus the indefinite article, plus a noun is used to refer to someone's profession, political affiliation, religious affiliation, or nationality—for example, "she's a doctor," or "he's a Protestant."

In Spanish, when the verb *ser* (to be) is used to introduce certain kinds of nouns, the indefinite article is *not* normally used. The nouns in question are:

▶ Nouns of profession

▶ Nouns of political affiliation

▶ Nouns of religious affiliation

▶ Nouns of nationality

◀ *SEE ALSO 15.2, "Two Forms of Being:* ser *vs.* estar" ▶

See the following examples:

Soy profesor.	I'm a professor.
Ella es abogada.	She's a lawyer.
Pedro es mexicano.	Pedro is a Mexican.
El es médico.	He's a doctor.

This is true when the noun is unmodified. However, if the noun is modified, the definite article *is* used. See the following examples:

Soy un buen profesor.	I'm a good professor.
Ella es una abogada muy capaz.	She's a very capable lawyer.
Pedro es un mexicano trabajador.	Pedro is a hard-working Mexican.
El es un médico que sabe lo que hace.	He's a doctor who knows what he's doing.

It is possible to use *ser* plus the indefinite article plus a noun of the types specified here, but the indefinite article is then stressed and the connotation is more emphatic. The meanings of such statements would be something like the following:

¡Ella es *una* abogada!	She's *quite* a lawyer!
¡El es *un* médico!	He's one *heck* of a doctor!

As you have seen, in many cases, the English and Spanish uses of both definite and indefinite articles coincide. You have also seen that in some instances, they do not. Spanish uses the definite article much more than English does, but the opposite occurs with the indefinite article: it is used more in English than in Spanish.

4
PRONOUNS

4.1 SUBJECT PRONOUNS

All Subject Pronouns

First Person Plural

Second Person

When we talk about people, including ourselves, we don't repeat the name over and over if we know who we're talking about. Instead, in both English and Spanish, we use a pronoun. If the **pronoun** refers to the person who is performing the action of the verb, we use the **subject** pronoun (I, you, he ...).

WORDS TO GO . . . WORDS TO GO . . . WORDS TO GO

The **subject** of a verb is the one who performs the action of that verb.

A **pronoun** is a word that takes the place of a noun.

The **subject pronoun** is a word that takes the place of a noun when that noun performs the action of the verb.

All Subject Pronouns

The English subject pronouns are *I, you, he, she, it, we, you,* and *they.* The first five are singular (they stand for one person); the last three are plural. It will help to review the grammatical terms for these persons, as listed here, before going on to the Spanish subject pronouns:

I	first person, singular
you	second person, singular
he	third person, singular, masculine
she	third person, singular, feminine
it	third person, singular, neuter
we	first person, plural
you	second person, plural
they	third person, plural, masculine/feminine/neuter

In modern English, the second person singular and plural are identical; this is not the case in Spanish. The subject pronoun is frequently omitted because the verb endings indicate who the subject is. The third-person subject pronouns (*él, ella, usted, ellos, ellas, ustedes*) use them more frequently than the other subject pronouns because the endings don't specify exactly which of the three singular subjects or of the three plural subjects is indicated. However, these are often omitted as well because of clues in the context and by pointing. The subject pronouns are used for emphasis or, in the case of the third person, for clarity.

The following table shows the Spanish subject pronouns.

4.1

TABLE OF SPANISH SUBJECT PRONOUNS

Subject Pronouns	Description	English Equivalent
yo	first person singular	I
tú	second person singular, familiar	you
usted	second person singular, formal	you
él	third person singular, masculine	he
ella	third person singular, feminine	she
nosotros	first person plural, masculine	we
nosotras	first person plural, feminine	we
vosotros	second person plural, masculine, familiar	you
vosotras	second person plural, feminine, familiar	you
ustedes	second person plural, formal	you
ellos	third person plural, masculine	they
ellas	third person plural, feminine	they

First Person Plural

As shown in the preceding chart, the first person plural has two forms: the masculine *nosotros* and the feminine *nosotras*. The feminine pronoun is used only when the person speaking and every other person she is including is female. Even if only one male is included in this group, the masculine pronoun is used.

Second Person

The last column of the previous table includes five listings of the English *you* (the second person). This is because they take into account whether you are speaking to one person (singular) or more than one (plural), as well as whether you are on familiar terms with the person(s) or are addressing the person(s) with a degree of formality.

Second Person: Familiar and Formal

The unwritten rules of familiar versus formal treatment in the second person vary from one Spanish-speaking area to another. For example, in Spain, much of the older generation (if they are not old friends or relatives, and especially if they have only recently met) address each other with the formal *usted* and its plural, *ustedes*; however, members of "younger" generations (from 50 years of age down) use the familiar *tú* and its plural *vosotros/-as* with almost everyone.

In the Caribbean region, just about everyone uses the familiar form for everyone else. Conversely, in Mexico, the formal *usted* and its plural, *ustedes*, are used widely. One would have to be a family member or a longtime close friend to be addressed as *tú*.

Various gradations of usage exist in all the far-flung regions of Spanish speech. If you visit a Hispanophone country, you will soon discover the local usage. Besides, the locals do not expect a foreigner to use these pronouns as they do. The term *foreigner* includes Spanish-speakers from other countries; natives will be even more tolerant of Anglophones.

Second Person: Plural

As shown in the preceding table, the form *vosotros* has a feminine form, *vosotras*. This is used only when every single person belonging to the group you are addressing is female. Even if the group has only one male, the masculine form is employed.

A difference in usage with regard to the second person (you) exists between the Spanish of the **Iberian Peninsula** and that of Latin America.

WORDS TO GO . . .WORDS TO GO . . .WORDS TO GO

The **Iberian Peninsula** consists of the two nations of Portugal and Spain. Iberian or Peninsular Spanish refers to the Spanish spoken in Spain as opposed to that of Latin America.

In Latin-American Spanish, *vosotros* and *vosotras* are not used in everyday conversation. They're found frequently in poetry and sometimes in political speeches. Still, most people today are not completely unfamiliar with the usage; they know it is used in Spain and they hear it frequently in motion pictures made in Spain. They also hear it in religious sermons when the Bible is quoted. The usual Latin-American plural of the familiar *tú* is the same as the plural of the formal: *ustedes*. The formal/familiar distinction in the second person singular disappears in the plural.

In Spain, the second person plural familiar subject pronoun, *vosotros/-as*, is commonly used in conversation; there's nothing special or strange about it.

4.1

Second Person Singular Variant

As the preceding table demonstrates, the second person singular familiar is *tú*. This is true in most Hispanophone areas. However, in Argentina and several Central American countries, a different term is used: *vos*. This subject pronoun has its own verb system as well.

WORDS TO GO . . .WORDS TO GO . . .WORDS TO GO

Voseo is the Spanish term for the practice of using the subject pronoun *vos* for the second person familiar instead of *tú*.

Tuteo is the Spanish term for the practice of using the subject pronoun *tú* as the second person familiar.

Even though the Argentine and Central American *vos* is singular and used in place of *tú*, its verb system is based on and very closely related to the plural *vosotros* of Spain.

However, those who use *voseo* in their normal speech patterns today are familiar with *tuteo*, which is used in most of the Spanish-speaking world. You will always be understood when using *tuteo* because of the influence of motion pictures and television programs emanating from other Hispanic countries. But keep in mind that you will always be safe using the formal *usted*.

4.2 OBJECT PRONOUNS

Direct vs. Indirect Object
Direct Object Pronouns
Indirect Object Pronouns
Placement of Object Pronouns
Clarifying the Identity of the Pronoun
Two Object Pronouns of the Same Verb

Object pronouns take the place of **object** nouns. If the person is on the receiving end of the action, he or she is the object of the verb, and we use the object pronoun (me, you, him ...). In English, the object pronouns are identical for the **direct** and the **indirect** objects. In Spanish, some are identical, but others are different. In this section, you will come to understand the difference and then learn the Spanish direct and indirect object pronouns.

WORDS TO GO . . . *WORDS TO GO . . .WORDS TO GO*

The **object** of a verb is the one who receives the action of the verb.
A **direct object** receives the action of the verb directly.
An **indirect object** receives the action of the verb indirectly.

Direct vs. Indirect Object

In both Spanish and English, the direct object receives the action of the verb directly; the indirect object receives the action of the verb indirectly. Consider the following sentence:

John gave the woman a telephone book.

The verb is *gave*. To determine what receives the action of this verb directly, ask yourself what John gave, the woman or the telephone book? He certainly did not give the woman to anyone! The telephone book is the direct object. Who or what was affected by this giving? The woman receives the action indirectly, so *woman* is the indirect object.

In English, the same sentence could be stated a second way without changing its meaning:

John gave a telephone book to the woman.

In each of these two sentences, the subject and the objects are nouns. There are no pronouns. If we changed all the nouns to pronouns, the sentence would be:

He gave it to her.

In Section 4.1, you can see how *he* and all the other subject pronouns of Spanish are formed. In this section, you learn how to form direct and indirect object pronouns in Spanish.

Direct Object Pronouns

4.2

The English direct object pronouns are *me, you, he, she, it, us, you,* and *them.* The first five are singular (they stand for one person); the last three are plural. It will help to review the grammatical terms for these persons, listed here, before going on to the Spanish object pronouns:

me	first person, singular
you	second person, singular
him	third person, singular, masculine
her	third person, singular, feminine
it	third person, singular, neuter
us	first person, plural
you	second person, plural
them	third person, plural, masculine/feminine/neuter

The following table shows the Spanish direct object pronouns.

TABLE OF DIRECT OBJECT PRONOUNS IN SPANISH

Direct Object Pronouns	Description	English Equivalent
me	first person singular	me
te	second person singular, familiar	you
lo	second person singular, formal, masculine	you
la	second person singular, formal, feminine	you
lo	third person singular, masculine	him, it
la	third person singular, feminine	her, it
nos	first person plural	us
os	second person plural, familiar	you
los	second person plural, formal, masculine	you

continues...

(continued)

TABLE OF DIRECT OBJECT PRONOUNS IN SPANISH

Direct Object Pronouns	Description	English Equivalent
las	second person plural, formal, feminine	you
los	third person plural, masculine	them
las	third person plural, feminine	them

In the case of *lo* and *la* meaning *you,* use the first one if you are speaking to a man and the second if you are speaking to a woman. In the case of *los* and *las* meaning *you* plural, use the first if you are speaking to men or mixed men and women. Use the second if you are speaking exclusively to women.

Indirect Object Pronouns

English direct object pronouns are identical to the English indirect object pronouns. In Spanish, some of the direct and indirect object pronouns are identical; others are different. See the following table for the Spanish indirect object pronouns.

TABLE OF INDIRECT OBJECT PRONOUNS IN SPANISH

Indirect Object Pronouns	Description	English Equivalent
me	first person singular	me
te	second person singular, familiar	you
le	second person singular, formal	you
le	third person singular	him, it
nos	first person plural	us
os	second person plural, familiar	you
les	second person plural, formal	you
les	third person plural	them

Unlike direct object pronouns, indirect object pronouns do not distinguish between masculine and feminine. The pronouns that are identical for direct and indirect objects are *me, te, nos,* and *os.*

Placement of Object Pronouns

The placement of the object pronoun in relation to the verb depends on whether the verb is **conjugated, infinitive,** the present participle, or a positive or negative command.

> **WORDS TO GO . . .WORDS TO GO . . .WORDS TO GO**
>
> A **conjugated** verb is a verb whose endings signal person, number, tense, and mood. An **infinitive** verb indicates only the action or state; it does not indicate person, number, tense, or mood.

With Conjugated Verbs

The object pronoun is always placed directly before the conjugated verb:

Tengo los libros.	I have the books.
Los tengo.	I have them.
Le hablé ayer.	I spoke to him/her/you yesterday.

The last two preceding sentences involve a pronoun that is the object of a conjugated verb. Because that verb is conjugated, the object pronoun is placed in front of it.

With Infinitives and Present Participles

If the object pronoun is the object of an infinitive verb or a present participle, it is attached to that infinitive verb or present participle:

Decirlo no es hacerlo.	Saying it is not doing it.
Al verme …	Upon seeing me …
Viéndola en ese estado …	Seeing her in that condition …
Pensándolo bien …	Thinking it over …

However, the infinitive verb and the present participle are often used in conjunction with a conjugated verb. In those cases, you have a choice:

▶ Place the object pronoun in front of the conjugated verb.

▶ Attach the object pronoun to the infinitive verb or the present participle.

Quiero decirlo.	I want to say it.
Lo quiero decir.	I want to say it.
Estoy pensándolo bien.	I'm thinking it over.
Lo estoy pensando bien.	I'm thinking it over.

No matter which form is used, the meaning is the same.

Do *not* place the object pronoun between the conjugated verb and the infinitive, or between the conjugated verb and the present participle.

◀ SEE ALSO 10.1, *"Forming the Present Participle"* ▶

With Commands

The placement of the pronouns as the object of a command depends on whether the command is **affirmative** or **negative.**

WORDS TO GO . . .WORDS TO GO . . .WORDS TO GO

An **affirmative** command orders a person to do something. A **negative** command orders a person not to do something.

In an affirmative command, attach the object pronoun to the end of the verb:

¡Hágalo!	Do it!
¡Hábleme!	Speak to me!

In a negative command, place the object pronoun in front of the command:

¡No lo haga!	Don't do it!
¡No me hable!	Don't speak to me!

Clarifying the Identity of the Pronoun

You have seen that *lo* and *la* can mean several things: *him, her,* or *it*. They both can mean *you* (formal). Their plural, *los* and *las*, can mean *you* (formal plural) or *them*. The indirect object pronoun *le* can mean *(to) him, (to) her, (to) you* (formal) or *(to) it*; the plural *les* can mean *(to) them* or *(to) you* (formal plural). Usually, the meaning is clear, for these reasons:

▶ The person or thing in question has already been mentioned.

▶ Pointing or hand gestures make explicit the person or thing indicated.

▶ The entire flow of the conversation makes it clear.

However, sometimes there is room for ambiguity with the third-person object pronouns. If the ambiguity is caused by the direct object pronoun, simply use the noun instead:

Lo veo.	I see him/it.
Veo el libro.	I see the book.
Veo al hombre.	I see the man.

If the ambiguity is caused by the indirect object pronoun, you can be crystal clear by using the preposition *a* followed by a noun, whether common or proper.

◄ *SEE ALSO 6.1, "Prepositions"* ►

See the following sentences to compare the first one, which could possibly be ambiguous, with the last two, which are precise:

Le dí mi paraguas.	I gave my umbrella to him/her/it.
Dí mi paraguas a Carlos.	I gave my umbrella to Carlos.
Dí mi paraguas a mi amigo.	I gave my umbrella to my friend.

Although the last two preceding sentences are grammatically correct, in normal usage, Spanish-speakers tend to leave the indirect object pronoun in the sentence even though they are specifying the exact indirect object noun. **Redundancy** is common in Spanish. Most of the time, then, the last two preceding sentences would be given as follows:

Le dí mi paraguas a Carlos.

Le dí mi paraguas a mi amigo.

WORDS TO GO . . .WORDS TO GO . . .WORDS TO GO

Redundancy, with reference to grammar or sentence structure, is the inclusion of superfluous, repetitive, or unnecessary words.

In the previous two sentences, the indirect object pronoun *le* is not translated into English.

Two Object Pronouns of the Same Verb

When a verb has two pronouns as its objects, one direct and the other indirect, the order is always and invariably as follows:

1. Indirect object pronoun
2. Direct object pronoun

See the following examples:

(Ella) me lo dio.	She gave it to me.
Los chicos nos la dieron.	The boys gave it to us.
Te lo dije.	I told it to you.

A special complication arises if both object pronouns are grammatically in the third person. An easier way to remember this is to realize that this would mean both object pronouns would begin with the letter *l*.

Consider the English sentence "She gave it (el libro) to him." You would logically expect to hear, "(Ella) le lo dio." But this *never, ever* happens. You will *never* have the combination *le* or *les* plus either *lo, la, los,* or *las.*

The rule is: If the two object pronouns begin with the letter *l*, change the first one to *se*. See the following sentences:

Pedro se la dio.	Pedro gave it to him/her/it/them.
María se lo dijo.	María told it to him/her/it/them.

As indicated in the preceding section, you can make the indirect object pronoun clearer by using the preposition *a* plus the prepositional object pronoun or, for even more specificity, the noun. See the following sentences:

Pedro se la dio a él.	Pedro gave it to him.
Pedro se la dio a ella.	Pedro gave it to her.
Pedro se la dio a Carlos.	Pedro gave it to Carlos.
Pedro se la dio a ellos.	Pedro gave it to them.
Pedro se la dio a los chicos.	Pedro gave it to the boys.
Pedro se la dio a Roberto y José.	Pedro gave it to Roberto and José.
Pedro se la dio a Ud.	Pedro gave it to you (singular).
Pedro se la dio a Uds.	Pedro gave it to you (plural).

But if the person you're speaking with knows whom you're referring to, the sentences do not need the addition of *a* plus the noun. They can be as simple as the first two sentences with Pedro and María as the subjects.

◀ **SEE ALSO 12.1, *"Reflective Object Pronouns"*** ▶

4.3 OBJECT PRONOUNS OF PREPOSITIONS

A pronoun can also replace the object noun in a prepositional phase. For example, instead of saying "I am driving *with John*," you can say "I am driving *with him*." "With John" and "with him" are both prepositional phrases. Almost all the prepositional object pronouns are identical to the subject pronouns in Spanish. See the following table comparing the subject pronouns to the prepositional object pronouns.

SUBJECT PRONOUNS COMPARED TO PREPOSITIONAL OBJECT PRONOUNS

Subject Pronouns	Prepositional Object Pronouns
yo	mí
tú	ti
él	él
ella	ella
usted	usted
nosotros/as	nosotros/as
vosotros/as	vosotros/as
ellos	ellos
ellas	ellas
ustedes	ustedes

◀ SEE ALSO 6.1, *"Prepositions"* ▶

Only *yo* and *tú* have a different form for the object of the preposition. The accent mark in *mí* distinguishes it in writing from the possessive adjective *mi* (*my*). There's no written accent on *ti* because no other word is spelled that way.

An additional complication arises: when *mí* or *ti* is an object of the preposition *con* (with), they combine into *conmigo* and *contigo*, respectively. See the following examples:

| Ellos van al teatro conmigo. | They're going to the theater with me. |
| No quieren hablar contigo. | They don't want to speak with you. |

◀ SEE ALSO 12.1, *"Reflective Object Pronouns"* ▶

5

DESCRIPTORS: ADJECTIVES, NOUNS, AND ADVERBS

5.1 DESCRIPTIVE NOUNS AND ADJECTIVES AS NOUNS

Nouns Described by Nouns

Adjectives Used as Nouns

All languages have ways to describe or modify nouns. In both English and Spanish, these include **adjectives, adjective clauses,** and other **nouns.**

WORDS TO GO . . . *WORDS TO GO . . . WORDS TO GO*

An **adjective** is a word that modifies a noun. A **clause** is a subdivision of a sentence that contains a subject and a predicate. An **adjective clause** functions as an adjective to modify the noun.

Nouns Described by Nouns

English uses nouns to modify other nouns much more commonly than does Spanish. In this section, you learn how nouns are modified in Spanish.

English often modifies a noun by using another noun. See the following examples:

- ► Chicken salad
- ► Gold ring
- ► Wool coat
- ► Cotton dress

And even:

- ► Wolf Man
- ► Bat Man
- ► Wonder Woman

In each of the first four cases, one noun (chicken, gold, wool, cotton) informs us of the *substance* of the second (salad, ring, coat, dress). This is the most common way nouns modify nouns in English.

In the last three cases, one noun (Wolf, Bat, Wonder) tells us something about the *qualities* of the second noun (Man, Man, Woman). An adjective could have done the job—"a wolfish man," "a batlike man," "an amazing woman"—or adjective phrases could have described these entities: "a man who turns into a wolf," "a man who takes on the form of a bat," "a woman who performs marvels." These last three cases represent a much rarer kind of noun-describing-noun combination.

In Spanish, it's rare to use a noun to modify another noun. No Spanish equivalents exist for the first four cases; instead, a prepositional phrase would be used; a "gold ring" would be "un anillo de oro"—literally, "a ring of gold."

The only times nouns modify nouns in Spanish are like the last three shown, such as *hombre-lobo* (werewolf). But even this type is very rare.

◀ *SEE ALSO 6.4, "Prepositional Phrases"* ▶

Adjectives Used as Nouns

Unlike in English, any Spanish adjective can be turned into a noun. When the noun can be assumed or implied, you can simply use the adjective without using the noun itself, essentially converting the adjective into a noun. The following table explains the process.

ADJECTIVE BECOMING A NOUN

Noun Plus Adjective	English	Adjective as Noun	English
el coche azul	the blue car	el azul	the blue one
los coches azules	the blue cars	los azules	the blue ones
el libro nuevo	the new book	el nuevo	the new one
los libros nuevos	the new books	los nuevos	the new ones

When the noun is deleted in English, the pronoun *one* or *ones* is put in its place, which doesn't save any words. But in Spanish, all that is left is the definite article and the adjective used as a noun.

Many adjectives in Spanish are used as though they were nouns, even though the true noun wasn't previously mentioned. See the following examples:

viejo/a (old)   el viejo (the old man)

viejo/a (old)   una vieja (an old lady)

rubio/a (blond)   la rubia (the blonde)

rubio/a (blond)	unas rubias (a few blondes)
joven (young)	el joven (the young man)
joven (young)	la joven (the young woman)

In Spanish, it is deemed unnecessary to say "el hombre viejo"; if it's singular and masculine, then, of course, *el viejo* means "the old man"—unless, of course, we were talking about cars or something else; then *el viejo* would mean "the old one."

5.2 ADJECTIVES IN AGREEMENT

Adjectives That End in -o

Adjectives of Nationality

Dual-Gender Adjectives

Adjectives Ending in -dor, -ón, and -ote

Pluralization of Adjectives

A house can be big or small, white or blue, old or new. A man can be tall or short, smart or unintelligent, good or bad. We can also modify nouns by referring to numbers or quantities, saying "many houses" or "a couple of men." In this section, you learn how to modify nouns in Spanish.

Nouns modified by adjectives are as common in Spanish as they are in English, but there is a fundamental difference in the way that Spanish adjectives are handled. In English, there is only one form of any given adjective. In Spanish, the adjective must be in **agreement** with the noun. The adjective must be adjusted to agree in number and gender with the noun it modifies, which means you must know the number and gender of the noun.

> **WORDS TO GO . . .WORDS TO GO . . .WORDS TO GO**
>
> **Agreement,** in the context of the relationship between nouns and adjectives, refers to the adjective having to reflect both the gender and number of the noun it modifies.

◀ SEE ALSO 3.1, *"Masculine and Feminine Nouns"* ▶

◀ SEE ALSO 3.2, *"Singular and Plural Nouns"* ▶

Adjectives That End in -o

If an adjective ends with -o, that is the masculine form of the adjective, used to modify a masculine noun. If (and *if* is the operative word) the masculine form of the adjective ends with -o, only then do you change the -o to an -a to make it feminine. Examples follow:

un libro bueno	a good book
una silla buena	a good chair

71

un hombre alto	a tall man
una mujer alta	a tall woman
un edificio tremendo	a tremendous building
una casa tremenda	a tremendous house
un hombre estúpido	a stupid man
una razón estúpida	a stupid reason

Adjectives of Nationality

If (and, again, *if* is a key word) you are using an adjective of nationality, and *if* that adjective ends with a consonant, you must add *-a* to that consonant to feminize it. Examples follow:

un libro español	a Spanish book
una silla española	a Spanish chair
un hombre francés	a French man
una mujer francesa	a French woman
un edificio inglés	an English building
una casa inglesa	an English house

Dual-Gender Adjectives

All other Spanish adjectives (those that do not end in *-o* in the masculine form, those that end in other vowels, and those that do not show nationality and at the same time end in a consonant) require no change to show gender. They are both masculine and feminine at the same time. Examples follow:

un hombre inteligente	an intelligent man
una mujer inteligente	an intelligent woman
un libro azul	a blue book
una mesa azul	a green table
un edificio espectacular	a spectacular building
una casa espectacular	a spectacular house
un escritorio verde	a green desk
una mesa verde	a green table
un hombre joven	a young man
una mujer joven	a young woman

Adjectives Ending in -dor, -ón, and -ote

Adjectives that end with *-dor* in the masculine form: add *-a* to feminize.

Adjectives that end with *-ón* in the masculine form: add *-a* to feminize.

Adjectives that end with *-ote* in the masculine form: change *e* to *a* to feminize.

These types of adjectives form a relatively small group. Consider some examples:

un hombre trabajador	a hard-working man
una mujer trabajadora	a hard-working woman
Pancho es muy mandón.	Pancho is very bossy.
María es muy mandona.	María is very bossy.
un tejano grandote	a great big Texan
una tejana grandota	a great big Texan (woman)

The *-dor/-a* endings refer to one who performs the action of the verb on which the adjective (or noun) is based, such as *trabajar* = "to work."

The *-ón/-ona* and *-ote/-ota* endings are **augmentative suffixes.**

WORDS TO GO . . .WORDS TO GO . . .WORDS TO GO

An **augmentative suffix** is an ending added to a noun or adjective to suggest the idea of bigness, of large size.

Pluralization of Adjectives

The rule for the pluralization of adjectives is exactly the same as the rule for pluralization of nouns: If the adjective ends with a vowel, add *-s* to make plural. If it ends with a consonant, add *-es* to make it plural. See the following examples:

el hombre bueno	the good man
los hombres buenos	the good men
el libro azul	the blue book
los libros azules	the blue books
la silla francesa	the French chair
las sillas francesas	the French chairs

un hombre trabajador	a hard-working man
unos hombres trabajadores	some hard-working men

If the adjective ends with the letter -*z*, change the -*z* to -*c* before adding -*es*. See the following examples:

Una mujer feliz.	A happy woman.
Unas mujeres felices.	Some happy women.
Una situación atroz.	An atrocious situation.
Unas situaciones atroces.	Some atrocious situations.

PLACEMENT OF ADJECTIVES

Quantitative Adjectives

Descriptive Adjectives

In English, adjectives are invariably placed in front of the nouns they modify, with a few exceptions for poetic license, like names of publications (*House Beautiful* and so on).

In Spanish, the placement of adjectives depends on various factors, such as whether we are dealing with a quantitative or a descriptive adjective.

5.3

Quantitative Adjectives

Quantitative adjectives normally precede the noun. See the following examples:

un libro	a book/one book
cinco mesas	five tables
mucho dinero	a great deal of money
muy pocas sillas	very few chairs

Descriptive Adjectives

Descriptive adjectives normally follow the noun, but there are exceptions.

Literal Meaning

As in English, some adjectives have both a literal meaning and a figurative meaning. When the meaning is literal, the adjective generally follows the noun it modifies. See these examples:

un hombre grande	a big man (physical size)
un amigo viejo	an old friend (an elderly friend)
mujeres puras	pure women (virgins)
un coche nuevo	a new car (this year's model)
el hombre pobre	the poor man (financially strapped)

DESCRIPTORS: ADJECTIVES, NOUNS, AND ADVERBS

Figurative Meaning

When the meaning is figurative, the adjective generally precedes the noun it modifies. Compare the following examples with the preceding:

un gran hombre	a great man (moral stature)
un viejo amigo	an old friend (a longtime friend)
puras mujeres	exclusively women, nothing but women
un nuevo coche	a new car (an additional car; replacement)
el pobre hombre	the poor guy (unfortunate)

Even if a descriptive adjective has only a literal meaning, its placement depends on whether you want to emphasize the adjective—in other words, demonstrate that the noun with the quality of this adjective is outstanding, and different from the nouns that do not have this quality. See the following examples:

la hierba verde	the *green* grass (as opposed to dried-up, brown grass)
la nieve blanca	the *white* snow (as opposed to the dirty snow)
las montañas altas de Suiza	the *high* mountains of Switzerland (as opposed to the low ones in the same country)

In these examples, *hierba*, *nieve*, and *montañas* are the nouns (grass, snow, and mountains).

5.4 ADJECTIVE CLAUSES AND RELATIVE PRONOUNS

Relative Pronouns

Relative Pronoun *Que*

Relative Pronoun *Quien*

Relative Pronouns *El Cual, El Que,* and So On

Adjective Functioning as Relative Pronoun

5.4

In this section, you will learn how to introduce a clause with a relative pronoun and how to describe a noun with an entire clause (adjective clause).

Relative Pronouns

Just as an adjective can describe a noun, a whole clause can perform the same task. A **relative pronoun** connects the main clause to a dependent clause and refers to a noun in that dependent clause. A main (or independent) clause forms a complete sentence in itself. A dependent (or subordinate) clause doesn't form a complete sentence in itself, but must be attached to the main clause.

WORDS TO GO . . .WORDS TO GO . . .WORDS TO GO

The part of speech that links the adjective clause to the noun it describes is the **relative pronoun**.

An **adjective clause** is a subordinate clause that modifies a noun in the main clause.

Here's an English example:

I know a restaurant that has good food.

The main clause could be a sentence in itself: "I know a restaurant." The dependent clause is not a sentence in itself ("has good food"); it has to be attached to the main clause to form part of a sentence. The sample sentence employs the relative pronoun *that* to introduce the dependent clause, which describes or modifies the restaurant. It performs the same duty that an adjective does; that's why it's called an **adjective clause.**

Relative Pronoun *Que*

The most commonly used relative pronoun in Spanish is *que*. Because of that, and because it can be used with humans as well as other things, it can be translated variously as "that," "which," or "who." The English sample sentence we considered in the last section would be this in Spanish:

Conozco un restaurante que tiene buena comida.

In this sentence, *que* refers to the restaurant.

This relative pronouns can be translated into English as "which" as well. See the following example:

El auto, que no anda,   The car, which isn't
está en el garaje.   running, is at the garage.

This relative pronoun is also used with reference to human beings, as in the following sentence:

Conozco al hombre que vive   I know the man who lives in
en esa casa.   that house.

Relative Pronoun *Quien*

The relative pronoun *quien* and its plural form, *quienes*, is used exclusively for reference to human beings. Its English counterpart is "who" or "whom." It is not used interchangeably with *que*. It is used only in **parenthetical expressions** or when it's in an adjective clause, when it refers exclusively to people, and when that clause begins with a preposition.

WORDS TO GO . . .WORDS TO GO . . .WORDS TO GO

A **parenthetical expression** is an expression that is not the main idea of the sentence and is not necessary for the sentence to be complete. This type of expression is usually found between commas, dashes, or parenthesis marks.

Consider these examples of *quien(es)* in parenthetical expressions:

Ese hombre, quien vive en   That man, who lives in
Madrid, no habla inglés.   Madrid, doesn't speak English.

Mi padre, quien es un   My father, who is a good
hombre bueno, trabaja   man, works hard.
mucho.

See these examples of *quien(es)* when following prepositions:

| El chico a quien se lo dí no está. | The boy I gave it to isn't here. (The boy to whom I gave it is not here.) |
| La chica de quien hablabas es bonita. | The girl you were talking about is pretty. (The girl about whom you were talking is pretty.) |

These are examples of *quien(es)* when following prepositions and in parenthetical expressions:

| Mis amigos, con quienes fui al cine, querían comer. | My friends, with whom I went to the movies, wanted to eat. |
| Ese hombre, de quien hablé ayer, es mi jefe. | That man, about whom I spoke yesterday, is my boss. |

5.4

Relative Pronouns *El Cual, El Que,* and So On

You can use the relative pronouns *el cual, la cual, los cuales,* and *las cuales,* as well as *el que, la que, los que,* and *las que,* with the same meanings and in the same circumstances as *que* and *quien(es).* The only difference is that *el/la/los/las* plus either *cual(es)* or *que* is usually used in writing or speech that is more formal. This construction is especially used after prepositions of more than one syllable, such as *encima de* and *debajo de,* as well as after the prepositions *sin, por,* and *para.*

If emphasis or greater clarity is desired, these prepositions can also be used after prepositions of only one syllable.

See these examples of sentences:

| Mis amigos, con los que fui al cine, querían comer. | My friends, with whom I went to the movies, wanted to eat. |
| Son las razones por las cuales lo digo. | They're the reasons (because of which) I say it. |

If you want to introduce an adjective clause that refers to a location *in which* or *where,* you can start that adjective clause with the relative pronoun *donde* or, *if it involves a verb of motion, adonde:*

| Arizona es el estado donde nací. | Arizona is the state I was born in. |
| No puedes ir adonde voy yo. | You can't go (to) where I'm going. |

79

Adjective Functioning as Relative Pronoun

The word *cuyo/a/os/as*, which means "whose," is technically an adjective but behaves like a relative pronoun. Like the relative pronouns, it can connect the main clause to an adjective clause. Because it is actually an adjective, it has to agree in number and gender with the noun it modifies. The noun it modifies is *not* the noun in the main clause, but rather the noun that follows it.

See these examples:

La mujer, cuyo libro tengo, está en el Japón.	The woman, whose book I have, is in Japan.
Mi amigo, cuyas maletas no han llegado, está preocupado.	My friend, whose suitcases haven't arrived, is worried.

◀ *SEE ALSO 5.2, "Adjectives in Agreement"* ▶

5.5 POSSESSIVES

Possessive Adjectives

Possessive Pronouns

In this section, you learn to use possessive adjectives (*my, your, her*, and so on) and possessive pronouns (*mine, yours, hers*, and so on) to attribute ownership of items to specific persons.

Possessive Adjectives

Possessive adjectives refer to ownership and, like all adjectives, must agree in number and gender with the nouns they modify. Spanish has two forms of possessive adjectives: the short form and the long form.

Short Form

The short form of the possessive adjectives is the most commonly used. The possessive adjectives for *nosotros/-as* and *vosotros/-as* have four forms. This is because the masculine singular form ends with *-o*. All the others have only two forms because their masculine form does *not* end with *-o* or any of the other endings that require a change to feminize it; they have only a singular and a plural form.

◀ SEE ALSO 5.2, *"Adjectives in Agreement"* ▶

Subject Pronoun	Possessive Adjective	English
yo	mi, mis	my
tú	tu, tus	your
nosotros/as	nuestro, nuestros, nuestra, nuestras	our
vosotros/as	vuestro, vuestros, vuestra, vuestras	your
él	su, sus	his
ella	su, sus	her
usted	su, sus	your
ellos	su, sus	their
ellas	su, sus	their
ustedes	su, sus	your

Possessive adjectives do *not* agree in number and gender with the possessor; like any other adjectives, they agree with the noun modified: the thing possessed. See the following examples:

Elena tiene sus libros.	Elena has her books.
Los chicos buscan a su amigo.	The boys are looking for their friend.

In the first sentence, the possessive adjective is plural (*sus*) to agree with libros. In the second sentence, the possessive adjective is singular (*su*) to agree with *amigo*.

Even though *su* and *sus* are the possessive adjectives for six different subject pronouns (él, ella, usted, ellos, ellas, and ustedes), usually the possessor is obvious from the context or situation. Ordinarily, if I say, "Elena no tiene su cuaderno," people assume I'm saying that Elena doesn't have her own notebook, not someone else's. In face-to-face conversation, pointing also clarifies this matter.

If, however, there is any chance of confusion or ambiguity, a more precise way exists for showing who the possessor is. The alternative is to use the combination of the preposition *de* plus the subject pronoun:

Es el libro de él.	It's his book.
Es el libro de ella.	It's her book.
Es el libro de usted.	It's your book.
Es el libro de ellos.	It's their book.
Es el libro de ellas.	It's their book.
Es el libro de ustedes.	It's your book.

Of course, you can be even more specific by using the person's name:

Es el libro de Roberto.	It's Roberto's book.
Es el libro de Carmen.	It's Carmen's book.

Or you can use an ordinary noun:

Es el libro del jefe.	It's the boss's book.
Es el libro de la chica.	It's the girl's book.

The last four sentences take an apostrophe-s in English. In Spanish, there is no apostrophe -s.

Long Form

You can use the long form of the possessive adjective to emphasize the possessor. English accomplishes this by stressing the possessor in oral communication and by underlining it or using italics in written form, as in "It's *my* book!" (no one else's). Spanish uses the long form to lend emphasis to the possessor:

Es mi libro.	It's my book.
Es el libro mío.	It's *my* book!

The following table shows the long form of the possessive adjectives.

LONG (EMPHATIC) FORM OF POSSESSIVE ADJECTIVES WITH NOUNS

Short Form	Long Form	English
mi libro	el libro mío	my book
mis libros	los libros míos	my books
mi silla	la silla mía	my chair
mis sillas	las sillas mías	my chairs
tu cuaderno	el cuaderno tuyo	your notebook
tus cuadernos	los cuadernos tuyos	your notebooks
tu casa	la casa tuya	your house
tus casas	las casas tuyas	your houses
su amigo	el amigo suyo	(see note)
sus amigos	los amigos suyos	(see note)
su casa	la casa suya	(see note)
sus casas	las casas suyas	(see note)
nuestro amigo	el amigo nuestro	our friend
nuestros amigos	los amigos nuestros	our friends
nuestra amiga	la amiga nuestra	our (female) friend
nuestras amigas	las amigas nuestras	our (female) friends
vuestro amigo	el amigo vuestro	your friend
vuestros amigos	los amigos vuestros	your friends
vuestra amiga	la amiga vuestra	your (female) friend
vuestras amigas	las amigas vuestras	your (female) friends

Note: You already know, from the previous "Short Form" section, that *su/sus* can stand for "his," "her," "your," and "their." The definite article is used with the long form of the possessive adjective.

Possessive Pronouns

As you know, a pronoun is a word that takes the place of a noun. If we already know what the noun in question is, we don't usually bother to repeat it. This is true in English as well as Spanish.

English uses a whole different set of possessive pronouns. In place of the adjective plus noun, such as "my book(s)," "your books(s)," "his book(s)," "her book(s)," "our book(s)," "their book(s)," we use the possessive pronouns *mine*, *yours*, *his*, *hers*, *ours*, and *theirs*.

◀ SEE ALSO 4.1, *"Subject Pronouns"* ▶

In Spanish, the possessive pronoun is formed like this:

1. Think of the long form of the possessive adjective with its noun.

2. Then drop the noun.

3. You are left with the definite article plus the possessive pronoun.

Long Form	Possessive Noun	English Translation Possessive Adjective
el libro mío	el mío	mine
los libros míos	los míos	mine
la casa mía	la mía	mine
las casas mías	las mías	mine
el amigo tuyo	el tuyo	yours
los amigos tuyos	los tuyos	yours
la amiga tuya	la tuya	yours
las amigas tuyas	las tuyas	yours

The same principle works with every one of the long-form possessive adjectives becoming possessive pronouns. Simply drop the noun and leave both the definite article and the possessive. In this way, both the definite article and the possessive pronoun will agree in number and gender with the noun you have in mind but are not stating. Look at the following sentences:

No tienes tus libros; tienes los míos.

You don't have your books; you have mine.

No veo a tu amiga; veo a la mía.

I don't see your friend; I see mine.

Because the third-person forms can be hazy, you can be more specific. For example, instead of saying "they're his" as "son suyos" or "son suyas," you can pinpoint the possessor by saying "son de él." Of course, you could be even more specific by using his name: "son de Roberto." (The preposition *a* in the last example is the "personal a").

◁ *SEE ALSO 6.1, "Prepositions"* ▷

There's one exception to keeping the definite article with the possessive pronoun: After any form of the verb *ser*, there is no need for the definite article with the possessive pronoun—for example, "No son tus libros; son míos."

5.5

5.6 ADVERBS AND ADVERBIAL PHRASES

Regular Adverbs

Irregular Adverbs

Adverbial Phrases

Adverbs and **adverbial phrases** are used for several purposes:

▶ To modify a verb (He speaks *well.*)

▶ To modify an adjective (It is *very* good.)

▶ To modify another adverb (He speaks *very* well.)

WORDS TO GO . . .WORDS TO GO . . .WORDS TO GO

An **adverb** is used to modify either a verb, an adjective, or another adverb.
An **adverbial phrase,** which combines a preposition and noun, performs the
same duties as an adverb.

◀ SEE ALSO 7.1, *"Present Tense: Regular Verbs"* ▶

In this section, you learn how to form adverbs and adverbial phrases.

Regular Adverbs

In English, regular adverbs are formed by adding the ending *-ly* to an adjective:
solemn + ly = solemnly.

In Spanish, regular adverbs are formed by adding the ending *-mente* to the *femi-nine* form of an adjective. See the following table.

FORMING REGULAR SPANISH ADVERBS

Masc. Adj.	Fem. Adj.	Ending	Adverb	English
rápido	rápida	-mente	rápidamente	rapidly
lento	lenta	-mente	lentamente	slowly
obvio	obvia	-mente	obviamente	obviously
alegre	alegre	-mente	alegremente	merrily
sutil	sutil	-mente	sutilmente	subtlely
veloz	veloz	-mente	velozmente	swiftly

The first three adjectives needed to have the ending changed from -o to -a to make them feminine before adding the adverbial termination -mente. The last three adjectives needed no change before adding the adverbial ending.

Irregular Adverbs

In English, some adverbs are not formed according to the adjective + -ly ending formula: *fast, soon, well, often, very,* and so on.

In Spanish as well, some adverbs are not formed according to the formula of feminine adjective + -mente.

bien	well
mal	badly, poorly, not well
pronto	soon
despacio	slowly

Because these adverbs and a few others like them do not follow the formula used for forming most adverbs, they are called irregular adverbs.

Adverbial Phrases

In English as well as in Spanish, adverbial phrases can be used instead of adverbs. The meanings are synonymous. In Spanish, however, it is more common to use adverbial phrases than it is in English. The Spanish adverbial phrase is almost always (although not exclusively) introduced with the preposition *con* (with) followed by the noun that is based on the adjective. See the following examples:

Celebraron con alegría.	They celebrated with joy.
Habló con sutileza.	He spoke with subtlety.
Corrió con rapidez.	She ran with speed.
Vienen a menudo.	They come often.

The third sentence sounds awkward in English, but not in Spanish. The same sentences could have been formed as follows:

Celebraron alegremente.	They celebrated joyfully.
Habló sutilmente.	He spoke subtlely.
Corrió rápidamente.	She ran fast.
Vienen repetidamente.	They come repeatedly.
Vienen muchas veces.	They come often (many times).

The sentence that uses "a menudo" employs an idiom. The closest we can come to a synonymous meaning in the form of an adverb is by using the one based on the adjective *repetido* (repeated), which is not that common. The expression *muchas veces* is the most common expression for this idea. The term "repetidas veces," literally "repeated times," although odd-sounding in English, is often used in somewhat more formal speech.

6
PREPOSITIONS

6.1 PREPOSITIONS

Common Prepositions

Preposition *a*

Prepositions, in English and in Spanish, are placed in front of a noun or pronoun to indicate its relationship with the rest of the sentence. For example, in the English sentence "I'm going to India," the preposition *to* indicates direction. It shows that the noun, India, is where I'm going. In the phrase "the interior of Brazil," the preposition *of* indicates that the "interior" we're referring to belongs to the proper noun called Brazil. In the phrase "the restaurant in the park," the preposition *in* tells us that the noun "park" is the location of the restaurant in question. In this section, you learn the meanings and uses of Spanish prepositions.

WORDS TO GO . . .WORDS TO GO . . .WORDS TO GO

A **preposition** is a word placed in front of a noun or pronoun to indicate the relationship between the noun or pronoun and the rest of the sentence.

Common Prepositions

This section presents the most common prepositions used in Spanish. The following prepositions offer no major problems and can simply be defined by their English counterpart.

COMMON PREPOSITIONS IN SPANISH AND ENGLISH

Spanish	English
a la derecha (de)	to the right (of)
a la izquierda (de)	to the left (of)
al lado de	beside; to the side (of)
alrededor de	around
arriba de	above, over
bajo	under, below
con	with

Spanish	English
de	of; from
debajo (de)	under, underneath, beneath
delante (de)	in front (of)
dentro (de)	inside (of); within
detrás (de)	behind, in back (of)
encima (de)	on top (of)
en	in; into; on
enfrente (de)	facing; across (from); in front (of)
entre	between; among
excepto	except
fuera (de)	outside (of)
junto a	next to
sin	without
sobre	on; on top of; over
según	according to

The preposition *en* can be synonymous with, but less specific than, *dentro de*, *encima de*, and *sobre*. All the terms showing the preposition *de* in parentheses need that *de* when mentioning the thing or place "in which," "under which," "behind which," "beside which," and so on.

◀ SEE ALSO 4.3, *"Object Pronouns of Prepositions"* ▶

In the following sections, you learn about prepositions that require more detailed explanations.

Preposition *a*

The preposition *a* is used in two distinctly different ways in Spanish. One of those ways translates into English; the other does not.

Translatable *a*

One use of the preposition *a* is to indicate direction or destination, just like the English preposition *to*. See the following examples:

Voy a Nueva York.	I'm going to New York.
Corren a la tienda.	They run to the store.
Ella fue a casa.	She went home.

The last sentence contains an idiom. Literally, the meaning is "She went to house." The idea of "her" house is implicit in the idiom.

This use of the preposition *a* is necessary after a verb of motion (*going, coming, running, flying, swimming,* and so on). But *a* is also used between certain conjugated verbs and the following infinitive verb. It is used after verbs of beginning, of inviting, of teaching, and of learning. See the following examples:

Me invitaron a cenar.	They invited me to dinner (to dine).
Empezó a llover.	It started to rain.
Aprendieron a tocar la guitarra.	They learned (how to) play (the) guitar.

Untranslatable *a*

The preposition *a* has another function with no parallel in English. Many textbooks refer to this as the personal *a*. Its function is to signal a specific **direct object,** usually human or at least personified.

◀ SEE ALSO 4.2, *"Object Pronouns of Verbs"* ▶

WORDS TO GO . . .WORDS TO GO . . .WORDS TO GO

A **direct object** is the person or thing directly affected by the verb. In the sentence "He gave Mary the book," the thing he actually gave was the book; it receives the action of the verb directly and, therefore, is the direct object.

The rule is this: When the direct object of a verb is a specific human being (or human beings), place the preposition *a* after the verb. Do *not* use this preposition with that function with inanimate objects. See the following examples:

Veo la silla.	I see the chair.
Veo la luna.	I see the moon.
Veo a la chica.	I see the girl.
Veo a María.	I see María.

The first two sentences lack the personal *a* because the object of the verb in each case is not a specific human being. The last two sentences have the personal *a* because the object of the verb in each case is a specific human being. This usage of the preposition *a* is not translatable into English.

The personal *a* is often used to personify nonhumans, such as family pets, as in, "Veo a mi perro" ("I see my dog").

Because Spanish sentence structure is very flexible, and because the subject can be placed almost anywhere in the sentence, it can sometimes be unclear which is the subject and which is the object. Use the personal *a* to mark the direct object, as in the following examples:

El policía mató al asesino.	The policeman killed the murderer.
Al policía mató el asesino.	The murderer killed the policeman. (It was the policeman [that] the murderer killed.)

The word *al* used here is a contraction; it is explained in the next section.

6.1

6.2 WRITTEN CONTRACTIONS

a + el = al

de + el = del

The Spanish language has no more than two written contractions. This brief section points them out. Unlike contractions in English, which are optional, the two Spanish contractions must always be written as contractions; the component parts must not be separated.

a + el = al

When the preposition *a* comes immediately before the masculine singular definite article *el*, the two words must combine into the contraction *al*. This holds true whether the preposition is the equivalent of the English *to* or whether it is the untranslatable personal *a*. The preposition *a* does *not* combine with the other definite articles (*los, la, las*) into contractions. See the following examples:

Llamé al profesor.	I called the professor.
Llamé a la profesora.	I called the (female) professor.
Llamé a los profesores.	I called the (male or mixed) professors.
Llamé a las profesoras.	I called the (female) professors.
Fueron al club.	They went to the club.
Fueron a la playa.	They went to the beach.

This contraction affects only the masculine singular definite article. The *a* does *not* combine with *él*, the third-person singular masculine subject pronoun (English *he, him*). Instead, it's used as "Le hablé a él" (I spoke to him).

de + el = del

When the preposition *de* ("of" or "from") comes immediately before the masculine singular definite article *el*, the two words combine into the contraction *del*.

The preposition *de* does *not* combine with any of the other definite articles or with the subject pronoun *él* (he, him). See the following examples:

Somos del Sur.	We are from the South.
Vuelve de la escuela.	He's returning from school.
Es de él.	It's his.

The last sentence is an example of using *de* to indicate possession.

◄ *SEE ALSO 5.5, "Possessives"* ▶

Other than *al* and *del*, there are no written contractions in the Spanish language.

6.3 USES OF *POR* AND *PARA*

Movement Through a Space: *por*

Movement Toward a Space: *para*

Cause: *por*

Aims: *para*

Instrument or Agent: *por*

Exchange: *por*

For the Sake of/On behalf of: *por*

Vague Location: *por*

Opinion: *para*

Considering the Fact That ...: *para*

The choice of the prepositions *por* and *para* represents an obstacle for many students of Spanish. Both can often be translated as "for" and, at other times, as "by." Yet these two Spanish prepositions are in no way interchangeable; each has its own particular use.

The problem for the Anglophone resides in trying to speak Spanish while thinking in English. Translation isn't much help because both prepositions can often be translated as the same English preposition. The best approach is to internalize the meanings and uses of *por* and *para*, to get inside the Spanish-speaker's mind and visualize the concepts, perhaps subconscious, that underlie the choice of preposition. This section helps you do just that.

Movement Through a Space: *por*

To picture the meaning of the preposition *por*, imagine an arrow, representing motion, inside or alongside a box. This preposition refers to movement within or alongside a specific space, depending on context.

The symbolic box can represent physical or geographical space. See the following examples:

Anduve por el parque.	I walked through the park
Viajé por México.	I traveled through Mexico.

Caminaba por la calle.	He/she was walking down the street.
Entraste por la puerta principal.	You came in through the main door.

The translation of the last two preceding sentences was partially arbitrary. The third sentence uses an English idiom involving the adverb *down* even though there is no literal meaning having to do with either up or down. That sentence could just as well have been translated as, "He/she was walking along the street."

The fourth sentence could have used *by* instead of *through*. It's the mental image, the "feel," that is important in learning the meaning and use of these prepositions.

The box does not have to represent physical or geographical space, either. It can also represent a block of time. In this case, the arrow passing through the box would represent movement through a specific period of time or duration. See the following examples:

Estuve en el parque por dos horas.	I was in the park for two hours.
Me quedé en México por un mes.	I stayed in Mexico for one month.
Caminé por tres horas.	I walked for three hours.
Hablaste por mucho tiempo.	You spoke for a long time.

Movement Toward a Space: *para*

The underlying concept involved with the preposition *para* can be conceptualized as an arrow moving *toward* a box. *Para* represents movement *toward* a specific space, in the direction of that space. See the following examples:

Me voy para España.	I'm leaving for Spain.
Salió para la oficina.	He/she left for the office.
Me fui para el parque.	I headed for the park.
Esta noticia es para todo el país.	This piece of news is for the whole country.

The third sentence could just as well have employed *toward* instead of *for*. The last sentence has no verb of motion, yet it uses *para* because the underlying meaning is "This piece of news is *destined for* the whole country" or "This piece of news is *aimed at* the whole country." The whole country is to be the recipient of the news. It still follows the mental image of the arrow aiming at the box.

Para can also be used to express destination, even when that destination is not a space. See these sentences:

Este regalo es para ti.	This gift is for you.
Compré el libro para mi padre.	I bought the book for my father.

In the first sentence, the gift is meant to end up in your possession. It is coming to you. In the second sentence, the book I bought is destined for my father; he is to be the recipient of the book. It is aimed at him.

The metaphorical box can again stand for a block of time, but the arrow is moving toward it or aiming to reach it. The arrow flying toward the space of time represents a deadline, a cutoff date. See the following examples:

Necesito recibir el cheque para el viernes.	I need to receive the check by Friday.
Déme los papeles para mañana.	Give me the papers by tomorrow.
Venga para las diez.	Come by ten o'clock.
Te querré para siempre.	I will love you forever.
Quiero tenerlo para la semana que viene.	I want to have it for next week.

The fourth sentence employs the idiom *forever* in the English translation. The literal meaning of the Spanish is "for always." The last sentence could substitute *by* for the preposition *for*, as could many other possible English sentences that refer to a deadline.

In each sentence, the preposition *para* represents a deadline, a cutoff date, a time you are aiming to reach, not pass through.

Cause: *por*

The box does not have to represent either a physical space or a block of time. It can represent something more abstract, such as the *cause* of the situation in which you find yourself. A cause, naturally, exists before an effect. Picture the arrow inside the box, representing the person or thing in the present situation. Then picture someone with a bow, the cause, who has launched that arrow into the box. See the following examples:

¿Por qué estudia Ud.?	Why do you study?
Estudio porque mis padres insistieron.	I study because my parents insisted (on my studying).

The question "¿Por qué?" asks for the cause of an action or state. This means it looks toward the past. In the example sentence, it asks who or what put the person into the situation of studying. The answer, which uses *porque* (because), names his/her parents' insistence as the cause. There are three possible ways to answer a "¿por qué?" question:

▶ Use *porque* plus a conjugated verb.

▶ Use *por* plus an infinitive verb.

▶ Use *por* plus a noun.

If a reporter were to ask a prisoner "¿Por qué está Ud. aquí?" ("Why are you here?"), the prisoner might answer in three possible ways:

Estoy aquí porque robé.	I'm here because I stole.
Estoy aquí por robar.	I'm here because of stealing.
Estoy aquí por robo.	I'm here for robbery.

The first preceding sentence uses *porque* plus a conjugated verb. The second sentence employs *por* plus an infinitive verb. The third sentence uses *por* plus a noun. In each case, the question and answer look toward the past. First the robbery occurred, then the thief landed in prison: cause and effect.

◀ **SEE ALSO 7.1, *"Present Tense: Regular Verbs"* ▶**

◀ **SEE ALSO 7.3, *"Asking Questions"* ▶**

If the thief were very conscious of grammatical nuances, the second sentence would most likely have used a compound tense:

Estoy aquí por haber robado.	I'm here for having stolen.

◀ **SEE ALSO 11.6, *"Haber Plus Past Participle for Compound Tenses"* ▶**

The last example sentence uses *por* because it comes before the helping verb (*haber*) in its infinitive form.

Aims: *para*

The question "¿Para qué?" does *not* look toward the past. On the contrary, it looks to the future. It could be translated as "Why?," but it would be more apt to translate it as "What for?" or "For what?" The point is, "¿Para qué?" asks for goals, purpose, aims. It asks about what box the arrow is aiming at. It asks about what a person is trying to accomplish. The answer has the preposition *para* in it. See the following examples:

¿Para qué trabajas?	Why (toward what goal) do you work?
Trabajo para vivir.	I work in order to live.
¿Para qué quiere Ud. hablar?	Why do you want to speak? (What do you hope to accomplish by speaking?)
Quiero hablar para persuadirlos.	I want to speak (in order) to persuade them.

Keep in mind that even when referring strictly to aims, goals, or purpose, the preposition *para* can be translated into English in several ways. The English expression "in order to" is an excellent translation, but remember that we usually shorten that expression to a simple *to*. The second preceding English sentence could have been expressed as "I work to live."

This often confuses English-speaking students of Spanish. If you're thinking in English and want to translate the English word *to* into Spanish, you have to try to think in Spanish. Try to grasp the underlying meaning of that *to*. See the following English sentences that use *to* and their Spanish equivalents:

I want to eat.	Quiero comer.
I went to Chicago.	Fui a Chicago.
I study to learn.	Estudio para aprender.

The *to* in the first English sentence here is simply part of the infinitive verb *to eat*, which is expressed by the Spanish infinitive *comer*; no preposition is involved. The *to* in the second English sentence expresses movement toward a destination and is expressed in Spanish by the preposition *a*.

◄ *SEE ALSO 6.1, "Prepositions"* ▶

However, the *to* of the third sentence is really a shortened form of the idiom "in order to." It speaks of what one is trying to accomplish. "I study (in order) to learn" means that my studying has learning as its goal. Learning is what I am aiming at; it's the target of my arrow.

Instrument or Agent: *por*

In some uses of *por*, the concept of the arrow within the box is not immediately obvious, although a deeper analysis will show it does apply. If the metaphor doesn't help you, learning the specific rules will suffice.

The preposition *por* introduces the instrument by which an action is performed or the agent of that action. In these cases, it is usually translated by the English preposition *by*. See the following examples:

Llegué por avión.	I arrived by (air)plane.
Me llamaron por teléfono.	They phoned me. (They called me by phone.)

You could think of the plane and the telephone not merely as instruments of the actions described, but, in a way, as the actual cause. The plane was what got me here—it is the arrow I rode into the box that represents the place where I am now. The telephone was the cause of their communicating with me; it is the instrument that shot their arrow (their message) at me (the box).

Strongly connected with the idea of the inanimate instrument by which something is accomplished is the idea of the human or other living creature being the agent of an action. See the following sentences:

Este libro, escrito por Borges ...	This book, written by Borges ...
Hamlet, por William Shakespeare ...	*Hamlet,* by William Shakespeare ...
La ventana fue rota por unos chicos.	The window was broken by some boys.
Las puertas serán cerradas por el portero.	The doors will be closed by the janitor.

The first, third, and fourth sentences contain past participles. The last two use the passive voice.

◀ *SEE ALSO 11.1, "Forming the Past Participle"* ▶

◀ *SEE ALSO 11.3, "Past Participle in the Passive Voice"* ▶

Exchange: *por*

The preposition *por* is used to mean "for" in the sense of "in exchange for." See the following examples:

Me dio sus zapatos por mi camisa.	He gave me his shoes (in exchange) for my shirt.
Pagué cincuenta por la chaqueta.	I paid fifty dollars for the jacket.

The use of *por* involving exchanges can also be thought of as similar to cause. The cause of my giving him my shirt was his giving me his shoes (or vice versa). The cause of my acquiring the jacket was having paid fifty dollars (or vice versa).

For the Sake of/On Behalf of: *por*

The preposition *por* is used to express "for the sake of" and "on behalf of." See the following examples:

Sacrificó su carrera por ella.	He sacrificed his career for her (for her sake).
Dio la vida por la patria.	He gave his life for (the sake of) his country.
Lo hago por ti.	I'm doing it for you (for your sake).

This use of *por* is closely related to the concept of cause. She was the cause of his giving up his career. She was the thing that propelled him (the arrow) into the situation of forsaking his career (the box). His homeland was the cause of his giving his life; it was the bow that shot him (the arrow) into the situation of giving his life (the box). Consider the following sentence:

Ella no pudo estar; lo acepto por ella.	She couldn't be present; I accept it for her (on her behalf).

Once more, there is a connection to the idea of cause and the concept of "for the sake of." I accept it for her, on her behalf, for her sake, and, ultimately, because of her.

Be aware, however, that a certain type of sentence in English, involving the preposition *for*, could have two possible Spanish translations: one that uses *para* and the other that uses *por*. Context and intent need to be considered. See the following English sentence:

I bought the chair for her.

If the sentence is taken to mean that I bought the chair to present to her as a gift, then we are referring to destination. The chair is destined to be in her possession. It will be going to her. It is being aimed at her, so to speak. The Spanish sentence would be:

Compré la silla para ella.

But if I mean that she was going to buy the chair for someone else, but she couldn't actually make the purchase herself, then I bought the chair *on her behalf*. It's not destined for her. It will be going to other people. The Spanish sentence would be:

Compré la silla por ella.

The same English sentence could come out two different ways in Spanish because the intentions are different. This last sentence (with por) means that I bought the chair on her behalf, for her sake. Once more, translation doesn't help. Understanding the underlying meaning is essential.

6.3

Vague Location: *por*

The preposition *por* is used to indicate a vague location rather than a specific point. When placed before an adverb of location, it implies that the person or thing you're referring to is in the general area. See the following examples:

Esa casa está por aquí.	That house is around here (somewhere).
Lo dejé por allá.	I left it somewhere out there.
Viven por acá.	They live (somewhere) around here.

You can conceptualize this as an arrow sweeping in a circular movement around the inside of the box.

Opinion: *para*

The preposition *para* can be used to indicate an opinion coming from someone. See the following examples:

Para mí, eso no vale nada.	As far as I'm concerned, that isn't worth anything.
Para Carlos, es imposible hacerlo.	In Carlos's opinion, it's impossible to do it.
Para ellos, no es importante.	It's not important to them.

Considering the Fact That ...: *para*

The preposition *para* can be translated by the English preposition *for* with the meaning of "considering the fact that ...." See the following examples:

Para (ser) norteamericanos hablan bien el castellano.	For (being) Americans, they speak Spanish well. (Considering the fact that they are Americans, they speak Spanish well.)
Es muy fuerte para (ser) un hombre tan flaco.	He's very strong for (being) such a thin man.
Para (ser) profesor, no sabe mucho.	Considering the fact that he's a professor, he doesn't know much.

The verb *ser* can follow the preposition or just be understood implicitly.

6.4 PREPOSITIONAL PHRASES

Prepositional phrases are used more often in Spanish than in English to take the place of adverbs. They take the form of a preposition plus noun for this purpose, as well as to show the origin of a person or thing, or to indicate the material of which anything is made. A preposition plus noun or pronoun is also used to indicate possession.

WORDS TO GO . . .WORDS TO GO . . .WORDS TO GO

A **prepositional phrase** is a noun or pronoun preceded by a preposition that indicates the function of the noun or pronoun within the sentence or phrase.

A preposition plus a noun can be used instead of an adverb. See the following examples:

Carlota habla sinceramente.	Carlota speaks sincerely.
Carlota habla con sinceridad.	Carlota speaks with sincerity.
Los estudiantes escuchan atentamente.	The students listen attentively.
Los estudiantes escuchan con atención.	The students listen with attention.

To show origin:

Carlos es de Guatemala.	Carlos is from Guatemala.

To show material:

La casa es de madera.	The house is made of wood.

To show possession:

Esta casa es de Carlos.	This house is Carlos's.
Es de él.	It's his.

◄ SEE ALSO 5.5, *"Possessives"* ▶

◄ SEE ALSO 5.6, *"Adverbs and Adverbial Phrases"* ▶

Chapters 5 and 15 have more detailed explanation, as well as more examples of the uses mentioned here.

7

VERBS: PRESENT TENSE, QUESTIONS, NEGATION

7.1 PRESENT TENSE: REGULAR VERBS

Function of Verb Endings

Regular -ar Verbs

Regular -er Verbs

Regular -ir Verbs

Meanings of the Present Tense

This section introduces you to the Spanish **verb** system. You will learn the meanings of the present tense and how to **conjugate** the present tense of the **regular verbs,** and you'll understand the function of the verb endings.

WORDS TO GO . . .WORDS TO GO . . .WORDS TO GO

A **verb** is a word that expresses action, such as *to walk, to eat, to sleep,* and so on.

To **conjugate** a verb is to give the verb its various forms, such as *I go, she goes,* and so on.

Regular verbs are verbs that are conjugated the way most verbs are conjugated. They follow the usual pattern.

Function of Verb Endings

The purpose of conjugating a verb is to specify and establish agreement with **person,** number, and **tense.** When Spanish verbs are conjugated, specific endings are attached to the verb **stem** that provide information about who the subject of the verb is (person), whether the subject is singular or plural, and whether the action of the verb occurs in the present, all the time, in the past, or in the future. Understanding how to conjugate verbs is indispensable.

WORDS TO GO . . .WORDS TO GO . . .WORDS TO GO

Person refers to first person (I, we), second person (you), and third person (he, she, it, they).

Tense refers to the action of the verb taking place in the past, present, or future.

Stem refers to the part of the verb that remains after the infinitive ending is removed. A verb that undergoes changes in the stem is called a "stem-changing" or "radically changing" verb.

To conjugate accurately (place the correct endings on the verbs), it is essential to know that all Spanish verbs fall into one of three types of conjugations. The conjugation to which a verb belongs depends on whether the **infinitive** form ends with an *-ar*, an *-er*, or an *-ir*.

WORDS TO GO . . .WORDS TO GO . . .WORDS TO GO

Infinitive is the unconjugated form of the verb. In English, all infinitives start with the word *to,* as in *to walk, to eat, to sleep,* and so on. In Spanish, all infinitives end with a vowel plus *-r.*

Regular *-ar* Verbs

Most verbs in Spanish have the infinitive ending of *-ar*. This is technically labeled the first conjugation. To conjugate a regular *-ar* verb, remove the infinitive ending (*-ar*), leaving the verb stem, and attach the ending that indicates person, number, and tense (in this case, present).

The following table shows how a typical *-ar* verb is conjugated in the present tense. The endings for *él*, *ella*, and *usted* are always exactly the same, no matter what verb or tense. Likewise, the endings for *ellos*, *ellas*, and *ustedes* are always the same.

7.1

REGULAR PRESENT TENSE OF *-AR* VERBS USING *HABLAR* (TO SPEAK)

Subject Pronoun	Verb Stem	Ending	Conjugated
yo	habl-	-o	hablo
tú	habl-	-as	hablas
él	habl-	-a	habla
ella	habl-	-a	habla
usted	habl-	-a	habla
nosotros/as	habl-	-amos	hablamos
vosotros/as	habl-	-áis	habláis
ellos	habl-	-an	hablan
ellas	habl-	-an	hablan
ustedes	habl-	-an	hablan

The verb endings are extremely important—much more so in Spanish than English—because in Spanish, the subject pronouns are usually left out. The verb endings tell us precisely who the subject is, so there is no need for a subject pronoun. See the following examples:

hablo	I speak.
hablas	You speak. (We can tell that this "you" is singular and familiar.)
hablamos	We speak.
habláis	You speak. (We can tell that this "you" is plural and familiar.)

In the other cases, at least we can tell that it is the third person and specify whether it is singular or plural. If the subject has already been mentioned (*él, ella, usted, ellos, ellas, ustedes,* or someone's name), there is no need to repeat it. For example, if we were just referring to Carlos, and someone adds, "Habla mucho," we know that it is Carlos who talks a lot. If we were just talking about your brother and sister, and someone says, "Hablan mucho," we understand that it is your brother and sister who talk a lot.

The subject pronoun is certainly used whenever clarity or emphasis is needed. Note the use of the subject pronoun for clarity in the following sentences:

Ustedes hablan bien.	You (pl.) (not they) speak well.
Ellos hablan bien.	They (not you) speak well.
Ella habla bien.	She (not he, not you) speaks well.

Note the use of the subject pronoun for emphasis in the following sentences:

Yo hablo bien.	*I* speak well. (not someone else)
Tú hablas bien.	*You* speak well. (not I, not they)

Placing the subject pronoun at the end of the sentence gives even greater emphasis or distinction:

Hablo bien yo.	I'm the one who speaks well.
Hablas bien tú.	You're the one who speaks well.

◄ SEE ALSO 4.1, *"Subject Pronouns"* ▶

To further familiarize yourself, study the following sample list of conjugated, regular, present-tense *-ar* verbs:

cantar (to sing): (yo) canto, (tú) cantas, (él) canta, (ella) canta, (usted) canta, (nosotros) cantamos, (vosotros) cantáis, (ellos) cantan, (ellas) cantan, (ustedes) cantan

mirar (to look [at]): (yo) miro, (tú) miras, (él) mira, (ella) mira, (usted) mira, (nosotros) miramos, (vosotros) miráis, (ellos) miran, (ellas) miran, (ustedes) miran

buscar (to look [for]): (yo) busco, (tú) buscas, (él) busca, (ella) busca, (usted) busca, (nosotros) buscamos, (vosotros) buscáis, (ellos) buscan, (ellas) buscan, (ustedes) buscan

viajar (to travel): (yo) viajo, (tú) viajas, (él) viaja, (ella) viaja, (usted) viaja, (nosotros) viajamos, (vosotros) viajáis, (ellos) viajan, (ellas) viajan, (ustedes) viajan

Regular -er Verbs

The second most numerous class of Spanish verbs has the infinitive ending -er. This class of verbs is called the second conjugation. The following table shows how a typical -er verb is conjugated in the present tense.

7.1

PRESENT TENSE OF -ER VERBS USING CREER (TO BELIEVE, THINK)

Subject Pronoun	Verb Stem	Ending	Conjugated Verb
yo	cre-	-o	creo
tú	cre-	-es	crees
él	cre-	-e	cree
ella	cre-	-e	cree
usted	cre-	-e	cree
nosotros	cre-	-emos	creemos
vosotros	cre-	-éis	creéis
ellos	cre-	-en	creen
ellas	cre-	-en	creen
ustedes	cre-	-en	creen

To further familiarize yourself, review the following sample list of conjugated, regular, present-tense -er verbs:

comer (to eat): (yo) como, (tú) comes, (él) come, (ella) come, (usted) come, (nosotros) comemos, (vosotros) coméis, (ellos) comen, (ellas) comen, (ustedes) comen

leer (to read): (yo) leo, (tú) lees, (él) lee, (ella) lee, (usted) lee, (nosotros) leemos, (vosotros) leéis, (ellos) leen, (ellas) leen, (ustedes) leen

beber (to drink): (yo) bebo, (tú) bebes, (él) bebe, (ella) bebe, (usted) bebe, (nosotros) bebemos, (vosotros) bebéis, (ellos) beben, (ellas) beben, (ustedes) beben

Regular *-ir* Verbs

A third class of Spanish verbs has the infinitive ending *-ir*; these are called the third conjugation. The following table shows how a typical *-ir* verb is conjugated in the present tense.

PRESENT TENSE OF *-IR* VERBS USING *RECIBIR* (TO RECEIVE)

Subject Pronoun	Verb Stem	Ending	Conjugated Verb
yo	recib-	-o	recibo
tú	recib-	-es	recibes
él	recib-	-e	recibe
ella	recib-	-e	recibe
usted	recib-	-e	recibe
nosotros	recib-	-imos	recibimos
vosotros	recib-	-ís	recibís
ellos	recib-	-en	reciben
ellas	recib-	-en	reciben
ustedes	recib-	-en	reciben

The endings for *-er* verbs and *-ir* verbs in the present tense are identical in all persons—*except* for *nosotros* and *vosotros*. The *-er* verb endings for these persons are *-emos* and *-éis*; the *-ir* verb endings for these persons are *-imos* and *-ís*.

Review the following list of conjugated, regular, present-tense *-ir* verbs.

vivir (to live): (yo) vivo, (tú) vives, (él) vive, (ella) vive, (usted) vive, (nosotros) vivimos, (vosotros) vivís, (ellos) viven, (ellas) viven, (ustedes) viven

decidir (to decide): (yo) decido, (tú) decides, (él) decide, (ella) decide, (usted) decide, (nosotros) decidimos, (vosotros) decidís, (ellos) deciden, (ellas) deciden, (ustedes) deciden

escribir (to write): (yo) escribo, (tú) escribes, (él) escribe, (ella) escribe, (usted) escribe, (nosotros) escribimos, (vosotros) escribís, (ellos) escriben, (ellas) escriben, (ustedes) escriben

Meanings of the Present Tense

The meanings of the present tense may seem self-evident, but don't be misled! You may also assume that the present tense in Spanish means the same as the present tense in English; this, too, would be misleading.

The term "present tense" as it applies to English is a misnomer. When you say "I watch TV," you aren't referring to what you're doing right now; you're referring to what you usually do. By the same token, if we want to know what someone is doing right now, we don't ask, "What do you do?" Instead, we ask, "What are you doing?"

The Spanish use of the present tense can have several meanings. Depending on the situation, these Spanish sentences could be translated in one of several ways:

Customary behavior (same as in English):

Trabajo.   I work.

True present (what is happening right now):

Trabajo.   I'm working.

Confession or insistence:

Trabajo.   I do work.

Near future (as in English):

Trabajo mañana.   I work tomorrow.

The meaning of the true present (the second sentence of the preceding group), "can be insisted upon," can emphasize the ongoing aspect by using the present tense of *estar* plus the present participle.

◀ *SEE ALSO 10.1, "Forming the Present Participle"* ▶

You will notice that the first and last sentences are used very much as we use the present tense in English, but the second and third sentences do not correspond to English usage.

7.2 PRESENT TENSE: IRREGULAR VERBS

Stem-Changing Verbs

Changes Applying to First Person Singular

Verbs with Interposed -y-

The Verb ver

Other Verbs with Irregular yo Form

You have already learned to conjugate regular verbs in the present tense. In this section, you learn how to use various types of irregular verbs in the present tense.

Stem-Changing Verbs

One type of irregularity in the conjugation of present-tense Spanish verbs affects the verb stem. Some grammar books use a different part of the plant to describe this part of the verb in question: the root.

From *e* to *ie*

One type of stem-changing verb contains the vowel *e* in the stem, which, for all forms of the present tense—except the *nosotros* and the *vosotros* forms—changes to the diphthong *ie*. See the following table for examples of these verbs' conjugation in the present tense. (In the table, *él* represents itself as well as *ella* and *usted*. The abbreviations N. and V. represent *nosotros* and *vosotros*, respectively. *Ellos* represents itself as well as *ellas* and *ustedes*.)

PRESENT TENSE OF *E* TO *IE* STEM-CHANGING VERBS

Pronoun	Cerrar (to close)	Perder (to lose)	Querer (to want)	Sentir (to feel)
yo	cierro	pierdo	quiero	siento
tú	cierras	pierdes	quieres	sientes
él	cierra	pierde	quiere	siente
N.	cerramos	perdemos	queremos	sentimos
V.	cerráis	perdéis	queréis	sentís
ellos	cierran	pierden	quieren	sienten

As you can see from the preceding table, all three conjugations (*-ar*, *-er*, *-ir*) have some verbs with this type of stem change.

◀ *SEE ALSO 7.1, "Present Tense: Regular Verbs"* ▶

The verb *querer* (to want), when taking a human being as object, usually means "to love." In fact, it is the most common Spanish verb used to mean "to love."

See this list of other common verbs that have a stem change of *e* to *ie:*

pensar (ie) (to think): pienso, piensas, piensa, pensamos, pensáis, piensan

comenzar (ie) (to begin): comienzo, comienzas, comienza, comenzamos, comenzáis, comienzan

empezar (ie) (to begin): empiezo, empiezas, empieza, empezamos, empezáis, comienzan

From this point on, verbs that have a stem change *e* to *ie,* when given as a vocabulary item, will show "(ie)" after the infinitive.

From *e* to *i*

In some verbs, the stem vowel *e* changes in all forms—except the *nosotros* and *vosotros* forms—to the vowel *i.* See the following table for examples of their conjugation in the present tense:

7.2

PRESENT TENSE OF *E* TO *I* STEM-CHANGING VERBS

Pronoun	pedir (to ask for)	medir (to measure)	elegir (to choose)	reir (to laugh)
yo	pido	mido	elijo	río
tú	pides	mides	eliges	ríes
él	pide	mide	elige	ríe
N.	pedimos	medimos	elegimos	reímos
V.	pedís	medís	elegís	reís
ellos	piden	miden	eligen	ríen

The first-person singular of *elegir* (*elijo*) contains the letter *j* instead of the letter *g* to preserve the correct sound.

◀ *SEE ALSO 1.3, "The Spelling System"* ▶

Here's a list of other common verbs that have a stem change of *e* to *i:*

gemir (i) (to moan, groan): gimo, gimes, gime, gemimos, gemís, gimen.

freír (i) (to fry): frío, fríes, fríe, freímos, freís, fríen

reñir (i) (to scold; quarrel; to fight): riño, riñes, riñe, reñimos, reñís, riñen

From this point on, verbs that have a stem change of e to i, when given as a vocabulary item, will show "(i)" after the infinitive.

From *o* to *ue*

One type of stem-changing verb contains the vowel o in the stem, which, for all forms of the present tense—except the *nosotros* and the *vosotros* forms—changes to the diphthong *ue*. See the following table for examples of their conjugation in the present tense:

PRESENT TENSE OF *O* TO *UE* STEM-CHANGING VERBS

Pronoun	sonar (to sound)	poder (to be able)	dormir (to sleep)	morir (to die)
yo	sueno	puedo	duermo	muero
tú	suenas	puedes	duermes	mueres
él	suena	puede	duerme	muere
N.	sonamos	podemos	dormimos	morimos
V.	sonáis	podéis	dormís	morís
ellos	suenan	pueden	duermen	mueren

From this point on, verbs with a stem change o to *ue*, when given as a vocabulary item, will show "(ue)" after the infinitive.

Here's a list of other common verbs that have a stem change of o to *ue*:

soñar (ue) (to dream): sueño, sueñas, sueña, soñamos, soñáis, sueñan

soler (ue) (to be in the habit of; to be accustomed to): suelo, sueles, suele, solemos, soléis, suelen

colar (ue) (to seep; to strain ([liquid]); to percolate): cuelo, cuelas, cuela, colamos, coláis, cuelen

oler (ue) (to smell): The verb *oler*, as in the case of any other verb that would have the o change to *ue* in the first syllable, would, in the present tense, have the first syllable spelled *hue-* and would be conjugated *huelo, hueles, huele, olemos, oléis, huelen*. Because the letter *h* is silent, this is simply a Spanish convention.

From *u* to *ue*

Only one verb in the Spanish language changes the consonant *u* to the diphthong *ue* for all forms of the present tense except *nosotros* and *vosotros*. This unique verb is *jugar* (ue) (to play), and it's conjugated like this:

jugar: juego, juegas, juega, jugamos, jugáis, juegan

This verb refers to playing games (sports, board games, playing with toys, and so on), not playing a musical instrument or a radio or a CD.

Changes Applying to First Person Singular

In some groups of verbs, the *yo* form alone is irregular.

Yo Form Ends in *-oy*

In a small group of verbs, the *yo* form of the present tense is irregular in the sense that, instead of ending with *-o*, it ends with *-oy*.

VERBS IN WHICH THE FIRST-PERSON SINGULAR OF THE PRESENT TENSE ENDS WITH *-OY*

Pronoun	ir (to go)	dar (to give)	estar (to be)	ser (to be)
yo	voy	doy	estoy	soy
tú	vas	das	estás	eres
él	va	da	está	es
N.	vamos	damos	estamos	somos
V.	vais	dais	estáis	sois
ellos	van	dan	están	son

In the case of *dar*, the present tense is completely regular except for the *yo* form; it is the only irregularity. The other verbs are irregular throughout, although some more than others. In addition to the *yo* form of *ir* having the *-oy* ending, the other forms don't look or sound anything like the infinitive. Yet once you arrive at the tú form (*vas*), the others are what you would expect to follow.

In addition to the *-oy* ending of the *yo* form of *estar*, the other forms are technically irregular only because of the stress (accentuation) on the last syllable (except, of course, for the *nosotros* form).

As you can see, the verb *ser* is completely irregular, like the very irregular English verb *to be* (be, am, is, are).

You may be wondering why there are two Spanish verbs in the table with the same meaning: "to be." They may both translate into English as the same verb, but in Spanish they have separate purposes. An entire chapter is devoted to the difference in use between these two verbs.

◄ SEE ALSO 15.2, *"Two Forms of Being:* ser *vs.* estar" ►

Yo Form Ending with *-zco*

Another group of verbs have, in the present tense, the irregularity of ending with the letters *-zco* in the yo form of the verb. The only irregularity for these verbs occurs in the yo form; the other forms are completely regular. See the following table for examples:

VERBS IN WHICH THE FIRST-PERSON SINGULAR OF THE PRESENT TENSE ENDS WITH *-ZCO*

Pronoun	conocer (to know)	producir (to produce)	crecer (to grow)
yo	conozco	produzco	crezco
tú	conoces	produces	creces
él	conoce	produce	crece
N.	conocemos	producimos	crecemos
V.	conocéis	producís	crecéis
ellos	conocen	producen	crecen

Here's a list of other common verbs in which the yo form of the present tense ends with the letters *-zco*:

ofrecer (to offer): ofrezco, ofreces, and so on.

obedecer (to obey): obedezco, obedeces, and so on.

parecer (to appear, to seem): parezco, pareces, and so on.

reconocer (to recognize): reconozco, reconoces, and so on.

traducir (to translate): traduzco, traduces, and so on.

nacer (to be born): nazco, naces, and so on.

Many of the *-zco* verbs have the infinitive ending *-cer*. But there are also several verbs like *producir* and *traducir*, whose infinitive also ends with *-ducir* and are related to verbs such as *conducir* (to conduct, to lead, to drive), *reducir* (to reduce), *seducir* (to seduce), *reducir* (to reduce), *deducir* (to deduce; to deduct), and so on. The yo form of all these verbs in the present tense ends with *-zco*.

Yo Form Ending with *-go*

Some verbs end with the letters *-go* in the present tense, only in the *yo* form. Some of these are completely regular in the other persons, but others have further peculiarities, such as belonging to the *e* to *ie* stem-change verbs or the *e* to *i* stem-change verbs. See the following table for verbs ending with *-go* that are also stem changing:

STEM-CHANGING VERBS IN WHICH THE FIRST-PERSON SINGULAR OF THE PRESENT TENSE ENDS IN *-GO*

Pronoun	tener (to have)	venir (to come)	decir (to say, tell)
yo	tengo	vengo	digo
tú	tienes	vienes	dices
él	tiene	viene	dice
N.	tenemos	venimos	decimos
V.	tenéis	venís	decís
ellos	tienen	vienen	dicen

Both *tener* and *venir* have a stem change, except in the *yo* form, from *e* to *ie*, while *decir* has the stem change from *e* to *i*. In each case, a *g* is **interposed** between the stem and the *-o* ending of the *yo* form.

WORDS TO GO . . .WORDS TO GO . . .WORDS TO GO

To **interpose** is to insert something between one item and another.

The next table shows verbs in which the *yo* form has an interposed *g* between the stem and the *-o* ending, but every other person (with one small exception) is completely regular. The small exception is that, in addition to the interposed *-g-* in the *yo* form of the verb *caer*, the letter *-i-* is inserted between the stem and the *-g-*.

OTHERWISE REGULAR VERBS IN WHICH THE FIRST-PERSON SINGULAR OF THE PRESENT TENSE ENDS WITH -GO

Pronoun	hacer (to do, make)	poner (to put)	salir (to leave)	caer (to fall)
yo	hago	pongo	salgo	caigo
tú	haces	pones	sales	cae
él	hace	pone	sale	cae
N.	hacemos	ponemos	salimos	caemos
V.	hacéis	ponéis	salís	caéis
ellos	hacen	ponen	salen	caen

The verb *valer* is conjugated like *salir: valgo, vales, vale,* and so on. In the case of *hacer,* the *c* is converted into a *g* in the *yo* form. In the cases of *poner* and *salir,* a -*g*- is interposed.

The verb *salir* does not mean "to leave" in the sense of leaving things or people where they are. That verb is *dejar* (which is perfectly regular) and is a near synonym of *abandonar* (to abandon). But *dejar* also has the meaning of "to let, allow." The verb *salir* means "to leave" only in the sense of "to go out of." In other words, "He leaves his wife" would be "Deja a su esposa" or "Abandona a su esposa." "He leaves (goes out of) the house" would be "Sale de la casa."

The verb *traer* (to bring) and its derivatives, *retraer* (to bring again, bring back; dissuade; retract), *atraer* (to attract, pull toward oneself), *detraer* (to detract, take away; defame, vilify), *sustraer* or *substraer* (to remove, take away; deduct, subtract; rob, steal), contraer (to contract), and so on are all conjugated like *caer* in the table.

Verbs with Interposed -y-

Another group of verbs, when conjugated, has an interposed -*y*- between the stem and present-tense endings (except in the *nosotros* and *vosotros* forms). This table shows the conjugations of this kind of verb:

PRESENT TENSE OF VERBS CONTAINING AN INTERPOSED -y-

Pronoun	construir (to build)	influir (to influence)	oír (to hear)
yo	construyo	influyo	oigo
tú	construyes	influyes	oyes
él	construye	influye	oye
N.	construimos	influimos	oímos
V.	construís	influís	oís
ellos	construyen	influyen	oyen

The verb *oír* has an additional peculiarity: the *yo* form does not have an interposed -y- but does have the letter *i* followed by the letter *g* between the stem and the ending.

All verbs whose infinitive ends with -*uir* follow the same pattern as *construir* and *influir*. Their relationship with English is obvious. Some others are in the following list:

concluir (to conclude, to end, to finish): concluyo, concluyes, and so on.

destruir (to destroy): destruyo, destruyes, and so on.

obstruir (to obstruct): obstruyo, obstruyes, and so on.

instruir (to instruct): instruyo, instruyes, and so on.

The Verb *ver*

Strictly speaking, the verb *ver* (to see) is irregular. This is because, when conjugated, it drops only the -*r* of the infinitive; it does *not* drop the -*e*-. It is conjugated as follows:

ver (to see): veo, ves, ve, vemos, veis, ven

Other Verbs with Irregular *yo* Form

Several other verbs of the present tense have an irregularity in the *yo* form of the verb only. All other forms are perfectly regular:

caber (to fit): quepo, cabes, cabe, and so on

saber (to know): sé, sabes, sabe, and so on

7.2

7.3 ASKING QUESTIONS

Eliciting Yes or No Answers

Using Interrogative Words

In this section, you learn how to ask questions. This involves sentence structure, **intonation,** and interrogative words such as *why, what, when, who,* and so on.

WORDS TO GO . . . WORDS TO GO . . . WORDS TO GO

Intonation refers to the rise and fall of voice pitch to convey various types of meaning.

Eliciting Yes or No Answers

English sentence structure is very rigid. It depends on this formula:

Subject + Verb + Object

Spanish sentence structure is very flexible.

Sentence Structure

The most typical way of asking a yes/no question is to reverse the order of the subject and verb.

Usted habla italiano.	You speak Italian.
¿Habla usted italiano?	Do you speak Italian?

However, because the sentence structure of Spanish is so flexible, the subject can come before the verb (as in English), right after the verb, or at the end of the sentence. Keep in mind that you can often dispense with the subject altogether, if the context makes it clear.

You notice that in Spanish questions are written with an upside-down question mark at the beginning and a regular question mark at the end.

You could just as well make the statement reversing the order of subject and verb, and ask the question starting with the subject:

¿Usted habla italiano?	Do you speak Italian?
Habla usted italiano.	You speak Italian.

The English sentence "Do they eat a great deal of meat?" could be asked in various ways:

¿Comen ellos mucha carne?

¿Ellos comen mucha carne?

¿Comen mucha carne ellos?

¿Comen mucha carne?

In the last sentence, the subject pronoun is completely left out.

Conversely, any of these four sentences could be used as a statement of fact. Keep in mind that, in Spanish, whatever comes toward the end of a sentence has more emphasis placed on it. This means that of the four preceding sentences— whether used as a question or as a statement—the first one places the emphasis on *carne* (meat). The second sentence does the same. The third sentence stresses *ellos*. The last one places the emphasis once more on *carne*.

Obviously, the sentence structure alone is not a foolproof way of determining whether a sentence is a statement or a question.

Intonation

The determining factor—at least, in speech—is the intonation. In writing, of course, the signal is in the punctuation: the inverted question mark before the question and the normal one at the end.

In oral delivery, the intonation indicating a question that demands a yes or no answer is, as in English, a rising one. However, the rise isn't as drastic as in English. The rise typically occurs on the last stressed syllable.

Using Interrogative Words

Just as in English, a question that uses an interrogative word does *not* end with a rising pitch. It has the same intonation as a statement. However, to ask this kind of question, you must know the interrogative words. The following table provides the Spanish interrogative words with their English equivalents:

Spanish Interrogative	English Equivalent
¿Qué?	What?
¿Quién?	Who(m)? (singular)
¿Quiénes?	Who(m)? (plural)
¿Cómo?	How?

continues...

(continued)

Spanish Interrogative	English Equivalent
¿Dónde?	Where?
¿Cuál?	Which (one)? (singular)
¿Cuáles?	Which (ones)? (plural)
¿Cuándo?	When?
¿Cuánto/a?	How much?
¿Cuántos/as?	How many?
¿Por qué?	Why? (cause)
¿Para qué?	What for? (goal, purpose)

The Spanish interrogatives for *who(m)* and for *which (one)* have a singular and a plural form. The plural *quiénes* is used when referring to more than one person. The plural *cuáles* is used when referring to more than one item.

Cuánto is an adjective that in the masculine form ends with *-o*. Therefore, it has four possible endings.

The difference in use between ¿*por qué?* and ¿*para qué?* specifically involves the difference in meaning and use of *por* as opposed to *para*.

◀ SEE ALSO 6.3, "Uses of **por** *and* **para**" ▷

You will notice in the table that every one of the interrogative words has a written accent. You should also remember that those words follow the rules of accentuation and, therefore, according to those rules, need no accent mark.

The reason for the accent marks is just a spelling convention. The interrogative words are also used as the answers to questions. When they are used to answer questions, they do not take the written accent. When they truly ask questions, they do. See the following examples:

¿Cómo puedo hacer eso?	How can I do that?
Puedes hacerlo como yo.	You can do it as I do it. ("like me")

In the first sentence, the word *cómo* is actually asking a question (how); therefore, it bears an accent mark on the vowel that would automatically be stressed even without the mark. In the second sentence, *como* is part of the answer to the question (as, like) and therefore does not have a written accent. See the following sentences:

El libro que tengo …	The book that I have …
Quien no come, no vive.	Who(ever) does not eat, does not live.
Come como un puerco.	He eats like a pig.
Está donde lo dejé.	It's where I left it.
La mesa, la cual es muy grande,	The table, which is very large,
Me llaman cuando llegan.	They call me when they arrive.
Lo hago porque quiero.	I do it because I want to.
Lo digo para que ustedes entiendan.	I say it so that you will understand.

The preceding sentences all contain interrogative words without written punctuation; this is because they are being used not to ask questions, but rather to answer them or make statements.

The next-to-last sentence has the word *porque*. When the question *¿por qué?* becomes the answer (because), it is written as one word and loses the accent mark.

The last sentence has an *-er* verb—*entender* (ie)—which has the vowel *a* in the ending rather than the expected *e*. This is because it is not in the present indicative tense, but is in the present subjunctive, which we'll talk about in subsequent chapters.

◁ **SEE ALSO 13.1, *"Formation of Regular Present Subjunctive"* ▷**

When the Spanish interrogative word is used to ask a question, sometimes the English equivalent of that question word is different from the English word used to translate that same Spanish word when it makes a statement (as in the first and third example sentences). In other cases, the English translation uses the same word in both cases (as in the fourth and sixth example sentences).

7.4 NEGATIVE AND POSITIVE LANGUAGE

Negative and Positive Expressions

Negative Sentence Structure

Every language has its own way of expressing the positive and the negative. There are ways to turn a positive statement into a negative one. Certain individual words and phrases convey positive ideas or negative ones. In this section, you learn to change positive statements into negative ones.

Negative and Positive Expressions

Translation often does not explain the true meaning and use of a word or expression. Because of this, the following table shows the positive Spanish expression alongside its opposite (negative) counterpart, in addition to the English equivalent.

SPANISH POSITIVE AND NEGATIVE EXPRESSIONS

Positive Spanish	English	Negative Spanish	English
sí	yes	no	no
alguien	someone	nadie	no one
algo	something	nada	nothing
alguno/a/os/as	some	ninguno/a/os/as	no, none
todo/a/os/as	all, every		
siempre	always	nunca	never
todo el tiempo	all the time	jamás	never
a veces	at times		
algunas veces	some times		
de vez en cuando	occasionally		
de cuando en cuando	once in a while		
de vez en vez	from time to time		

The words *nunca* and *jamás* are synonyms, but *nunca* is used much more frequently. The combination *nunca jamás* is a very emphatic expression, equivalent to the English combination *never ever*.

The last five expressions in the preceding list are synonyms; there are no real differences in meaning among them, just like their English counterparts. Those five positive expressions, plus *siempre* and *todo el tiempo*, even though different in meaning, are the opposite of the negative *nunca* and *jamás*.

The list includes two positive adjectives: *alguno* and *todo*. This is why they have four possible endings. Their negative opposite, *ninguno*, is also an adjective and, for the same reason, theoretically has four possible endings. But good usage dictates that the plural form of *ninguno/a* not be used, because the true meaning is "not one," and logically there can't be a plural to a zero.

◀ *SEE ALSO 5.2, "Adjectives in Agreement"* ▶

A fifth form exists for the adjectives *alguno* and *ninguno*. When either one of them is placed before a masculine, singular noun, these adjectives are shortened by dropping the final *-o*. The rules of accentuation then make it necessary to place an accent mark over the *-u-*.

Be careful, though! This happens only if the following three conditions are met:

7.4

1. One of these adjectives is placed *in front*
2. of a *singular,*
3. *masculine* noun.

See these examples of *alguno* used with nouns:

algún hombre	some man
algunos hombres	some men
alguna mujer	some woman
algunas mujeres	some women

You can see from the preceding table that the Spanish *no* is the negative of *sí*. This means that if you want to say "No human can fly," you do not say "No humano puede volar." This is not Spanish. You use the opposite of *alguno* and say "Ningún humano puede volar."

Negative Sentence Structure

A basic rule is this: In Spanish, any negative statement must have a negative word *before* the verb. No matter what comes after the verb, that rule must always be obeyed.

General Negation

The most basic way to turn a positive statement into a negative one in Spanish is simply to place the word *no* in front of the verb. See the following examples:

María viene pronto.   María is coming soon.

María no viene pronto.   María is not coming soon.

Tengo mucho tiempo.   I have a lot of time.

No tengo mucho tiempo.   I don't have a lot of time.

Specific Negation

Often, as in English, you will want to use a very specific negative word or expression, like the ones listed in the preceding table on the negative column (the third column). In that case, you have a choice:

You can place that *specific* negative word or expression in front of the verb. See the following examples:

Nada tengo.	I have nothing./I don't have anything.
Nunca voy al cine.	I never go to the movies./ I don't ever go to the movies.
Ningún hombre sabe hacerlo.	No man knows how to do it.
Nadie quiere salir.	No one wants to leave.

Or you can place the *general* negative word (*no*) in front of the verb, and the *specific* negative word or expression after the verb. See the following examples:

No tengo nada.	I have nothing./I don't have anything.
No voy al cine nunca.	I never go to the movies./ I don't ever go to the movies.
No sabe hacerlo ningún hombre.	No man knows how to do it.
No quiere salir nadie.	No one wants to leave.

Double negatives are perfectly correct in Spanish.

In the last two sentences, it is not only a matter of placing the specific negative word after the verbs (*sabe hacerlo*; *quiere salir*), it is also part of the flexible Spanish sentence structure in which the subject can go before or after the verb.

Always remember that, in a negative statement, some negative word or expression must always be placed *before* the verb, no matter what comes after it.

8

VERBS: PRETERIT AND IMPERFECT PAST TENSES

8.1 PRETERIT TENSE: REGULAR VERBS

Regular Preterit *-ar* Verbs

Regular *-er* Verbs

Regular *-ir* Verbs

The **preterit tense** of verbs is used to indicate that a specific action took place—began and ended—in the past.

In this section, you learn how to form the regular preterit tense. The term *regular* refers to the fact that most verbs in any given tense are conjugated in this manner. Using this tense will enable you to refer to events that took place in the past.

WORDS TO GO . . . *WORDS TO GO* . . . *WORDS TO GO*

Preterit tense refers to an action, event, or state that was completed at some point in the past. The Spanish word for this tense is *pretérito*.

In addition to the endings on the preterit verbs being different from the endings of the present tense, there is a difference in stress. Whereas the stress falls on the next-to-last syllable in the present tense, except for the vosotros forms, this is not the case with the regular preterit forms. The regular preterit tense in the yo, él, ella, and usted forms stress the last syllable.

Regular Preterit *-ar* Verbs

Just as in the present tense, we form the preterit tense by first removing the last two letters of the infinitive verb. To conjugate a regular *-ar* verb in the preterit tense, remove the infinitive ending (*-ar*), leaving the verb stem, and attach the ending that indicates person, number, and tense.

The following table will help you understand the various forms of the regular preterit *-ar* verbs.

REGULAR PRETERIT TENSE OF *-AR* VERBS USING *HABLAR* (TO SPEAK)

Subject Pronoun	Verb Stem	Ending	Conjugated Verb
yo	habl-	-é	hablé
tú	habl-	-aste	hablaste
él	habl-	-ó	habló
nosotros	habl-	-amos	hablamos
vosotros	habl-	-asteis	hablasteis
ellos	habl-	-aron	hablaron

Note that the *nosotros* form of the preterit tense of *-ar* verbs is exactly the same as the *nosotros* form of the present tense. This is not a problem; meaning is easy to infer from the context. We have similar situations in English—for example, "I hurt right now" and "I hurt myself yesterday."

In the preceding table, as in conjugation tables throughout the rest of this book, the pronoun *él* is used to represent itself plus *ella* and *usted*. The pronoun *ellos* is used to represent itself plus *ellas* and *ustedes*.

The following list shows four sample conjugated regular preterit-tense *-ar* verbs:

8.1

> **cantar** (to sing): canté, cantaste, cantó, cantamos, cantasteis, cantaron.
>
> **mirar** (to look at): miré, miraste, miró, miramos, mirasteis, miraron
>
> **buscar** (to look for): busqué, buscaste, buscó, buscamos, buscasteis, buscaron
>
> **viajar** (to travel): viajé, viajaste, viajó, viajamos, viajasteis, viajaron

Notice the spelling of *busqué* above.

◄ *SEE ALSO 1.3, "The Spelling System"* ▷

Regular *-er* Verbs

Just as in the present tense, we form the preterit tense by first removing the last two letters of the infinitive verb. To conjugate a regular *-er* verb in the preterit tense, remove the infinitive ending (*-er*), leaving the verb stem, and attach the ending that indicates person, number, and tense (preterit).

The following table shows the various forms of the regular preterit *-er* verbs.

REGULAR PRETERIT TENSE OF -*ER* VERBS USING *COMER* (TO EAT)

Subject Pronoun	Verb Stem	Ending	Conjugated Verb
yo	com-	-í	comí
tú	com-	-iste	comiste
él	com-	-ió	comió
nosotros	com-	-imos	comimos
vosotros	com-	-isteis	comisteis
ellos	com-	-ieron	comieron

Unlike -*ar* and -*ir* verbs, the *nosotros* form of -*er* verbs in the preterit tense is different from its form in the present tense.

Below is a list of sample regular preterit-tense -*er* verbs conjugated:

beber (to drink): bebí, bebiste, bebió, bebimos, bebisteis, bebieron

coger (to take, seize): cogí, cogiste, cogió, cogimos, cogisteis, cogieron

escoger (to choose, select): escogí, escogiste, escogió, escogimos, escogisteis, escogieron

conocer (to know, be acquainted with): conocí, conociste, conocimos, conocisteis, conocieron

mover (to move [something]): moví, moviste, movió, movimos, movisteis, movieron

Regular -*ir* Verbs

Just as in the present tense, we form the preterit tense by first removing the last two letters of the infinitive verb. To conjugate a regular -*ir* verb in the preterit tense, remove the infinitive ending (-*ir*), leaving the verb stem, and attach the ending that indicates person, number, and tense (preterit).

The following table provides the various forms of the regular preterit -*er* verbs.

REGULAR PRETERIT TENSE OF -*IR* VERBS USING *VIVIR* (TO LIVE)

Subject Pronoun	Verb Stem	Ending	Conjugated Verb
yo	viv-	-í	viví
tú	viv-	-iste	viviste
él	viv-	-ió	vivió
nosotros	viv-	-imos	vivimos
vosotros	viv-	-isteis	vivisteis
ellos	viv-	-ieron	vivieron

The *nosotros* form of the preterit tense of *-ir* verbs has an ending identical to the ending it had in the present tense. Context clarifies the meaning.

The following list shows a sample of regular preterit-tense *-ir* verbs conjugated.

salir (to leave, go out): salí, saliste, salió, salimos, salisteis, salieron

escribir (to write): escribí, escribiste, escribió, escribimos, escribisteis, escribieron

sufrir (to suffer): sufrí, sufriste, sufrió, sufrimos, sufristeis, sufrieron

recibir (to receive): recibí, recibiste, recibió, recibimos, recibisteis, recibieron

See the verbs listed here:

describir (to describe)

inscribir (to inscribe)

reescribir (to rewrite)

proscribir (to proscribe, to outlaw)

Just as in the present tense, all verbs based on *escribir* are conjugated the way *escribir* is in all tenses.

8.1

8.2 PRETERIT TENSE: IRREGULAR VERBS

-u- Verbs

-duj- Verbs

Other Verbs Containing *-j-*

Internal *-i-* Verbs

Verbs with Interposed *-y-*

The Verb *decir*

Stem Changers

Preterit of *ser* and *ir*

You have seen that a group of irregular verbs has various types in the present tense. A somewhat larger group of irregular verbs has various types in the preterit tense. In this section, you learn how to conjugate those irregular preterit verbs.

Except for those verbs whose irregularity is based on stem changes, all other irregular preterit-tense verbs—unlike the regular ones—are stressed on the next-to-last syllable. Therefore, they do not use accent marks.

-u- Verbs

A large group of verbs contains the letter *u* in the stem when in the preterit tense, no matter what their stem was in the infinitive and the present tense. These verbs are stressed on the next-to-last syllable in all persons of the preterit tense.

The following table shows verbs that have the letter *u* in the stem when in the preterit tense.

PRETERIT TENSE OF VERBS CONTAINING *-U-* IN THE STEM

Pronoun	estar (to be)	tener (to have)	poder (to be able)	poner (to put)
yo	estuve	tuve	pude	puse
tú	estuviste	tuviste	pudiste	pusiste
él	estuvo	tuvo	pudo	puso
nosotros	estuvimos	tuvimos	pudimos	pusimos
vosotros	estuvisteis	tuvisteis	pudisteis	pusisteis
ellos	estuvieron	tuvieron	pudieron	pusieron

The following three verbs also belong to this -*u*- category:

andar (to walk, ride, go): anduve, anduviste, anduvo, anduvimos, anduvisteis, anduvieron

saber (to know): supe, supiste, supo, supimos, supisteis, supieron

caber (to fit): cupe, cupiste, cupo, cupimos, cupisteis, cupieron

Note that the verb *saber* in the preterit tense usually means "found out."

-*duj*- Verbs

The group of verbs whose infinitive ends with -*ducir* have a peculiarity in the yo form of the present tense. They have another peculiarity in the preterit tense: they all contain -*duj*- in the preterit stem. The following table shows the conjugation in the preterit tense of this type of verb.

PRETERIT TENSE OF VERBS CONTAINING -*DUJ*- IN THE STEM

Pronoun	conducir (to conduct)	traducir (to translate)
yo	conduje	traduje
tú	condujiste	tradujiste
él	condujo	tradujo
nosotros	condujimos	tradujimos
vosotros	condujisteis	tradujisteis
ellos	condujeron	tradujeron

Conducir also means "to lead" and "to drive (a car)." In this type of verb, the *ellos* form of the verb does not have the -*ieron* ending typical of -*er* and -*ir* verbs in the preterit tense; instead, it ends with -*dujeron*. In other words, the letter *i* is dropped after the *j*.

The following verbs are also of the same type:

reducir (to reduce): reduje, redujiste, redujo, redujimos, redujisteis, redujeron

deducir (to deduce, deduct): deduje, dedujiste, dedujo, dedujimos, dedujisteis, dedujeron

producir (to produce): produje, produjiste, produjo, produjimos, produjisteis, produjeron

Other Verbs Containing -j-

One verb and its derivatives are, in the preterit tense, irregular and contain the letter *j* between the verb stem and the verb ending.

traer (to bring): traje, trajiste, trajo, trajimos, trajisteis, trajeron

In the *ellos* form, just like the *-duj* verbs, the *i* drops out after the letter *j* and before the *-eron* ending.

Several verbs are derivatives of *traer* (such as *atraer, distraer, retraer,* and so on). All are conjugated in the same way. In the present tense, the *yo* form of these verbs ends with *-go*.

Internal -i- Verbs

In a handful of verbs, the *-a-* or the *-e-* of the infinitive is converted into the consonant *-i-* in the preterit tense. See the following table.

VERBS WITH INTERNAL CONSONANT -I- IN THE PRETERIT STEM

dar (to come)	hacer (to do, make)	venir (to come)	querer (to want, love)
di	hice	vine	quise
diste	hiciste	viniste	quisiste
dio	hizo	vino	quiso
dimos	hicimos	vinimos	quisimos
disteis	hicisteis	vinisteis	quisisteis
dieron	hicieron	vinieron	quisieron

The verb *dar* in the preterit behaves peculiarly. It is an *-ar* verb that, in the preterit tense, is conjugated like a regular *-er* or *-ir* verb.

The *él/ella/usted* form of *hacer* in the preterit tense substitutes the letter *-z-* for the letter *-c-*. This is to avoid signaling the *k* sound in the combination *co*. The derivatives of *hacer* are conjugated the same way:

rehacer (to redo, to remake)

deshacer (to undo, take apart, untie, diminish, destroy)

satisfacer (to satisfy)

The verb *satisfacer* is conjugated in all tenses just like *hacer*. The *-f-* is a throwback to Old Spanish, in which the verb *hacer* was spelled *facer*.

Verbs with Interposed -y-

The same verbs that, in the present tense, had the letter -y- between the stem and the present-tense endings have the -y- between the stem and the preterit-tense endings. These are all the verbs whose infinitive ends with -uir. In the present tense, this happened in all forms except *nosotros* and *vosotros*.

However, in the preterit tense, the letter y is interposed *only* in the *él, ella, usted, ellos, ellas,* and *ustedes* forms. These are typical examples:

construir (to build, construct): construí, construiste, construyó, construimos, construisteis, construyeron

destruir (to destroy): destruí, destruiste, destruyó, destruimos, destruisteis, destruyeron

The process is simply one of substituting the letter y for the usual letter i before the -ó of the *él* form and before the -eron ending of the *ellos* form in the preterit ending of -ir verbs.

The Verb *decir*

The verb *decir* (i) and its derivatives are unique. They behave peculiarly in the preterit tense. The vowel -e- of the infinitive changes to the vowel -i- just as it does in the stem change of the present tense of this verb. However, unlike its present tense, this same change affects the *nosotros* and *vosotros* forms. In the present tense, this does not happen.

In addition, *decir* in the preterit tense undergoes a transformation of the -c- of the stem into the consonant -j-, similar to the -duj- verbs. See the following preterit-tense conjugation:

decir (to say, tell): dije, dijiste, dijo, dijimos, dijisteis, dijeron

Once more, there is no i between the -j and -eron. Several verbs are based on *decir* and are conjugated the same way in all tenses:

bendecir (i) (to bless)

maldecir (i) (to curse)

contradecir (i) (to contradict)

Stem Changers

Many verbs undergo a stem change in the present tense. You have seen that some change from -e- to -ie or from -e- to -i-, while others change from -o- to -ue-.

One verb changes from -u- to -ue-. Some of these verbs carry stem changes into the preterit tense; most do not.

-ar and -er Verbs

The -ar or -er verbs (first and second conjugations) that have a stem change in the present tense do not have any type of stem change in the preterit tense. For example, even though the verb cerrar (to close) is a stem-changing verb in the present tense (cierro, cierras, cierra, cerramos, and so on), it is absolutely regular in the preterit tense (cerré, cerraste, cerró, cerramos, and so on).

-ir Verbs

The -ir verbs (third conjugation) that have a stem change in the present tense definitely do have a stem change in the preterit. However, keep in mind two major points:

▶ No matter what the stem change is in the present tense, the stem change in the preterit tense is always from -e- to -i- and from -o- to -u-.

▶ In the preterit tense, this stem change takes place solely with relation to the third person singular and plural. No other grammatical person is affected.

Even though usted and its plural, ustedes, are conceptualized semantically as the second person, they are third person grammatically. This is why usted has the same verb forms as él and ella, while ustedes takes the same verb forms as ellos and ellas.

See the following table for a comparison of the present tense with the preterit tense for stem-changing -ir verbs.

PRESENT AND PRETERIT TENSES OF STEM-CHANGING -IR VERBS

sentir (ie, i) (to feel)		dormir (ue, u) (to sleep)	
Present	Preterit	Present	Preterit
siento	sentí	duermo	dormí
sientes	sentiste	duermes	dormiste
siente	sintió	duerme	durmió
sentimos	sentimos	dormimos	dormimos
sentís	sentiste	dormís	dormisteis
sienten	sintieron	duermen	durmieron

When an infinitive verb is listed as a vocabulary item, if it has a different stem change in the preterit from the present tense, it will show both changes in parentheses, such as "*sentir* (ie, i)."

Preterit of *ser* and *ir*

The verb *ser* (to be) and the verb *ir* (to go) have entirely different meanings and have different verb forms in the present tense. Those present-tense verb forms are extremely irregular. Stranger still, in the preterit tense, *ser* has exactly the *same* verb forms as *ir*. Here's the conjugation of these two verbs in the preterit tense.

PRETERIT TENSE OF *SER* AND *IR*

Subject Pronoun	ser (to be)	ir (to go)
yo	fui	fui
tú	fuiste	fuiste
él	fue	fue
nosotros	fuimos	fuimos
vosotros	fuisteis	fuisteis
ellos	fueron	fueron

8.2

Although the form is identical, the context makes the meaning clear in most cases. For example, "Lincoln fue un gran presidente" can only mean "Lincoln was a great president." But "Lincoln fue a Wáshington" obviously means "Lincoln went to Washington." There can be no confusion between the meanings "Lincoln went to Washington" and "Lincoln was in Washington."

◀ *SEE ALSO 15.2, "Two Forms of Being:* ser *vs.* estar" ▶

Beyond the fact that you would use the preposition *a* in the first case but the preposition *en* in the second case, you would not use the verb *ser* for the second sentence. Instead, you would use the verb *estar* because you would be referring to a physical location.

◀ *SEE ALSO 7.2, "Present Tense: Irregular Verbs"* ▶

◀ *SEE ALSO 1.3, "The Spelling System"* ▶

8.3 IMPERFECT TENSE

Regular Imperfect -ar Verbs

Regular Imperfect -er Verbs

Regular Imperfect -ir Verbs

Irregular Imperfect Verbs: *ser, ir, ver*

Spanish has two past tenses. These are not interchangeable; they are used to express different concepts. One is the preterit tense, which we discussed earlier in this chapter. The other is the imperfect tense, which expresses continuous or repeated actions in the past.

In the Spanish imperfect tense, the vast majority of verbs are regular. In fact, there are only three irregular verbs. However, there are two types of regular verbs in the imperfect tense. The *-ar* verbs are conjugated in one way, while the *-er* and *-ir verbs* are conjugated in a different manner. In this section, you learn how to conjugate the regular verbs of the imperfect tense.

Regular Imperfect *-ar* Verbs

To form the imperfect tense of the *-ar* verbs, detach the *-ar* ending of the infinitive and attach the endings *-aba, -abas, -aba, -ábamos, -abais*, and *-aban* to the stem. See the following table for an example of *-ar* verbs in the imperfect tense.

IMPERFECT TENSE CONJUGATION OF *-AR* VERBS USING *HABLAR*

Subject Pronoun	Verb Stem	Imperfect Ending	Conjugated Verb
yo	habl-	-aba	hablaba
tú	habl-	-abas	hablabas
él	habl-	-aba	hablaba
nosotros	habl-	-ábamos	hablábamos
vosotros	habl-	-abais	hablabais
ellos	habl-	-aban	hablaban

All *-ar* verbs, without exception, work this way. There are no irregular *-ar* verbs in the imperfect tense.

In the imperfect tense, the yo form is identical to the form for *él, ella,* and *usted.*

Here are a few other -ar verbs conjugated in the imperfect tense:

llamar (to call): llamaba, llamabas, llamaba, llamábamos, llamabais, llamaban

llegar (to arrive): llegaba, llegabas, llegaba, llegábamos, llegabais, llegaban

estar (to be): estaba, estabas, estaba, estábamos, estabais, estaban

pasar (to pass, happen): pasaba, pasabas, pasaba, pasábamos, pasabais, pasaban

Regular Imperfect -er Verbs

To form the imperfect tense of the -er verbs, detach the -er ending of the infinitive and attach the endings -ía, -ías, -ía, -íamos, -íais, and -ían to the stem. See the following table for an example of -er verbs in the imperfect tense.

IMPERFECT-TENSE CONJUGATION OF -ER VERBS USING COMER (TO EAT)

Subject Pronoun	Verb Stem	Imperfect Ending	Conjugated Verb
yo	com-	-ía	comía
tú	com-	-ías	comías
él	com-	-ía	comía
nosotros	com-	-íamos	comíamos
vosotros	com-	-íais	comíais
ellos	com-	-ían	comían

Only two -er verbs do not fit this pattern (ser and ver); all the others do. Here are other examples of -er verbs in the imperfect tense:

poner (to put): ponía, ponias, ponía, poníamos, poníais, ponía

volver (ue) (to return, go back, come back): volvía, volvías, volvía, volvíamos, volvíais, volvían

correr (to run): corría, corrías, corría, corríamos, corríais, corrían

Regular Imperfect -ir Verbs

To form the imperfect tense of the -ir verbs, detach the -ir ending of the infinitive and attach the endings -ía, -ías, -ía, -íamos, -íais, and -ían to the stem. See the following table for an example of -ir verbs in the imperfect tense.

IMPERFECT-TENSE CONJUGATION OF -*IR* VERBS USING *DECIR* (TO SAY, TELL)

Subject Pronoun	Verb Stem	Imperfect Ending	Conjugated Verb
yo	dec-	-ía	decía
tú	dec-	-ías	decías
él	dec-	-ía	decía
nosotros	dec-	-íamos	decíamos
vosotros	dec-	-íais	decíais
ellos	dec-	-ían	decían

Here are some examples of other -*ir* verbs in the imperfect tense:

vivir (to live): vivía, vivías, vivía, vivíamos, vivíais, vivía

salir (to leave): salía, salías, salía, salíamos, salíais, salían

dormir (to sleep): dormía, dormías, dormía, dormíamos, dormíais, dormían

Only one -*ir* verb does not fit this pattern (*ir*); all others are regular.

Irregular Imperfect Verbs: *ser, ir, ver*

Only three verbs in the imperfect tense are irregular. Those verbs are *ser* (to be), *ir* (to go), and *ver* (to see). See the following for their conjugation in the imperfect tense:

ser (to be): era, eras, era, éramos, erais, eran

ir (to go): iba, ibas, iba, íbamos, ibais, iban

ver (to see): veía, veías, veía, veíamos, veíais, veían

The verb *ser* is conjugated very differently from other verbs in the imperfect tense, although it is similar to *tú eres* in the present tense.

The verb *ir* is peculiar in that it seems to combine the vowels of the imperfect -*ir* verbs (*í-a*) while at the same time sharing the ending -*ba* with -*ar* verbs. The verb *ver* doesn't look very irregular but technically is because it drops only the -*r* of the infinitive ending before adding the imperfect endings, rather than dropping the -*er*. In other words, its irregularity consists in retaining the -*e*- of the infinitive.

◀ SEE ALSO 8.1, *"Preterit Tense: Regular Verbs"* ▶

◀ SEE ALSO 8.2, *"Preterit Tense: Irregular Verbs"* ▶

8.4 IMPERFECT VS. PRETERIT

Use of the Preterit Tense
Use of the Imperfect Tense
Different Tense, Different Meaning

The two Spanish past tenses are not interchangeable; they express different concepts. Understanding the distinctions may be difficult for English-speakers because English doesn't necessarily have to show these distinctions, yet every time Spanish-speakers talk about the past, they choose either the preterit or the imperfect tense. The difference between the two tenses is based on **aspect.**

WORDS TO GO . . .WORDS TO GO . . .WORDS TO GO

Aspect: If you view the action or state as having started or finished at a specific point in the past, that aspect calls for the preterit tense. If you view the action or state as having been in progress ("was doing") or habitually repeated ("used to do") in the past, that aspect calls for the imperfect tense.

All actions, events, or states can be divided into three parts: beginning, middle, and end. To understand the two Spanish past tenses, you have to know which part(s) the speaker has in mind.

Use of the Preterit Tense

If the Spanish-speaker can visualize either the beginning or the end (or both) of the action or state being described, he/she will employ the preterit tense. Read the following sentences:

Hablé con Mercedes (esta tarde a las cinco.)	I spoke with Mercedes (this afternoon at 5:00).
Llamé al médico (ayer a las ocho).	I called the doctor (yesterday at 8:00).

The preterit tense is used in these sentences because we see the actions (speaking and calling) as having been completed at a specific time, whether that time is actually mentioned or not.

Use of the Imperfect Tense

On the other hand, if the speaker does not visualize either the beginning or the end, but "sees" only the middle going on, he or she will use the imperfect tense. The concept of visualizing only the middle going on can be divided into three categories:

▶ Repeated, habitual past actions

▶ Past actions in progress

▶ Setting the scene

Imperfect for Repeated, Habitual Past Actions

You have to learn to think like Spanish-speakers; you can't depend on translation to understand the two past tenses, because English can use the ordinary past tense to express either concept. It is perfectly acceptable and normal in English to say the following sentences:

I spoke with Mercedes at 5:00 when we were in college.

I called the doctor whenever I had a fever.

Both sentences use the English simple past tense. This might mislead you into using the Spanish preterit. Do *not* use the preterit. Use the imperfect tense. The first sentence, even though it mentions a specific time (5:00), talks about repeated habitual action. We don't see when the practice of calling at 5:00 began or ended. It was habitually repeated all the time they were in college.

The second sentence also refers to repeated habitual action ("whenever I had a fever"). We don't see a beginning or an end of the practice.

It is possible to obtain a clue from English. Ask yourself if you can substitute the following pair of statements *without changing the meaning:*

I used to speak with Mercedes at 5:00 when we were in college.

I used to call the doctor whenever I had a fever.

The last part of the second sentence could have read "… whenever I used to have a fever." It would be correct but sound awkward with too many "used to" instances involved.

Those "used to" sentences make perfectly good sense and do not change the meaning of the previous two sentences.

Clue: If you can employ "used to" with the verb, this means you are referring to repeated, habitual action. Whether you use the "used to" form of the verb or the plain past tense in English, this kind of repeated, habitual action, with no beginning or end discussed, requires the imperfect tense. The Spanish for these two sentences would be this:

(Yo) hablaba con Mercedes a las cinco cuando estábamos en la universidad.

(Yo) llamaba al médico cuandoquiera que tenía fiebre.

It would *not* make sense in English, however, to say this:

I used to speak with Mercedes this afternoon at 5:00.

I used to call the doctor yesterday at 8:00.

The preceding sentences obviously do not make sense in English because they refer to completed actions that happened on one occasion each. We cannot use "used to" in these circumstances in English, so we cannot use the imperfect tense in Spanish. We must use the preterit tense.

Imperfect for Past Actions in Progress

When referring to an action, event, or state that we think of as being in the middle of happening—we see neither its beginning nor its end—you will want to use the imperfect tense as well.

Sometimes there is a clue in English. Whenever the English would use *was* or *were* plus a verb ending with *-ing*, we are describing a past action or state in progress. See the following sentences:

We were speaking.	Hablábamos.
She was calling the doctor, when ...	(Ella) llamaba al médico, cuando ...

These sentences use the imperfect tense in Spanish because, in our mind's eye, we do not see the beginning or end of the actions. We do not see the completion of the events. We are left in the middle of these ongoing acts.

Imperfect for Setting the Scene

Descriptions of the past that set the scene for narration are given in the imperfect tense. This is because these descriptions are the background, the stage props, against which the events will unfold. See this sentence:

It was a cold, dark night, when ...	Era una noche fría y oscura cuando ...

We aren't saying that it just got cold and dark, or that it stopped being cold and dark. The events of the narration will take place in this setting.

If description is *not* being used to set the scene for narration in the past, but is merely making a summation, you use the preterit tense. You are not describing or placing action in the ongoing middle; the cold, dark night happened, and it's over. A specific point in time is either implied or stated:

It was a cold, dark night.   Fue una noche fría y
                               oscura.

In this case, the cold, dark night is not setting the scene; it is merely presented as having happened, period. We see the end of it.

Different Tense, Different Meaning

Certain verbs, by their nature, tend to be stated in the imperfect tense. Verbs expressing emotional states or thoughts come under this heading. If you say "I was glad," usually you're not describing the beginning or the end of it. Of course, if you mean that just at that moment you felt gladness (someone told you something) but in the next moment that gladness disappeared (you realized it was not what you thought), you would use the preterit tense.

Also, the verb *tener* (to have), when referring to the past, is usually in the imperfect tense because one usually doesn't refer to the beginning or the end of having something; one is usually in the middle of having it.

The following table shows that the **denotations** or **connotations** of some verbs can differ widely, depending on whether the preterit tense or the imperfect tense is used.

WORDS TO GO . . .WORDS TO GO . . .WORDS TO GO

Denotation is the meaning of the word or term.
Connotation is the idea and association suggested or implied by a word or term.

SEMANTIC CONTRASTS BETWEEN IMPERFECT AND PRETERIT TENSES

Infinitive	Imperfect	English	Preterit	English
saber	sabías	you knew	supiste	you found out
poder	podías	you were able	pudiste	you managed to
querer	querías	you wanted to	quisiste	you tried to
no querer	no querías	you didn't want	no quisiste	you refused to

Usually, when you say you knew something, you don't describe the beginning of knowing it or the end of knowing it; you are describing being in the middle of knowing it (imperfect). However, if you are referring to the beginning of knowing something (preterit), you usually say, "I found out," or "I learned." See the following sentences:

Yo sabía que era verdad.	I knew (all along) that it was true.
Yo supe que era verdad.	I found out it was true.
Quería hacerlo, pero no podía.	I wanted to do it, but didn't have the ability.
Quise hacerlo, pero no pude.	I tried to do it but didn't manage to do it.
No quería ir.	I didn't want to go.
No quise ir.	I refused to go.

Naturally, you could translate both "no podía" and "no pude" in the third and fourth sentences as "I couldn't." But the underlying feeling is that expressed in the translations.

In the first two sentences above, *era* (imperfect of *ser*) is used; we're not referring to the beginning of it being true or the end of it. We're referring to the ongoing nature of its being true.

8.4

9

VERBS: FUTURE AND CONDITIONAL TENSES

9.1 FUTURE TENSE

Regular Future Verbs

Irregular Future Verbs

Substitute for Future Tense

The English language uses the **auxiliary verb** *will* in front of other verbs to express the future. Spanish has verb conjugations that serve the same purpose. In this section, you learn how to express actions, events, and states that will take place in the future.

WORDS TO GO . . . *WORDS TO GO . . . WORDS TO GO*

Auxiliary verbs are verbs that are used in combination with another verb to add further meaning to the other verb—for example, *will, may, must.*

Regular Future Verbs

In the future tense, regular verbs do *not* first remove the infinitive ending and then attach endings to the stem. Unlike the verbs in the present, preterit, and imperfect tenses, the future tense is conjugated by attaching endings to the infinitive form of the verb. See the following process for the *yo* form of the verb *hablar:*

> Infinitive verb *hablar* plus first person singular ending *é* = *hablaré* = "I will speak"

This process is the same for all regular verbs, whether of the *-ar, -er,* or *-ir* conjugations.

See the following table for the future conjugation of *hablar.*

FUTURE-TENSE CONJUGATION OF THE REGULAR VERB *HABLAR* (TO SPEAK)

Pronoun	Infinitive	Future Ending	Conjugated Verb
yo	hablar	-é	hablaré
tú	hablar	-ás	hablarás
él	hablar	-á	hablará
nosotros	hablar	-emos	hablaremos

Pronoun	Infinitive	Future Ending	Conjugated Verb
vosotros	hablar	-éis	hablaréis
ellos	hablar	-án	hablarán

The process is exactly the same for all regular verbs; it does not matter whether they belong to the *-ar*, *-er*, or *-ir* conjugation. The following are examples of several other regular verbs in the future tense:

trabajar (to work): trabajaré, trabajarás, trabajará, trabajaremos, trabajaréis, trabajarán

comer (to eat): comeré, comerás, comerá, comeremos, comeréis, comerán

vivir (to live): viviré, vivirás, vivirá, viviremos, viviréis, vivirán

cerrar (ie) (to close): cerraré, cerrarás, cerrará, cerraremos, cerraréis, cerrarán

entender (ie) (to understand): entenderé, entenderás, entenderá, entenderemos, entenderéis, entenderán

ir (to go): iré, irás, irá, iremos, iréis, irán

Keep in mind that just because a verb is irregular in one tense, it is not necessarily irregular in any other tense. The verbs *cerrar* and *entender* are both stem-changing verbs in the present tense; this stem change does not take place in those verbs in any other tense.

The crucial point to remember is that the future-tense endings are attached not to the stem, but to the *infinitive* form of the verb.

Irregular Future Verbs

Several groups of verbs in the future tense depart somewhat from the usual (the "regular") procedure. This section shows how to conjugate these irregular verbs in the future tense.

Infinitive Vowel Drops

One small group of irregular verbs share one feature in the future tense: the vowel of the infinitive ending drops out before the future endings are added. See the following example:

1. Infinitive: *poder* (to be able, can)
2. Drop the infinitive vowel: *pod-r*

9.1

3. Close up: *podr*

4. Add future ending for yo: *podré*

See the following table of commonly used vowel-dropping future verbs:

poder (ue, u) (to be able)

querer (ie, i) (to want)

saber (to know)

TABLE OF VOWEL-DROPPING VERBS IN THE FUTURE TENSE

Pronoun	poder	querer	saber
yo	podré	querré	sabré
tú	podrás	querrás	sabrás
él	podrá	querrá	sabrá
nosotros	podremos	querremos	sabremos
vosotros	podréis	querréis	sabréis
ellos	podrán	querrán	sabrán

Note: When the vowel of the infinitive drops out of *querer*, you have a double *-rr-*.

Infinitive Vowel Transformed into *d*

A small group of verbs in the future tense not only drop the vowel of the infinitive ending, but replace it with the consonant *d*:

1. Infinitive: *tener*

2. Drop the infinitive vowel: *ten-r*

3. Place the letter *d* where the vowel had been: *tendr*

4. Add future ending for yo: *tendré*

Study the following table of verbs that in the future substitute the letter *d* for the infinitive vowel:

tener (ie, u) (to have)

venir (ie, i) (to come)

salir (to leave)

TABLE OF VERBS IN FUTURE TENSE THAT CHANGE THE INFINITIVE VOWEL INTO LETTER D

Pronoun	Tener	Venir	Salir
yo	tendré	vendré	saldré
tú	tendrás	vendrás	saldrás
él	tendrá	vendrá	saldrá
nosotros	tendremos	vendremos	saldremos
vosotros	tendréis	vendréis	saldréis
ellos	tendrán	vendrán	saldrán

Another commonly used verb that in the future tense substitutes -d- for the infinitive vowel is *poner*.

poner (to put): pondré, pondrá, pondrá, pondremos, pondréis, pondrán

The Verb *hacer*

The verb *hacer* undergoes a drastic change in the future tense. Before attaching the future endings to the -r of the infinitive ending, the -c- and the -e- are removed. This means that you add the future endings to a base of *har-*.

hacer (to do, make): haré, harás, hará, haremos, haréis, harán

The Verb *decir*

The verb *decir* also suffers a drastic transformation in the future tense. Before adding the future endings to the -r of the infinitive ending, the -e- and the -c- are removed. You add the future endings to a base of *dir-*.

decir (to say, tell): diré, dirás, dirá, diremos, diréis, dirán

Regardless of the conjugation (*-ar, -er, -ir*) and regardless of the irregularity that may take place in the stem and/or the infinitive ending, the future endings added to the letter -r of the infinitive are always identical from one verb to any other in the future tense.

Substitute for Future Tense

There are substitutes for the future tense in English and Spanish. This section deals with those substitutes.

English has a substitute for the future tense that's actually used more than the future tense itself. That future substitute is a sort of **circumlocution** for the future tense. For example, instead of saying "I will have dinner" or even "I'll have

9.1

dinner," we often say "I'm going to have dinner." That is, we use "to be going to" plus the main verb instead of the auxiliary verb *will* plus the main verb. This can be carried out in the present tense and in the imperfect tense.

WORDS TO GO . . .WORDS TO GO . . .WORDS TO GO

Circumlocution is a roundabout way of making a statement.

Using the Present Tense of *ir*

The Spanish substitute for the future tense parallels its English counterpart. Instead of affixing the future-tense endings to the infinitive verb (the true future), Spanish speakers often use the combination of the verb *ir* (to go) in the present tense, plus the preposition *a*, plus the infinitive of the main verb. See these examples of the same statement made in the true future tense and in the future substitute:

Ahora hablaré.	Now I will speak.
Ahora voy a hablar.	Now I'm going to speak.
Elena llegará tarde.	Elena will arrive late.
Elena va a llegar tarde.	Elena is going to arrive late.
El tren saldrá a las ocho.	The train will leave at eight o'clock.
El tren va a salir a las ocho.	The train is going to leave at eight o'clock.

In both English and Spanish, the future substitute is principally used—although not entirely—for something that *is going to* happen in the relatively near future. Of course, there is yet another way to substitute for the future, especially if we're speaking of the near future: the present tense.

◀ SEE ALSO 7.1, *"Present Tense: Regular Verbs"* ▶

Using the Imperfect Tense of *ir*

This substitute for the future, in both English and Spanish, can also be used in speaking of the past. In English, instead of saying "He's going to …," we can refer to his intention in the past by saying "He was going to …." In Spanish, you use the imperfect tense of the verb *ir* to express this concept, as shown in the following sentences:

(Yo) iba a hablar.	I was going to speak.
Elena iba a llegar tarde.	Elena was going to arrive late.
El tren iba a salir . a las ocho	The train was going to leave at eight.

The similarity between the English and the Spanish expressions should make them easy to learn.

◄ *SEE ALSO 8.3, "Imperfect Tense"* ▶

9.2 CONDITIONAL TENSE

Regular Conditional Verbs

Irregular Conditional Verbs

Substitute for Conditional Tense (*ir a* ...)

In both English and Spanish, the conditional tense speaks of what *would* happen *if* certain *conditions* were to be in force—hence, the name *conditional*. This tense is expressed in English by using the auxiliary verb *would* being placed before the main verb—for example "I would go ...." Whether stated or not, the implication is "... if something were to happen." For example: "I would go if they invited me."

In this section, you learn how to form the conditional tense in Spanish.

Regular Conditional Verbs

Regular verbs in the conditional tense do *not* first remove the infinitive ending and then attach endings to the stem. Instead, the process is exactly the same as with the future tense (see the preceding section). That is, the conditional endings are attached directly to the infinitive endings. See the process indicated here for the *yo* form of the verb *hablar*:

Infinitive verb *hablar* plus the first-person singular ending *ía* = *hablaría*, "I would speak."

This process is the same for all regular verbs, whether of the -*ar*, -*er*, or -*ir* conjugations. See the following table for the conditional conjugation of *hablar*.

CONDITIONAL-TENSE CONJUGATION OF THE REGULAR VERB *HABLAR* (TO SPEAK)

Pronoun	Infinitive	Conditional Ending	Conjugated Verb
yo	hablar	-ía	hablaría
tú	hablar	-ías	hablarías
él	hablar	-ía	hablaría
nosotros	hablar	-íamos	hablaríamos
vosotros	hablar	-íais	hablaríais
ellos	hablar	-ían	hablarían

Exactly as in the case of the future tense, the conditional-tense endings are attached not to the stem, but to the *infinitive* form of the verb.

Irregular Conditional Verbs

In several groups of verbs, the conditional tense departs somewhat from the usual (the "regular") procedure. In this section, you learn to conjugate these irregular verbs in the conditional tense. As you will see, the very same verbs that are irregular in the future tense are also irregular in the conditional tense, and in precisely the same manner.

Infinitive Vowel Drops

One small group of irregular verbs shares one feature in the conditional tense: the vowel of the infinitive ending drops out before the conditional endings are added. See the following example:

1. Infinitive: *poder* (to be able, can)

2. Drop the infinitive vowel: *pod-r*

3. Close up: *podr*

4. Add conditional ending for *yo: podría*

See the following table of commonly used vowel-dropping conditional verbs:

poder (ue, u) (to be able)

querer (ie, i) (to want)

saber (to know)

9.2

TABLE OF VOWEL-DROPPING VERBS IN THE CONDITIONAL TENSE

Pronoun	poder	querer	saber
yo	podría	querría	sabría
tú	podrías	querrías	sabrías
él	podría	querría	sabría
nosotros	podríamos	querríamos	sabríamos
vosotros	podríais	querríais	sabríais
ellos	podrían	querrían	sabrían

When the vowel of the infinitive drops out of *querer*, you have a double *-rr-*.

Infinitive Vowel Transformed into *d*

Just as in the future tense, a small group of verbs in the conditional tense not only drop the vowel of the infinitive ending, but replace it with the consonant *d:*

1. Infinitive: *tener*

2. Drop the infinitive vowel: *ten-r*

3. Place the letter *d* where the vowel had been: *tendr*

4. Add conditional ending for *yo: tendría* = "I would have"

Study the following table of verbs that in the future substitute the letter *d* for the infinitive vowel:

tener (ie, u) (to have)

venir (ie, i) (to come)

salir (to leave)

TABLE OF VERBS IN CONDITIONAL TENSE THAT CHANGE THE INFINITIVE VOWEL INTO LETTER D

Pronoun	tener	venir	salir
yo	tendría	vendría	saldría
tú	tendrías	vendrías	saldrías
él	tendría	vendría	saldría
nosotros	tendríamos	vendríamos	saldríamos
vosotros	tendríais	vendríais	saldríais
ellos	tendrían	vendrían	saldrían

Another commonly used verb that in the conditional tense substitutes the letter -*d*- for the infinitive vowel is *poner.*

poner (to put): pondría, pondrías, pondría, pondríamos, pondríais, pondrían

The Verb *hacer*

The verb *hacer* undergoes a drastic change in the conditional tense. Before attaching the conditional endings to the -*r* of the infinitive ending, the -*c*- and the -*e*- are removed. This means that you add the conditional endings to a base of *har*-.

hacer (to do, make): haría, harías, haría, haríamos, haríais, harían

The Verb *decir*

The verb *decir* also suffers a drastic transformation in the conditional tense. Before adding the conditional endings to the *-r* of the infinitive ending, the *-e-* and the *-c-* are removed. You add the conditional endings to a base of *dir-*.

decir (to say, tell): diría, dirías, diría, diríamos, diríais, dirían

Regardless of the conjugation (*-ar, -er, -ir*) and regardless of the irregularity that may take place in the stem and/or the infinitive ending, the future endings added to the letter *-r* of the infinitive are always identical from one verb to any other in the future tense.

Substitute for Conditional Tense (*ir a ...*)

If *ir a* + infinitive in the present tense is a substitute for the future tense, theoretically, *ir a* + infinitive in the imperfect tense should be a substitute for the conditional tense. This is true in theory in both English and Spanish, but we don't use the conditional tense as a synonym for the *iba a* + infinitive (was going to) construction unless certain circumstances are present.

These circumstances involve the "was going to" clause being preceded by a clause referring to communication or observation ("he said that ..."; "they found out that ..."; "we knew that ..."; "she saw that ..."; etc.). See the following examples:

9.2

Dijeron que hablarías.	They said (that) you would speak.
Dijeron que ibas a hablar.	They said (that) you were going to speak.
Sabían que Elena llegaría tarde.	They knew (that) Elena would arrive late.
Sabían que Elena iba a llegar tarde.	They knew (that) Elena was going to arrive late.
Supe que hablarían.	I found out (that) they would speak.
Supe que iban a hablar.	I found out (that) they were going to speak.

For all intents and purposes, the preceding pairs of conditional/*iba a* sentences are synonymous, in the same way that the pairs of future/*va a* sentences in the preceding section are synonymous.

You can see, in the preceding sentences, a typical discrepancy between Spanish and English: in English, the relative pronoun *that* can be dispensed with; it is understood without stating it explicitly. The Spanish equivalent, *que*, can never be dropped in normal Spanish.

9.3   WONDERING AND PROBABILITY

Wondering and Probability in the Present

Wondering and Probability in the Past

In addition to indicating an action, event, or state in the future, the future tense can also be used to express wondering or probability *in the present*. And in addition to referring to a potential action, event, or state under certain conditions, the conditional tense can also be used to express wondering or probability *in the past*.

Wondering and Probability in the Present

Depending on context, the future tense can indicate that someone is wondering about something that might be happening in the *present*. This can happen when it is in the form of a question. Compare a straightforward question with wondering here:

¿Dónde está Roberto?	Where is Roberto?
¿Dónde estará Roberto?	I wonder where Roberto is?/ Where can Roberto be?
¿Qué quiere ella?	What does she want?
¿Qué querrá ella?	I wonder what she wants?/ What can she want?

9.3

The first and third sentences are straightforward questions that usually demand an answer. The second and fourth sentences (wondering) are less pointed, don't necessarily demand an answer, and can often be what someone says to him/herself.

The future tense in the preceding sentences expresses wondering when posed as questions. There are at least two ways in English to express the thought. One way is in the form of a statement (I wonder …); the other is in the form of a question (what can …?).

Again, depending on context, the future tense can be the answer to a question if made as a statement rather than a question. In this case, it indicates probability

163

rather than absolute certainty. Compare these direct statements with indications of probability:

Roberto está en la oficina.	Roberto is at the office.
Roberto estará en la oficina.	Roberto is probably at the office./Roberto must be at the office.
Ella quiere ir a un restaurante.	She wants to go to a restaurant.
Ella querrá ir a un restaurante.	She probably wants to go to a restaurant./She must want to go to a restaurant.

Again, as you can see in the preceding sentences, there is more than one way to express the same thought in English.

Keep in mind that whether the future tense is used for wondering or showing probability, or straightforwardly asking a question or making a statement about the future, depends entirely on context.

◄ SEE ALSO 9.1, *"Future Tense"* ▷

Wondering and Probability in the Past

Depending on context, the conditional tense can indicate that someone is wondering about something that might have happened in the *past*. This can happen when it is in the form of a question. Compare a straightforward question with wondering here:

¿Dónde estuvo Roberto?	Where was Roberto?
¿Dónde estaría Roberto?	I wonder where Roberto was./Where could Roberto have been?
¿Qué quería ella?	What did she want?
¿Qué querría? ella	I wonder what she wanted./What could she have wanted?

With regard to the verb *querer*, the only structural difference between the imperfect past tense and the conditional tense is that the former contains only one *-r-*, while the latter contains a double *-rr-*. This difference is important because of the **semantic** change.

The first and third sentences are straightforward, blunt questions that usually demand an answer. The second and fourth sentences (wondering) are less pointed, don't necessarily demand an answer, and can often be what someone says to him- or herself.

The conditional tense in the preceding sentences expresses wondering about the past when posed as questions. There are at least two ways in English to express the thought. One way is in the form of a statement (I wonder …); the other is in the form of a question (what could …?).

Again, depending on context, the conditional tense can be the answer to a question about the past if made as a statement rather than a question. In this case, it indicates probability rather than absolute certainty. Compare these direct statements with indications of probability:

Roberto estuvo en la oficina.	Roberto was at the office.
Roberto estaría en la oficina.	Roberto was probably at the office./Roberto must have been at the office.
Ella quería ir a un restaurante.	She wanted to go to a restaurant.
Ella querría ir a un restaurante.	She probably wanted to go to a restaurant./She must have wanted to go to a restaurant.

9.3

Again, as you can see in the preceding sentences, there is more than one way to express the same thought in English.

Keep in mind that whether the conditional tense is used for wondering or showing probability in the past, or straightforwardly asking a question or making a statement about a potential action, event, or state depends entirely on context.

◄ *SEE ALSO 8.3, "Imperfect Tense"* ►

10

VERBS: PRESENT PARTICIPLE/ PROGRESSIVE TENSES

10.1 FORMING THE PRESENT PARTICIPLE

-ar Verbs

-er Verbs

-ir Verbs

Spanish has a verbal form called the present participle that is used very much like the English verb forms that end in *-ing*, except that it is never used as a gerund, or noun. The Spanish present participle always ends in *-ndo*.

The exact form of the Spanish present participle depends on the conjugation to which a verb belongs. See the following sections on forming the present participle in the three conjugations.

-ar Verbs

The procedure for producing the present participle of verbs of the first conjugation (*-ar* verbs) is as follows:

1. Remove the infinitive ending of the verb.
2. Add *-ando* to the stem.

See the example using *hablar*:

1. hablar
2. habl-
3. habl + ando
4. hablando

The meaning and uses of the present participle are clarified in further sections of this chapter.

◄ SEE ALSO 7.1, *"Present Tense: Regular Verbs"* ►

-er Verbs

The procedure for producing the present participle of verbs of the second conjugation (*-er* verbs) is as follows:

1. Remove the infinitive ending of the verb.

2. Add *-iendo* to the stem.

See the example using *comer*:

1. comer

2. com-

3. com + iendo

4. comiendo

Even though *ver* and *ser* are such short verbs, they are completely regular in the present participle:

1. ver

2. v-

3. v + iendo

4. viendo

and:

1. ser

2. s-

3. s + iendo

4. siendo

The verbs *ver* and *ser* follow the rules precisely for forming the present participle.

-ir Verbs

The procedure for producing the present participle of verbs of the third conjugation (*-ir* verbs) is as follows:

1. Remove the infinitive ending of the verb.

2. Add *-iendo* to the stem.

See the example using *vivir*:

1. vivir

2. viv-

3. viv + iendo

4. viviendo

The verb *ir*, as well as verbs whose stems end in a vowel, is irregular. See Section 10.2, "*-yendo* Verbs."

10.2 IRREGULAR PRESENT PARTICIPLES

From -*o*- to -*u*-

From -*e*- to -*i*-

-*yendo* Verbs

Almost all the irregular participles are -*ir* verbs, although a small number of -*er* verbs are affected as well. However, *none* of the -*ar* verbs is irregular.

From -*o*- to -*u*-

All -*ir* verbs that have a stem change in the present tense from -*o*- to -*ue*- or to -*u*- have a stem change from -*o*- to -*u*- in the present participle. Here are a few examples:

dormir (ue): durmiendo

morir (ue): muriendo

The same process takes place in one -*er* verb:

poder (ue): pudiendo

The verbs of the -*o*- to -*u*- category in the present participle undergo the same stem change in the preterit tense.

From -*e*- to -*i*-

10.2

All -*ir* verbs that have a stem change from -*e*- to -*ie*- or to -*i*- in the present tense have a stem change from -*e*- to -*i*- in the present participle. Here are a few examples:

venir (ie, i): viniendo

decir (i, i): diciendo

pedir (i, i): pidiendo

The verb *reír* is somewhat peculiar; the -*e*- does change to -*i*-, but instead of adding the ending -*iendo* to the stem *ri*-, just add -*endo*, to avoid having one -*i*- after another. The result is *riendo*.

The verbs of the -e- to -i- category in the present participle undergo the same stem change in the preterit tense.

-*yendo* Verbs

A group of verbs in the -er and -ir conjugations end with -yendo instead of -iendo.

Vowel Stem Ending

In the case of all -er and -ir verbs whose stem ends with a vowel, the ending begins with -y- instead of -i-. So instead of adding -iendo to the stem, add -yendo, as follows:

1. caer
2. ca-
3. ca- + yendo
4. cayendo

Other verbs in this category:

oír: oyendo

traer: trayendo

leer: leyendo

creer: creyendo

huir: huyendo

construir: construyendo

destruir: destruyendo

The -y- is inserted into these same verbs in the preterit tense in the third person singular and plural.

The Verb *ir*

The verb ir is in a class by itself when used as a present participle. Technically, it is not a verb whose stem ends with a vowel because it has no stem. When the infinitive ending (ir) is removed, nothing is left. However, this verb follows the rule for -er and -ir verbs whose stem ends with a vowel. Think of the process like this:

1. ir
2. -

3. -- + yendo

4. yendo

The present participle of the verb *ir* is *yendo*.

◀ *SEE ALSO 7.2, "Present Tense: Irregular Verbs"* ▶

10.3 PRESENT PARTICIPLE USED ALONE

Since, Because ...

While Doing Something

Cause and Effect

The present participle is often used with a conjugated or infinitive verb (see Section 10.4), but it's also used without one. When it is used alone, it can have several meanings.

Since, Because ...

One use of the present participle is very much like one of its uses in English. In English, instead of saying "Because (since) I was in Peru, I decided to ...," we can use the present participle, saying, "Being in Peru, I decided to ...." The same structure can be used in Spanish. See the following examples:

Estando en el Perú, decidí ...	Being in Peru, I decided to ...
Teniendo delante de mí el vaso, bebí	Having the glass before me, I drank.
Sabiendo que llegaría pronto, esperé.	Knowing (that) she would soon arrive, I waited.

The first sentence uses *estar* because it refers to physical location.

◀ *SEE ALSO 15.2, "Two Forms of Being:* ser *vs.* estar*"* ▶

While Doing Something

In English, we often use the present participle alone as an abbreviated form of *while* (plus the subject plus a conjugated form of *to be*) plus the present participle. For example, instead of saying "I fell asleep while (I was) watching television," we can say, "I fell asleep watching television." The same can be done in Spanish. See the following examples:

Me dormí viendo la televisión.	I fell asleep (while) watching television.
Sonreí pensando en sus palabras.	I smiled (while) thinking of his words.

These English sentences could also be stated, "I fell asleep while I was watching television" and "I smiled while I was thinking of his words."

Cause and Effect

One use of the present participle by itself conflicts with English usage. In English, if we want to use the present participle to show cause and effect, we precede the present participle with the preposition *by*—for example, "We learn by studying." In Spanish, this cause and effect never uses the equivalent of *by*; it uses the present participle and the conjugated verb *without* the preposition. See the following examples:

Aprendemos estudiando.	We learn by studying.
Progresamos trabajando.	We progress by working.
Apreciamos la música escuchándola.	We appreciate music by listening to it.

In the third sentence, the object pronoun is attached to the present participle and a written accent mark is used to keep the stress where it belongs.

As in English, in sentences that show cause and effect, it does not matter whether the cause or effect is stated first. The preceding sentences, in both languages, could just as well have been stated in reverse order, as in the following sentences:

Estudiando, aprendemos.	By studying, we learn.
Trabajando, progresamos.	By working, we progress.
Escuchándola, apreciamos la música.	By listening to it, we appreciate music.

10.3

The meaning is the same, whether the cause or the effect is stated first. In both languages, the subtle, almost imperceptible, difference is in the emphasis.

◀ SEE ALSO 1.4, *"Accentuation (Stress) and Capitalization"* ▶

◀ SEE ALSO 4.2, *"Object Pronouns of Verbs"* ▶

10.4 FORMING THE PROGRESSIVE TENSES

Present Progressive

Preterit Progressive

Imperfect Progressive

Future Progressive

Conditional Progressive

The progressive tenses in Spanish parallel the tenses of the same name in English. In English, we form the progressive tenses by using the verb *to be* plus the present participle—for example, "I am working," "I was working," "I will be working," and so on. In Spanish, the progressive tenses are formed by using the verb *estar* plus the present participle.

Never, ever use the verb *ser* for this purpose.

In English, we can use any tense of the helping verb *to be* with the present participle, which results in the different progressive tenses. The same is true of the helping verb *estar* in Spanish plus the present participle to form the various progressive tenses.

In the following sections, you learn to form the various progressive tenses of Spanish.

Present Progressive

The present progressive tense is formed by conjugating the verb *estar* in the present tense (*estoy, estás, está, estamos, estáis, están*) and then following it with the present participle. See the following examples:

Estoy leyendo.	I am reading.
Estamos hablando.	We are speaking.
¿Qué estás diciendo?	What are you saying?

Be careful: the present participle of the verb *ir* (*yendo*) is *not* generally used in the progressive tenses. Instead, the simple tenses are used—for example *va, iba,* and so on. It *is* used by itself, however, in any of the situations mentioned in Section 10.3.

One of the various possible translations of the Spanish present tense would seem to be the same as that of the present progressive tense. One of the possible meanings of *hablamos*, for example, is "we are speaking." You may wonder what the difference is, then, between the present tense and the present progressive tense.

The use of the present progressive tense simply puts more emphasis on the ongoing nature of the verb. The present tense doesn't emphasize this ongoing quality; in context, it merely takes it for granted. Suppose you come upon a friend in the post office. You know he doesn't work there. You say to him, "¿Qué haces aquí?" He knows that you know he doesn't work there, so he realizes you're not asking what he generally does there ("What do you do here?"), but "What are you doing here?"

You could just as well have asked, "¿Qué estás haciendo aquí?" There would be no actual difference in denotation. You would simply be putting more emphasis on the ongoing nature of what he is doing.

Preterit Progressive

You can use the preterit progressive tense to sum up an action that was ongoing in the past. It is not used as much as the imperfect progressive tense (see the next section) for mentally viewing the middle of the ongoing situation.

You form the preterit progressive tense by conjugating the verb *estar* in the preterit tense (*estuve, estuviste, estuvo, estuvimos, estuvisteis, estuvieron*) and then following it with the present participle. See the following examples:

Estuve leyendo.	I was reading.
Estuvimos hablando.	We were speaking.
¿Qué estuviste diciendo?	What were you saying?

10.4

You use this tense to sum up a past ongoing action or situation. You mentally "see" the end of that ongoing situation. You do not use it to set the scene for narration.

Imperfect Progressive

You use the imperfect progressive tense to emphasize the continuation of an action or situation in the past. You form the imperfect progressive tense by conjugating the verb *estar* in the imperfect tense (*estaba, estabas, estaba, estábamos, estabais, estaban*) and following it with the present participle.

See the following examples:

(Yo) estaba leyendo, cuando ella entró.	I was reading, when she came in.
Estábamos hablando, y el teléfono sonó.	We were speaking and the telephone rang.
¿Qué estabas diciendo mientras el estudiaba?	What were you saying while he was studying?

You would use the preceding sentences to conjure up a mental image of someone in the midst of an action or situation in the past. You can set the scene for the narration, either action or dialogue, by using the imperfect progressive tense.

One of the various possible translations of the Spanish imperfect tense would seem to be the same as that of the imperfect progressive tense. One of the possible meanings of *hablábamos*, for example, is "We were speaking." So what's the difference between the imperfect tense and the imperfect progressive tense?

◀ *SEE ALSO 8.4, "Imperfect vs. Preterit"* ▶

In the first preceding sentence, I was in the middle of reading. This ongoing act, with no indication of beginning or end, was interrupted by her entering the room. We can mentally picture both the beginning and the end of her entry. That is why the preterit *entró* is used. That sentence could just as well have been "(Yo) leía cuando ella entró," using the imperfect tense of *leer* rather than the imperfect progressive tense. In using the progressive form of the verb, you are emphasizing more forcefully the ongoing nature of the reading. It's merely a matter of emphasis.

The second sentence is another case of an ongoing act in the past being interrupted by narrative. The phone rang (preterit because we visualize the start of the ringing) in the middle of our speaking. The imperfect progressive tense puts more emphasis on the ongoing nature of the speaking than the imperfect tense would have, but the basic denotation is the same.

The third sentence is somewhat different. We have the case of an ongoing action being emphasized by the use of the imperfect progressive (*estabas diciendo*) taking place at the same time as someone else's studying (*estudiaba*), rather than an event starting in the middle of this studying, which would have required the preterit tense. To add to the notion of simultaneity the word *mientras* ("while") links the two acts.

The imperfect tense (*decías*) could have been used instead of the imperfect progressive without changing the meaning. Conversely, the imperfect progressive (*estaba estudiando*) could have been used instead of the imperfect tense in the second part of the sentence. It is not a question of meaning, but of emphasis.

The use of the imperfect progressive tense simply puts more emphasis on the ongoing nature of the verb. The use of the imperfect tense doesn't emphasize this ongoing quality; in context, it merely takes it for granted. The imperfect progressive tense is more emphatic, more insistent in "stretching out" the past action or situation in the mind's eye.

The imperfect progressive tense, of course, does *not* share another use of the imperfect tense: that of referring to repeated, habitual actions.

Future Progressive

The purpose of the future progressive tense is to refer to an action or state that will be ongoing in the future. This tense is formed by conjugating the verb *estar* in the future tense (*estaré, estarás, estará, estaremos, estaréis, estarán*) and following it with the present participle. See the following examples:

Estaré leyendo el libro esta noche.	I'll be reading the book tonight.
Estaremos hablando de eso.	We'll be speaking about that.
¿Qué estarás diciendo en la reunión?	What will you be saying at the meeting?

In each of these cases, we are referring to an activity that will be in progress at some time in the future.

10.4

Conditional Progressive

If you speak in the conditional progressive, you are referring to an act or situation that someone *would* be in the middle of *if* certain conditions were to prevail. To form this tense, you have the present participle follow the conditional tense of the helping verb *estar* (*estaría, estarías, estaría, estaríamos, estaríais, estarían*). See the following examples:

Estaría leyendo si hubiera tiempo.	I would be reading if there were time.
Estaríamos hablando de eso si él no estuviera.	We would be talking about that if he weren't here.

¿Qué estarías diciendo si no te hubieran interrumpido?	What would you be saying if they hadn't interrupted you?

The last of the preceding sentences contains an example of the imperfect subjunctive compound tense (*hubieran interrumpido*).

◀ *SEE ALSO 14.1, "Formation of Imperfect Subjunctive"* ▶

10.5 VARIANT WAYS TO FORM PROGRESSIVE TENSES

Gradual Progression

From Beginning to Present

Negative Connotation

Continuing Actions or Conditions

Although the use of *estar* plus the present participle is the most common way of forming the progressive tenses, you can form these tenses by using verbs of motion (*ir*, *venir*, and so on) or of continuation (*continuar*, *seguir*, and so on) plus the present participle. The connotation varies, depending on the verb of motion you use. In this section, you learn how to use these other ways of forming the progressive to obtain varying connotations.

Gradual Progression

If you want to produce the feeling of a steady, gradual quality in the progression, use the verb *ir* plus the present participle. See the following examples:

Manuel va vendiendo libros cada vez más.	Manuel is (gradually) selling more and more books.
Ella iba buscando el mejor candidato.	She was (gradually) searching for the best candidate.

10.5

From Beginning to Present

If you want to create the feeling that something has been happening for a long time and is still happening, you can use the verb *venir* plus the present participle. See the following examples:

Manuel viene vendiendo libros desde 1985.	Manuel has been selling books since 1985.
Vengo estudiando chino por mucho tiempo ya.	I've been studying Chinese for a long time now.

As you can see, English usually expresses this feeling by using the three-part "have/has-been-doing" form of the verb. In other words, English uses the present tense of the helping verb *to have* plus the past participle of the verb *to be* plus the present participle of whatever verb we want to be the main idea. This can be done in Spanish as well (present tense of *haber* plus the past participle of *estar* plus the present participle of the verb we want to be the main idea). For example, the two previous Spanish sentences could have been expressed as the following:

> Manuel ha estado vendiendo libros desde 1985.

> He estado estudiando chino por mucho tiempo.

These forms are not incorrect, but they are somewhat awkward. It is better to use the verb *venir* plus the present participle to provide the sensation that something has been occurring for quite a while and is continuing to occur.

Negative Connotation

Another verb of motion, *andar*, can be used with the present participle to show progression. But using this construction often produces a negative connotation. See the following examples:

Esa mujer anda hablando mal de todos.	That woman goes around badmouthing everybody.
Ese hombre andaba arruinando todo.	That man went around (used to go around) ruining everything.

Continuing Actions or Conditions

When you want to demonstrate that an action or condition is, was, will be, or would be continuing, you can use either the verb *continuar* or the verb *seguir* plus the present participle. See the following examples:

Continúan comiendo a pesar de todo.	They continue to eat in spite of everything.
Siguen comiendo a pesar de todo.	They keep on eating in spite of everything.
Continuará durmiendo.	He'll continue to sleep.
Seguirá durmiendo.	He'll keep on sleeping.

It is important to note that no matter what the form of the English is, in Spanish you can use only the infinitive form of the verb after the verb *continuar* or the verb *seguir*—they each have the meaning of continuing to do something, to keep on doing something.

10.6 PROGRESSIVE FOR WONDERING AND PROBABILITY

Wondering and Probability in the Present

Wondering and Probability in the Past

Verbs in the future tense can be used to refer to wondering and to probability in the present. The conditional tense can be used to refer to wondering and to probability in the past.

Wondering and Probability in the Present

Just as verbs in the future tense can also be used to refer to wondering and probability in the present, verbs in the future progressive tense can be used to refer to wondering and probability about acts or situations in progress in the present. See the following examples of wondering about the present:

◀ *SEE ALSO 9.3, "Wondering and Probability"* ▶

¿Qué estará haciendo Miguel?	I wonder what Miguel is doing. (What can Miguel be doing?)
¿Dónde estarán trabajando mis amigos?	I wonder where my friends are working. (Where can my friends be working?)
¿Qué estará diciendo el jefe?	I wonder what the boss is saying. (What can the boss be saying?)

Two possible ways of expressing the Spanish thought are given for each Spanish sentence here. The same thought could be expressed in English in several ways. The thought is what is important.

Depending on context, the future progressive tense, like the future tense, can be the answer to a question if made as a statement rather than a question. In this case, it indicates probability rather than absolute certainty. Compare these direct statements with indications of probability:

Miguel está viendo la televisión.	Miguel is watching television.

10.6

183

Miguel estará viendo la televisión.	Miguel is probably watching television. (Miguel must be watching television.)
Están trabajando en el mercado.	They are working at the market.
Estarán trabajando en el mercado.	They are probably working at the market. (They must be working at the market.)

Wondering and Probability in the Past

Just as verbs in the conditional tense can also be used to refer to wondering and probability in the past, verbs in the conditional progressive tense can be used to refer to wondering and probability about acts or situations in progress in the past. See the following examples of wondering about the present:

¿Qué estaría haciendo Miguel ayer?	I wonder what Miguel was doing yesterday.
¿Dónde estarían trabajando mis amigos el domingo pasado?	I wonder where my friends were working last Sunday.
¿Qué estaría diciendo el jefe?	I wonder what the boss was saying.

Depending on context, the conditional progressive tense, like the conditional tense, can be the answer to a question if made as a statement rather than a question. In this case, it indicates probability rather than absolute certainty. Compare these direct statements with indications of probability about the past:

Miguel estuvo viendo la televisión ayer.	Miguel was watching television yesterday
Miguel estaría viendo la televisión ayer.	Miguel was probably watching television yesterday. (Miguel must have been watching television yesterday.)
Estuvieron trabajando el domingo pasado.	They were working last Sunday.
Estarían trabajando el domingo pasado.	They probably were working last Sunday. (They must have been working last Sunday.)

Estuvo diciendo que tú no trabajas.	He was saying (that) you don't work.
Estaría diciendo que tú no trabajas.	He was probably saying that you don't work. (He must have been saying that you don't work.)

11

PAST PARTICIPLE/ PASSIVE VOICE/ COMPOUND TENSES

11.1 FORMING THE PAST PARTICIPLE

Regular Past Participles

Irregular Past Participles

The past participle in Spanish has many uses. In this section, you learn how to form the past participle. In the following sections, you learn the various uses of the past participle.

Regular Past Participles

Regular past participles—in other words, the vast majority of past participles—are formed by first removing the infinitive ending of the verb. When that is done, the rest depends on whether you are dealing with an *-ar*, *-er*, or *-ir* verb.

-ar Verbs

The past participles of *-ar* verbs are formed using the following formula:

1. Remove the infinitive ending of the verb.

2. Add *-ado* to the stem.

See the following example, using the verb *hablar* (to speak):

1. hablar

2. habl - ar

3. habl

4. habl + ado

5. hablado

There are no irregular *-ar* verbs in the past participle. Every *-ar* verb follows this pattern.

◀ *SEE ALSO 7.1, "Present Tense: Regular Verbs"* ▶

-er Verbs

The past participles of regular -er verbs are formed using the following formula:

1. Remove the infinitive ending of the verb.
2. Add -ido to the stem.

See the following example, using the verb *comer* (to eat):

1. comer
2. com - er
3. com
4. com + ido
5. comido

Even though the verb *ser* is so short, it is completely regular in the past participle. It is formed according to the same principle given for *comer*. See the following example of forming the past participle of *ser*.

1. ser
2. s - er
3. s
4. s + ido
5. sido

All regular -er verbs follow this pattern. The irregular -er past participles are treated in the next section.

11.1

-ir Verbs

The past participles of regular -ir verbs are formed using the following formula:

1. Remove the infinitive ending of the verb.
2. Add -ido to the stem.

See the following example, using the verb *vivir* (to live):

1. vivir
2. viv - ir
3. viv

4. viv + ido

5. vivido

Even though the verb *ir* is so short, it is completely regular in the past participle. It is formed according to the same principle given for *vivir*. See the following example of forming the past participle of *ir*:

1. ir

2. ___ - ir

3. ___

4. ___ + ido

5. ido

The pattern for the formation of regular *-ir* verb past participles is exactly the same as that of regular *-er* verb past participles. The irregular *-ir* past participles are treated in the next section.

Irregular Past Participles

A small group of *-er* and *-ir* verbs are irregular in the past participle and do not follow the formulas shown in the previous section. Every one of these irregular past participles ends in either *-to* or *-cho*. See the following table for irregular past participles that end in *-to*.

IRREGULAR PAST PARTICIPLES THAT END IN *-TO*

Infinitive	English	Past Participle
abrir	to open	abierto
cubrir	to cover	cubierto
escribir	to write	escrito
morir	to die	muerto
poner	to put	puesto
romper	to break	roto
volver	to return (go back)	vuelto
ver	to see	visto

See the following table for irregular past participles that end in *-cho*.

IRREGULAR PAST PARTICIPLES THAT END IN *-CHO*

Infinitive	English	Past Participle
decir	to say, tell	dicho
hacer	to do, make	hecho

Many verbs are based on the verbs in the two preceding tables. The meanings are changed somewhat by adding prefixes. See the following list and their past participles:

reabrir (to reopen): reabierto

describir (to describe): descrito

descubrir (to discover, to uncover): descubierto

recubrir (to surface, coat, re-cover): recubierto

contradecir (to contradict): contradicho

componer (to compose): compuesto

descomponer (to disturb, upset; put out of order, put out of commission): descompuesto

devolver (to return, give back): devuelto

exponer (to expose, display): expuesto

predecir (to predict): predicho

redecir (to say over and over): redicho

rehacer (to do over): rehecho

satisfacer (to satisfy): satisfecho

These verbs have the same past participles as the core verbs on which they are based, with, of course, the addition of the prefixes, so the past participles are *reabierto, descrito, descubierto,* and so on.

The last verb listed, *satisfacer,* is based on the verb *hacer* and is conjugated exactly the same in all tenses and in the past participle. The only difference is that *satisfacer* has the letter *f* instead of *h* in all forms. The past participle, then, is *satisfecho*.

11.2 PAST PARTICIPLE USED AS AN ADJECTIVE

As in English, one of the uses of the past participle is to describe a noun or nouns. In other words, it can be used as an adjective. As is the case with all adjectives, the past participle, when used as an adjective, must agree in number and gender with the noun(s) it describes.

◀ *SEE ALSO 5.2, "Adjectives in Agreement"* ▶

◀ *SEE ALSO 5.3, "Placement of Adjectives"* ▶

See the following examples:

el libro cerrado	the closed book
los libros cerrados	the closed books
la ventana cerrada	the closed window
las ventanas cerradas	the closed windows
un lápiz roto	a broken pencil
unos lápices rotos	some broken pencils
una mesa rota	a broken table
unas mesas rotas	some broken tables

Note: The plural of *lápiz* is *lápices* because of Spanish spelling rules.

◀ *SEE ALSO 1.4, "The Spelling System"* ▶

When used with the function of an adjective, the past participle does not have to be right next to the noun it modifies; it can be separated from it by one of the two verbs in Spanish that are equivalent to the English *to be*—that is, *ser* to form the passive voice or *estar* for describing the condition of the noun. See Sections 11.3 and 11.4.

11.3 PAST PARTICIPLE IN THE PASSIVE VOICE

Explanation of the Passive Voice

Formation of the Passive Voice

In both English and Spanish, an action can be expressed by a sentence formed either in the active voice or in the passive voice. In this section, you learn how to form the passive voice in Spanish.

Explanation of the Passive Voice

In a sentence in the **active voice,** the subject is the performer of the action expressed by the verb, the one who *does*. The object of an active sentence receives the action expressed by the verb. Take the following example of an active sentence:

The policeman arrested the criminal.

The subject is the policeman, because he is the one who is doing the arresting; he is *performing* the action of the verb *arrested*. The object of the sentence is the criminal because he is the one being arrested; the criminal is *receiving* the action of that same verb.

On the other hand, in a sentence in the **passive voice,** the grammatical subject receives the action of the verb. You can express the same thought as the one in the active sentence with a passive sentence. See the following example:

The criminal was arrested by the policeman.

11.3

In this sentence in the passive voice, the grammatical subject is the criminal, but he is not doing the arresting; he is being arrested. He is receiving the action of the verb.

Another way to express this difference is to say that the person or thing that is the object of an active sentence (the criminal) is the subject of a passive sentence. In addition, the person or thing that was the subject of an active sentence (the policeman) does not necessarily have to be mentioned in a passive sentence. See the following example:

The criminal was arrested.

If the performer of the act is mentioned at all, he/she/it is introduced by the preposition *by* to indicate this fact—for example, "by the policeman."

WORDS TO GO . . .WORDS TO GO . . .WORDS TO GO

In a sentence in the **active voice,** the subject performs the action of the verb, and the object receives the action of the verb.

In a sentence in the **passive voice,** the subject receives the action of the verb.

Formation of the Passive Voice

In English, we express the passive voice by using some form of the verb *to be* plus the past participle—for example, "was arrested."

In Spanish, the process is the same. However, two verbs in Spanish can be translated into English as "to be": *ser* and *estar.* They cannot both be used to form the passive voice. The verb *estar* is *never* used to form the passive voice; it has another function (see section 11.4). The only one of these two verbs that can be used to form a sentence in the passive voice is *ser.*

The formula for the passive voice in Spanish is:

1. The verb *ser* in whatever tense is needed (like English *is, was, will be, would be* and so on)

Followed by:

2. The past participle

The following list shows the conjugation of *ser* in the simple tenses:

Present: soy, eres, es somos, sois, son

Preterite: fui, fuiste, fue, fuimos, fuisteis, fueron

Future: seré, serás, será, seremos, seréis, serán

Imperfect: era, eras, era, éramos, erais , eran

Conditional: sería, serías, sería, seríamos, seríais, serían

Present Subjunctive: sea, seas, sea, seamos, seáis, sean

Imperfect Subjunctive: fuera, fueras, fuera, fuéramos, fuerais, fueran

In English the verb *to be* can be used in any tense with the past participle to form the passive voice—for example, *is arrested, was arrested, will be arrested*, and so on. The same is true in Spanish. It is important, then, to know how to conjugate the helping verb *ser* in all tenses.

See the following table for examples of sentences in the active voice and their counterparts in the passive voice.

SENTENCES IN THE ACTIVE VOICE COMPARED TO SENTENCES IN THE PASSIVE VOICE

Active Sentences	Passive Sentences
El policía arrestó al criminal.	El criminal fue arrestado (por el policía).
The policeman arrested the criminal.	The criminal was arrested (by the policeman).
Roberto lee estos libros.	Estos libros son leídos (por Roberto).
Roberto reads these books.	These books are read (by Roberto).
Ella leerá esta revista.	Esta revista será leída (por ella).
She will read this magazine.	This magazine will be read (by her).
Ella va a leer esta revista.	She is going to read this magazine.
Esta revista va a ser leída (por ella).	This magazine is going to be read (by her).
He visto a las chicas.	I've seen the girls.
Las chicas han sido vistas (por mí).	The girls were seen (by me).

The sentences in the preceding table appear in several different tenses; this is why the verb *ser* is conjugated in various tenses (*fue, son, será, va a ser, han sido*, and so on).

The past participles in the preceding passive sentences have endings that indicate the gender and number of the noun they modify (*-ado, -ídos, -ída, vistas*).

It is important to remember that, when used with *ser* to form the passive voice, the past participle is considered to be an adjective and, therefore, agrees in number and gender with the noun it modifies.

The second, third, and fourth preceding sentences involve the use of **demonstrative adjectives** (*estos, esta*). Demonstrative adjectives and pronouns are described in detail in Chapter 17.

◀ SEE ALSO 5.2, *"Adjectives in Agreement"* ▶

◀ SEE ALSO 17.2, *"Demonstrative Adjectives"* ▶

WORDS TO GO . . .WORDS TO GO . . .WORDS TO GO

A **demonstrative adjective** is a demonstrative pronoun that is used as an adjective to modify a noun.

A **demonstrative pronoun** is a pronoun that points out one or more persons or things (in English, *this, these, that, those*).

Because sentences in the passive voice express the same ideas that can be expressed in the active voice, the sentences in this voice never merely describe someone or something; they always involve action, someone or something doing something. To put this passively, it's something being done by someone or something.

11.4 PASSIVE VOICE VS. DESCRIPTION OF CONDITION

The passive voice uses some form of the verb *ser* plus the past participle. It involves action. The same thought can be expressed by a sentence in the active voice. (See 11.3.)

On the other hand, you use the verb *estar* with the past participle to simply describe the state or condition of someone or something. This state or condition could be the result of a previous action, but the sentence that uses *estar* plus a past participle does not depict that action; it merely describes the condition or state that the person or thing is in at the moment the sentence describes.

◀ *SEE ALSO 15.2, "Two Forms of Being:* ser *vs.* estar*"* ▶

Unfortunately, the English translation of a sentence in the passive voice turns out the same as a sentence that merely describes a state or condition. See the following examples:

Las puertas fueron cerradas.	The doors were closed.
Las puertas estaban cerradas.	The doors were closed.
La ventana será rota.	The window will be broken.
La ventana estará rota.	The window will be broken.

Although the English sentences here do not distinguish between passive voice and description, they can be made to do so by context or by adding words. In the first sentence (passive voice), if the context of the conversation does not make it clear, the words "by the janitor" or "by someone" can be added to not only tell us exactly who closed the doors, but also make it clear that we are de-picting action, not description. This cannot be done with the second sentence; the Spanish sentence shows that the sentence does not refer to anyone doing anything. It just provides a description of the condition the doors were in.

In the third English sentence, if context does not make it clear that we are refer-ring to future action (passive voice), we could tell who we think will do it by adding words such as "by the children playing baseball" or the vague "by some-one." We could not do that in the case of the last sentence. The third Spanish

11.4

sentence tells us that it is referring not to future action, but to a future condition of the window, possibly as a result of previous action.

Of course, it is possible to use both the passive voice and the descriptive sentence together to show explicitly that an action led to a resulting condition. See the following:

Las puertas fueron cerradas a las siete. Entonces ya estaban cerradas cuando llegué.	The doors were closed (by someone) at seven o'clock. So they were already (in a) closed (condition) when I arrived.
La ventana será rota por los chicos muy pronto. Por eso, estará rota la semana que viene.	The window will be broken by the children very soon. Therefore, it will be (in a) broken (condition) next week.

It is important to remember that, when used with the verb *estar* to describe a state or condition, the past participle is being used as an adjective. Because of this, the past participle must agree in number and gender with the noun it modifies.

11.5 THE VERB *HABER* TO SHOW PRESENCE/EXISTENCE

The common English idioms that indicate the presence or existence of someone or something are *there is* and *there are* in the present tense. This expression can be used in all tenses: *there was, there were; there will be; there would be; there had been*; and so on. These expressions are idioms because the direction *there* is not really involved.

The Spanish language has a common idiom for showing existence as well. The Spanish idiom in question has nothing to do with the direction *there* or with the verb *to be*. The Spanish idiom denoting existence uses the verb *haber*. To denote existence, this verb is conjugated only in the third person singular.

When it shows existence, the verb *haber* is conjugated as follows:

CONJUGATION OF *HABER* FOR DENOTING EXISTENCE IN VARIOUS TENSES

Present	hay	there is, there are
Preterit	hubo	there was, there were
Imperfect	había	there was, there were
Future	habrá	there will be
Substitute future	va a haber	there is going to be
Conditional	habría	there would be
Present subjunctive	haya*	
Imperfect subjunctive	hubiera*	
Present perfect	ha habido	there has been
Preterit perfect	hubo habido	there had been
Past perfect	había habido	there had been
Future perfect	habrá habido	there will have been
Conditional perfect	habría habido	there would have been
Present subjunctive perfect	haya habido*	
Imperfect subjunctive perfect	hubiera habido*	

*A simple translation into English of the items marked with asterisks is not possible. Chapters 13 and 14 explain this.

11.5

199

You can also use the verb *haber* as a present participle (*habiendo*) and in the infinitive form (*haber*).

See the following examples using *haber* in various ways to express existence:

Hay muchos libros aquí.	There are many (a lot of) books here.
Había muchos libros aquí.	There used to be many books here.
Habría muchos libros aquí, si ...	There would be many books here, if ...
Habiendo muchos libros aquí ...	There being many books here ...
Va a haber muchos libros aquí.	There are going to be many books here.

11.6 *HABER* PLUS PAST PARTICIPLE FOR COMPOUND TENSES

Present Perfect

Past Perfect

Past Anterior

Future Perfect

Conditional Perfect

Infinitive Perfect

Progressive Perfect

Spanish, like English, has compound tenses. These tenses are also referred to as the perfect tenses. In both languages, there are two parts to these tenses: the helping verb, which is conjugated, and the past participle.

When used as the helping verb in a compound tense, unlike when it is used to show existence (see Section 11.5), the verb *haber* can be conjugated in any of the persons (first, second, third) and in the singular or plural, like any other verb.

It is important to remember that, when used as part of a compound tense, the Spanish past participle does *not* agree with anything in number or gender. It is not considered an adjective when used with the helping verb; it is part of a verb construction. When the past participle has this function, it always ends with the letter *-o*.

11.6

Present Perfect

You know that the present perfect tense in English is formed by using the present tense of the helping verb *to have* before the past participle ("I have eaten," "you have eaten," "he has eaten," "she has eaten," and so on). This tense refers to an action or state that took place or existed at some time before the present moment. It doesn't specify exactly when.

In Spanish, the present tense is formed by conjugating the helping verb *haber* in the present tense and placing it before the past participle. (Section 11.1 covers the formation of the past participle.) The verb *haber* is irregular in the present tense. See the following for the present tense of *haber:*

yo	he
tú	has
él	ha
ella	ha
Ud.	ha
nosotros/as	hemos
vosotros/as	habéis
ellos	han
ellas	han
Uds.	han

As you can see, the only form of *haber* that is regular in the present tense is the one that you would use with *vosotros/as*.

When the verb *haber* is used to show existence in the present (see Section 11.5), the third-person singular form (the only one used to denote existence) is conjugated as *hay*. In the previous list, note that when used as the helping verb, the third-person singular form is conjugated as *ha*. In other words, the third-person singular form of *haber* is conjugated in two different ways, depending on use.

See these sample sentences in the present perfect tense:

He comido.	I've eaten.
¿Has oído?	Have you heard?
Carlota ha venido.	Carlota has come.
Hemos abierto las puertas.	We have opened the doors.
¿Habéis roto los platos?	Have you broken the dishes?
No me han visto.	They haven't seen me.

Note that when the past participle is used with the helping verb *haber*, it is part of a verb form, a compound tense. For that reason, it is not being used as an adjective and always ends with the letter *-o*.

Past Perfect

In English, the past perfect (also called the pluperfect) is formed by using the past tense of *to have* plus the past participle ("I had eaten," "you had eaten," "he had eaten," "she had eaten," and so on). This tense refers to an action or state that occurred or existed at some unspecified time before a specific time in the past. ("By 6:00 P.M. yesterday, I *had* already *eaten*.")

The Spanish past perfect tense is formed by conjugating the helping verb *haber* in the imperfect tense and placing it in front of the past participle. The conjugation of *haber* in the imperfect tense is: *había, habías, había, habíamos, habíais, habían.*

See the following examples of sentences in the past perfect tense:

(Yo) había comido.	I had eaten. (I'd eaten.)
¿Habías oído?	Had you heard?
Carlota había venido.	Carlota had come.
Habíamos abierto las puertas.	We had opened the doors.
¿Habíais roto los platos?	Had you broken the dishes?
No me habían visto.	They hadn't seen me.

The preceding sentences refer vaguely to an unspecified time that occurred before a specific time, even though that specific time is not stated in the previous sentences. The first sentence could have been "A las seis de la tarde yo ya había comido." The specified time is 6:00, but the event (eating) took place at some unspecified time before then. It could have been an hour before, or it could have been two weeks before. The speaker who uses the past perfect tense does not consider the time he or she ate to be important. The important thing is that by 6:00, he or she had already done this.

Past Anterior

In practice, this tense is not used as much as the preterit tense or the past perfect tense in ordinary conversation. This tense is used in Spanish chiefly in **temporal clauses** when the verb of the **main clause** is in the preterit tense. In other words, you use this tense if two things are present:

1. The main clause informs us that something was done at some specific point in time and, therefore, uses the preterit tense—for example, "I picked up the phone."

2. The **subordinate clause** is a temporal clause; that is, it begins with an adverb having to do with time (*when, as soon as, after,* and so on)—for example, "after they had arrived."

In Spanish, this compound tense is used especially when the action or state of the main clause, which is expressed in the preterit tense ("I picked up the phone"), takes place after the action or state of the subordinate clause ("they had arrived"). In other words, "they" had already arrived when I picked up the phone.

The English sentence would then be "I picked up the phone after they had arrived."

WORDS TO GO . . .WORDS TO GO . . .WORDS TO GO

A **temporal clause** is an adverbial clause that indicates the time a particular action or state occurs. It is introduced by an adverb of time (*when, while, before, after, as soon as,* and so on).

The **main clause** (also called independent clause) is a clause that forms a complete sentence in itself, as opposed to the subordinate clause.

The **subordinate clause** (also called the dependent clause) is a clause that cannot form a complete sentence in itself, but has to be connected to a main clause.

It doesn't matter, of course, which clause comes first. See the following examples of sentences that use the past anterior tense:

Descolgué el teléfono después (de) que hubieron llegado.	I picked up the phone after they had arrived.
Después (de) que hubieron llegado, descolgué el teléfono.	After they had arrived, I picked up the phone.

It is notable that English uses the past perfect tense, as seen in these examples, both where Spanish uses the past perfect tense and where Spanish might use the past anterior tense.

You form the past anterior tense by conjugating the helping verb *haber* in the preterit tense and placing it before the past participle. *Haber* is one of those verbs that, in the preterit tense, contains the vowel *-u-* in the stem.

The conjugation of the preterit tense of *haber* is: *hube, hubiste, hubo, hubimos, hubisteis, hubieron.*

In colloquial English, the preterit tense usually is used in both clauses. In ordinary colloquial conversation, most Spanish-speakers today simply use the preterit tense for both verbs as well:

Descolgué el teléfono despúes (de) que llegaron.	I picked up the phone after they arrived.
Despúes (de) que llegaron, descolgué el teléfono.	After they arrived, I picked up the phone.

The Spanish past anterior is used only in very careful speech and careful writing. The preterit tense and the past perfect tense are more common in these situations.

Future Perfect

As in English, you use the Spanish future perfect tense to express the idea that an action or state will take place or exist at some vague, unspecified time before another very specific time in the future.

In English, you might say, "By nine o'clock tomorrow morning, I will already have eaten." In that case, "nine o'clock tomorrow morning" is the very specific time in the future. "I will … have eaten" is the statement that your eating will have taken place at some vague, unspecified time, but whatever time that will be, the important thing is that it will be before that specific future time ("nine o'clock tomorrow morning"). Spanish usage is the same as English usage in the future perfect tense.

The future perfect tense is formed by conjugating the helping verb *haber* in the future tense and placing it before the past participle.

The conjugation of the helping verb *haber* in the future tense is: *habré, habrás, habrá, habremos, habréis, habrán*.

See the following examples of sentences that make use of the future perfect tense:

Ya habré desayunado a las nueve.	I will have already had breakfast at (by) nine o'clock.
La semana que viene habremos salido.	Next week we'll have left.

11.6

| ¿Habrás terminado para el próximo mes? | Will you have finished by next month? |
| El viernes a las cinco lo habrán visto. | (By) five o'clock Friday they will have seen it. |

You can see that the verb *haber* is one of those verbs that drops the vowel *-e-* from the infinitive ending before adding the future endings.

Conditional Perfect

As in English, you use the Spanish conditional perfect tense to express the idea that an action or state would have taken place or would have existed had certain other factors existed.

In English, you might say, "I would have gone, if they had invited me." In this case, the factor that would have determined your going is the nonexistent invitation. Spanish usage is the same as English usage in the conditional perfect tense.

The conditional perfect tense is formed by conjugating the helping verb *haber* in the conditional tense and placing it before the past participle.

The conjugation of *haber* in the conditional tense is: *habría, habrías, habría, habríamos, habríais, habrían*.

See the following examples of sentences that use the conditional perfect tense:

Ya habría desayunado si hubiera habido tiempo.	I would have had breakfast if there had been time.
Habrían salido si eso hubiera pasado.	They would have left if that had happened.
¿Habrías terminado si no te hubieran interrumpido?	Would you have finished if they had not interrupted you?
El viernes a las cinco lo habría visto, si me hubieran avisado.	I would have seen it at five o'clock on Friday if they had let me know.

◁ **SEE ALSO 14.1**, *"Formation of the Imperfect Subjunctive"* ▷

In the preceding sentences, the main clause has a verb in the conditional perfect tense, but in each case, the dependent clause has a verb in the imperfect subjunctive compound tense. Chapter 14 explains why this is necessary.

Infinitive Perfect

The infinitive is the only form of the verb that can be used as a noun in Spanish. If a verb is used with the same function as a noun, it will be either the subject or the object of a verb. See the following examples of the infinitive used as a noun:

(El) viajar es un placer.	Traveling is a pleasure.
Prefiero salir.	I would rather leave.

In the first preceding sentence, the infinitive is the subject of the verb *es*. When the infinitive is the subject of a verb, it doesn't matter whether the definite article *el* is used with it. If it is used, the definite article always is masculine singular.

◁ *SEE ALSO 15.3, "Verbs as Nouns"* ▷

In English, when a verb is used as a noun, it very often takes the form of the present participle, as in the first preceding sentence. This can never happen in Spanish. The only form of the verb that can be used as a noun, whether subject or object, is the infinitive.

The second sentence could just as well have come out in English as "I prefer to leave" or "I prefer leaving." But in Spanish, it must be the infinitive form of the verb.

The same is true when the helping verb *haber* is used with a past participle to form a compound tense. If this compound tense is used as a noun—the subject or object of a sentence—the helping verb must be in the infinitive. See the following examples:

(El) haber asistido a la reunión resultó en conocer a muchas personas.	Having attended the meeting resulted in meeting many people.
Habrían preferido no haber ido.	They would have preferred not to have gone.
(El) haber comido demasiado me hizo incómodo.	Having overeaten made me uncomfortable.
Quiero haberlo hecho ya.	I want to have already done it. (I want to have it over and done with.)

11.6

In the first and third sentences, the infinitive compound verb is the subject of the verb ("haber asistido" and "haber comido"). In each of the second and last of those sentences, the infinitive compound verb is the object of the verb ("no haber ido" and "haberlo hecho").

(The *lo* attached to the helping verb *haber* in the last preceding sentence is the direct object pronoun.)

◀ *SEE ALSO 4.2, "Object Pronouns"* ▶

No matter what form the verb takes in English, if the verb is being used in the same manner in which a noun is used, as the subject or object of another verb, the only form it can have in Spanish is the infinitive. This is true of the helping verb *haber* as well.

Progressive Perfect

The progressive perfect tense consists of the present participle of the helping verb (*habiendo*) being used before the past participle. The Spanish usage is basically the same as the English usage of the same construction. See the following examples:

Habiendo hablado, bajó de la plataforma.	Having spoken, he came down from the platform.
Habiéndome visto, tuvo que saludarme.	Having seen me, he had to greet me.

The progressive perfect tense is also used to show that by having done something, something else happened as a result. See the following example:

Habiendo estudiado, hice bien en el examen. By having studied, I did well on the exam.

◀ *SEE ALSO 10.3, "Present Participle Used Alone"* ▶

As in English, the clauses could have been reversed, as follows:

Hice bien en el examen, habiendo estudiado.	I did well in the exam by having studied.

In cause-and-effect statements, Spanish does not use the preposition equivalent to English *by* or any other preposition.

11.7 WONDERING AND PROBABILITY IN COMPOUND TENSES

Before the Present Moment

Before a Past Moment

Just as the future tense, depending on context, can be used to denote wondering and probability about an action or state in the present, the future perfect tense can also, depending on context, show wondering and probability concerning an action or state that took place at some time before the present moment.

In the same way that the conditional tense, depending on context, can be used to demonstrate wondering and probability about an action or state that took place in the past, the conditional perfect tense can, depending on context, show wondering and probability about an action or state that took place at some time before a moment in the past.

◀ SEE ALSO 9.3, *"Wondering and Probability"* ▶

Before the Present Moment

The future perfect tense can be used to express wondering or probability about an action or state that has taken place at some indefinite time before the present moment. See the following examples that contrast the present perfect with the future perfect used to express wondering or probability:

¿Qué ha hecho?	What has he done?
¿Qué habrá hecho?	I wonder what he has done. (What could he have done?)
No ha hecho nada.	He hasn't done anything.
No habrá hecho nada.	He probably hasn't done anything. (He must have done nothing.)
¿Adónde han ido?	Where have they gone?
¿Adónde habrán ido?	I wonder where they've gone. (Where could they have gone?)
Han ido al cine.	They've gone to the movies.

11.7

Habrán ido al cine.	They've probably gone to the movies. (They must have gone to the movies.)

Before a Past Moment

The conditional perfect tense can express wondering or probability about an action or state that had taken place at some indefinite time before a specific time in the past. See the following examples that contrast the past perfect with the conditional perfect used to express wondering or probability:

¿Qué había hecho?	What had he done?
¿Qué habría hecho?	I wonder what he had done.
No había hecho nada.	He hadn't done anything.
No habría hecho nada.	He probably hadn't done anything.
¿Adónde habían ido?	Where had they gone?
¿Adónde habrían ido?	I wonder where they had gone.
Habían ido al cine.	They had gone to the movies.
Habrían ido al cine.	They probably had gone to the movies.

Keep in mind that *haber* is one of those verbs that, in the future and conditional tenses, drops the infinitive vowel (letter *-e-* in this verb) before adding the future or the conditional endings.

◄ SEE ALSO 9.2, *"Conditional Tense"* ►

You can see in the preceding sentences that the imperfect form of the verb *haber* is *había*, and the conditional form of this verb is *habría*. They may look similar to the English-speaker, but you can see the great difference in meaning that the presence or absence of the letter *-r-* after the letter *-b-* makes.

12

REFLEXIVE VERBS

12.1 REFLEXIVE OBJECT PRONOUNS

Reflexive verbs in Spanish serve several purposes. You will learn about these purposes and how to use them further in this chapter. This first section shows how to form them. Later you'll learn how to use them when someone or something does something to him-/her-/itself/themselves, when the subjects do things to each other, and when you don't want to specify who is performing an action, but instead just want to refer to the action.

Reflexive verbs share some but not all of the same object pronouns—direct and indirect—as nonreflexive verbs. In this section, you learn the object pronouns that are used with reflexive verbs.

WORDS TO GO . . .WORDS TO GO . . .WORDS TO GO

Reflexive verbs are verbs of which the subject is identical to the object. The subject is doing something that *reflects back* on him-/her-/itself.

◄ SEE ALSO 4.2, *"Object Pronouns"* ▶

◄ SEE ALSO 4.3, *"Object Pronouns of Prepositions"* ▶

The following table shows the reflexive object pronouns of both verbs and prepositions.

REFLEXIVE OBJECT PRONOUNS

Subject Pronoun	Reflexive Object of Verbs	Pronouns of Prepositions
yo	me	mí
tú	te	ti
él, ella, Ud.	se	sí
nosotros/as	nos	nosotros/as
vosotros/as	os	vosotros/as
ellos, ellas, Uds.	se	sí

Look at the reflexive object pronoun used as the object of verbs (second column). The first- and second-person pronouns, both singular and plural, are exactly the same as the object pronouns for the direct object and the indirect object: *me, te, nos, os*. The only ones that differ are in the third person. The reflexive object pronoun for the third person, whether singular or plural, is *se*.

The third column presents the reflexive prepositional object pronouns. You can see that the reflexive prepositional object pronouns *nosotros/as* and *vosotros/as* are identical to the subject pronouns. The others are different: *mí, ti,* and *sí.*

The prepositional object pronoun *mí* has an accent mark over the letter *i* only to distinguish it in writing from the possessive adjective *mi* (my). The reflexive prepositional object pronoun *sí* carries an accent mark as well, to distinguish it from *si,* meaning "if." Of course, the Spanish word for "yes," *sí,* also has an accent mark.

◄ *SEE ALSO 5.5, "Possessives"* ▶

In the next few sections, you learn how to use the reflexive verbs.

12.2 THE TRUE REFLEXIVE

In General

With Parts of the Body

With Clothing

The original and basic function of a reflexive verb is to indicate that the subject of the verb is exactly the same person or thing that is the object of that verb. In other words, the one who performs the action of the verb in question is also the one who receives the action. The one who does it is doing it to him-, her-, or itself. In English, if you use a verb reflexively, the object word always contains the **morpheme** *-self* or the plural *-selves*.

In English and in Spanish, any **transitive verb** can be used reflexively. This is the same as saying that any transitive verb can become a reflexive verb. By its nature, an **intransitive verb** cannot be turned into a reflexive verb because it cannot take an object.

WORDS TO GO . . .WORDS TO GO . . .WORDS TO GO

A **morpheme** is the smallest unit of meaning. For example, the word *boyishness,* while being one word, contains three morphemes: *boy + ish + ness.*

A **transitive verb** is a verb that can take an object—for example, *to hear.*

An **intransitive verb** is a verb that cannot take an object—for example, *to shudder.*

In General

As an example of a transitive verb, consider the English verb *to see.* It is a transitive verb because it can take an object. You can see people and things. You can construct sentences such as the following:

Mary sees a bird.

Mary sees her uncle.

Mary sees Bob.

Mary sees him.

In each of these sentences, Mary is the subject of the verb *sees;* she is performing the action of the verb.

In Spanish, the verb *ver* is transitive because it can take an object. You can translate the preceding sentences with this verb as follows:

Mary ve un pájaro.

Mary ve a su tío.

Mary ve a Bob.

Mary lo ve.

(The one-letter word in sentences two and three, *a,* is the "personal *a.*")

◄ SEE ALSO 6.1, *"Prepositions"* ▷

The preceding English and Spanish sentences are not reflexive because the subject (Mary) is not the same person as any of those four objects.

But the following sentence *is* reflexive:

Mary se ve (en el espejo).   Mary sees herself (in the mirror).

These sentences are reflexive because Mary is both the subject and the object of the verb *ve* (see). In the Spanish sentence, we know this because of the reflexive object pronoun *se* placed before the verb.

The rules for placing reflexive object pronouns of a verb follow exactly the same rules for placing any object pronoun of a verb: direct, indirect, or reflexive.

◄ SEE ALSO 4.2, *"Object Pronouns"* ▷

See the following sentences that use *verse:*

(Yo) me veo.	I see myself.
(Tú) te ves.	You see yourself.
María se ve.	María sees herself.
Pedro se ve.	Pedro sees himself.
El gato se ve.	The cat see itself.
Ud. se ve.	You see yourself.
(Nosotros) nos vemos.	We see ourselves.*
(Vosotros) os veis.	You see yourselves.*

12.2

| Ellos se ven. | They see themselves.* |
| Uds. se ven. | You see yourselves.* |

* The sentences with plural subjects (the last four sentences) could have another meaning.

◀ **SEE ALSO 12.3, *"Reflexive as Reciprocal"* ▶**

When a reflexive verb is shown in the infinitive form the way it would in a dictionary—without reference to a specific person or thing—it has the object pronoun *se* attached to it: for example, *verse* = "to see oneself." However, if you want to be specific about who or what is seeing him-, her-, or itself, you must use the corresponding reflexive object pronoun. See the following examples:

Quiero verme.	I want to see myself.
Quieres verte.	You want to see yourself.
María quiere verse.	María wants to see herself.
Pedro quiere verse.	Pedro wants to see himself.
Ud. quiere verse.	You want to see yourself.
Queremos vernos.	We want to see ourselves.*
Queréis veros.	You want to see yourselves.*
Quieren verse.	They want to see themselves.*
Uds. quieren verse.	You want to see yourselves.*

* The sentences with plural subjects (the last four sentences) could have another meaning.

Any verb that can take an object—in other words, any transitive verb—can be made into a reflexive verb. If you can do something to someone or something, you can also do it to yourself—for example, *mirarse* (to look at oneself), *lavarse* (to wash oneself, to "wash up"), *decirse* (to tell oneself), *matarse* (to kill oneself), and so on.

Often you will see reflexive verbs defined as if they had no relation to the same verb when it is not reflexive. For example, you might see *levantarse* translated as "to get up," even though there is no *get* or *up* in the verb itself. But then you might come upon the verb *levantar* in a different context, in which it is defined as "to raise" or "to lift." You might wonder what the connection is between the seemingly different meanings.

Because *levantar* means "to raise" or "to lift," when this transitive verb is made reflexive (*levantarse*), it literally means "to raise oneself, to lift oneself." Of course, this is what we really mean when we use the English idiom *to get up*. Less idiomatically, we could also translate this reflexive Spanish verb as "to rise."

The verb *llamar* means "to call"—for example, "Me llamaron por teléfono" ("They called me by telephone, they phoned me.") When reflexive, *llamarse* literally means "to call oneself," which we often translate as "to be called" or "to be named." The sentence "Me llamo Pablo" literally means "I call myself Pablo." We usually translate this as "My name is Pablo," even though there is no equivalent of *my* or *name* or *is*. The sentence could also be translated as "I am called Pablo," using the passive voice in English.

◄ *SEE ALSO 11.3, "Past Participle in the Passive Voice"* ►

See the following table, which shows representative Spanish verbs as transitive and as reflexive, with their idiomatic English translation:

SPANISH VERBS TRANSITIVE/REFLEXIVE, WITH ENGLISH IDIOMATIC EQUIVALENTS

Transitive	English	Reflexive	English
levantar	to raise, lift	levantarse	to get up, rise
acostar (ue)	to put to bed	acostarse	to go to bed
despertar (ie)	to awaken (someone)	despertarse	to awaken (oneself)
bañar	to bathe, give a bath	bañarse	to take a bath
duchar	to give a shower	ducharse	to take a shower
poner	to put, place	ponerse	to put on (clothing)
quitar	to take away, remove	quitarse	to take off (clothing)
lavar	to wash (something)	lavarse	to wash (oneself)
llamar	to call	llamarse	to call oneself, to be called, to be named

For the verb to be reflexive, the subject and the object of the verb must be identical. The one who does it is the one to whom it is done.

With Parts of the Body

In English, we refer to acts performed on our bodies by using the possessive adjective—for example, "I hurt *my* foot." In Spanish, the usual way of expressing the same thought is to use the definite article plus an indirect object pronoun instead of the possessive adjective. In a sentence like "I hurt my foot," the reflexive object pronoun must be used because the subject (I) is the same person as the object (myself).

WORDS TO GO . . .WORDS TO GO . . .WORDS TO GO

A **possessive adjective** is an adjective that shows possession (*my, your, his,* and so on.)

A **definite article** is a word placed in front of a noun to show that the noun refers to a specific member of the class named by the noun. In English, the definite article is *the.* In Spanish, the definite articles are *el, la, los,* and *las.*

This is an example of a nonreflexive verb:

Me lastimaron el pie.	They hurt my foot.

This example is nonreflexive because the subject, *ellos* (understood), is not the same as the object (*me*). The subject is *they* (understood), while the object is *me.* These are two different people.

See the following for examples of reflexive verbs involving parts of the body:

Me lastimé el pie.	I hurt my foot.
Ella se lavó el cuello.	She washed her neck.
Se peinaron (el cabello).	They combed their hair.*

*The last sentence could have another meaning.

Of course, the preceding sentences literally mean "I hurt myself the foot," "She washed herself the neck," and "They combed themselves (the hair)."

In the last sentence, the words *el cabello,* referring specifically to the hair of the head, is not necessary in Spanish. When you use the verb *peinar,* it is assumed to refer to hair. Without specifying *el cabello*—and this is the most normal way of doing it—the sentence would literally mean "I combed myself."

With Clothing

In English, we refer to activities involving our clothing by using the possessive adjective—for example, "I put on *my* shirt" or "I put *my* shirt on." In Spanish, the usual way of expressing the same thought is to use the definite article plus an indirect object pronoun instead of the possessive adjective. In a sentence like "I put on my shirt," the reflexive object pronoun must be used because the subject (I) is the same person as the object (myself).

This is an example of a nonreflexive verb:

Ella me arruinó el abrigo.   She ruined my coat.

This example is nonreflexive because the subject, *ella*, is not the same person as the object (*me*). The subject, consisting of *ella*, did it to *me*.

See the following for examples of reflexive verbs involving articles of clothing:

Me puse el sombrero.   I put on my hat.

Carlos se quitó el
abrigo.   Carlos took off his coat.

¿Te manchaste el
suéter?   Did you stain your
sweater?

Of course, the preceding sentences literally—or as close to literally as we can get—mean "I put to myself the hat," "Carlos removed from himself the coat," and "Did you stain (to) yourself the sweater?"

12.3 REFLEXIVE AS RECIPROCAL

When the reflexive form of a verb is used in a sentence in which the subject of the verb is plural, two possible meanings result, depending on context. One meaning is the truly reflexive meaning, as described in section 12.2. In that case, the following Spanish sentences are expressed in English by these English sentences:

(Nosotros) nos vemos.	We see ourselves.
(Vosotros) os veis.	You see yourselves.
Ellos se ven.	They see themselves.
Uds. se ven.	You see yourselves.
Queremos vernos.	We want to see ourselves.
Queréis veros.	You want to see yourselves.
Quieren verse.	They want to see themselves.
Uds. quieren verse.	You want to see yourselves.
Se peinaron (el cabello).	They combed their hair.

However, remember that this applies only to sentences in which the subject is plural, as in the previous sentences—when the subject is plural, the reflexive form of the verb can represent **reciprocal** rather than strictly reflexive behavior.

WORDS TO GO . . .WORDS TO GO . . .WORDS TO GO

A **reciprocal** verb is a verb used to represent mutual action by two or more subjects.

If the plural subjects of a verb are engaging in reciprocal actions, they are doing things not to *themselves*, but to *each other*.

If the preceding sentences were meant to represent reciprocal action, they would have different English translations from the ones presented. They would be as follows:

(Nosotros) nos vemos.	We see each other.
(Vosotros) os veis.	You see each other.
Ellos se ven.	They see each other.

Uds. se ven.	You see each other.
Queremos vernos.	We want to see each other.
Queréis veros.	You want to see each other.
Quieren verse.	They want to see each other.
Uds. quieren verse.	You want to see each other.
Se peinaron (el cabello).	They combed each other's hair.

So sentences using the reflexive form of the verb—as long as the subjects are plural—can be either truly reflexive (they do it to themselves) or reciprocal (they do it to each other). Because the Spanish sentences are exactly the same for the reflexive and for the reciprocal, the context, the flow of the conversation, even hand motions make clear which idea you are conveying.

If any possibility of confusion or ambiguity exists, however, the meaning can be made clear by using the expression "El uno (la una) al otro (a la otra)" if only two people are involved. If many people are involved, the expression is "Los unos (las unas) a los otros (a las otras)." See the following examples:

Nos vemos los unos a los otros.	We see each other.
Uds. se ven los unos a las otras.	You see each other.
Nos vemos el uno al otro.	We see each other.
Uds. se ven el uno a la otra.	You see each other.

These examples include more information than the English translation provides:

▶ In the first two sentences, at least four people are involved.

▶ In each of the third and fourth sentences, only two people are involved.

▶ In the first sentence, the groups involved are either all men, or mixed men and women.

▶ In the second sentence, one group consists of either all men or mixed men and women, whereas the other group consists strictly of women.

▶ In the third sentence, each of the two people involved is a man.

▶ In the fourth sentence, one of the persons is a man and the other is a woman.

12.3

A Spanish sentence that contains a plural subject of a reflexive verb can be ambiguous without the addition of expressions such as "el uno al otro" because of the literal meaning. For example, the literal meaning of *Nos vemos* is "We see us." This last English sentence is something we would never say in English; it isn't English. But that is the literal meaning of the Spanish sentence. This literal meaning, then, could come out in English as either reflexive or reciprocal. Context or the situation or gestures usually make the intended meaning clear to the Spanish-speaker. When the meaning might not be clear, you use the expressions of the "el uno al otro" type.

13

VERBS: PRESENT SUBJUNCTIVE AND COMMANDS

13.1 FORMATION OF REGULAR PRESENT SUBJUNCTIVE

The subjunctive **mood** of verbs is, for all practical purposes, almost nonexistent in modern English; it has almost disappeared from general use. But the subjunctive mood in Spanish is very much alive.

Spanish has only two grammatical moods: **indicative** and **subjunctive.** Whatever is not subjunctive is indicative. The tenses we call present, preterit, imperfect, future, conditional, and so on are all indicative. In upcoming sections, you will learn the various uses of the subjunctive mood in Spanish and how they contrast with the uses of the indicative tenses; in this section, you learn how to form the regular present subjunctive.

WORDS TO GO . . . WORDS TO GO . . . WORDS TO GO

Mood is a variation in the conjugation of a verb that shows the way in which the action or state of the verb is carried out or exists.

Indicative is the verbal mood that indicates that the action or state of the verb is considered to be a fact.

Subjunctive is the verbal mood that indicates that the action or state of the verb is considered to be hypothetical.

The regular present subjunctive is formed in this way:

1. Start with the *yo* form of the present indicative tense.

2. Remove the ending that indicates present tense and first person (*-o* or *-oy*).

3. Add the "opposite" endings to the stem.

◀ SEE ALSO 7.1, *"Verbs: Present Tense"* ▶

By "opposite" endings, we mean this: if the verb is an *-ar* verb, use the letter *e* in conjugating it. If the verb is an *-er* or *-ir* verb, use the letter *a* in conjugating it.

See this example using the verb *hablar:*

1. **Infinitive:** *hablar*

2. Yo form, present tense: *hablo*

3. Remove ending: *habl*

4. Add "opposite" ending: *hable*

Whether the verb in question is regular in the present indicative has no bearing on whether it is regular in the present subjunctive. For example, the verb *tener* is irregular in the *yo* form of the present indicative (*tengo*), but follows the rules for the regular present subjunctive:

1. Infinitive: *tener*

2. Yo form, present tense: *tengo*

3. Remove ending: *teng*

4. Add "opposite" ending: *tenga*

The same is true of stem-changing verbs, such as *cerrar:*

1. Infinitive: *cerrar*

2. Yo form, present tense: *cierro*

3. Remove ending: *cierr*

4. Add "opposite" ending: *cierre*

The following table shows the full conjugation of regular present subjunctive verbs.

EXAMPLES OF REGULAR PRESENT SUBJUNCTIVE VERBS CONJUGATED

Subject	hablar	vivir	tener	cerrar
yo	hable	viva	tenga	cierre
tú	hables	vivas	tengas	cierres
él, ella, Ud.	hable	viva	tenga	cierre
nosotros/as	hablemos	vivamos	tengamos	cerremos
vosotros/as	habléis	viváis	tengáis	cerréis
ellos, ellos, Uds.	hablen	vivan	tengan	cierren

13.1

Notice that, in the present subjunctive, the *yo* form is identical to the *él, ella, Ud.* forms. Also notice that, just in the present indicative, the stem-changing verbs (*cerrar* is the example in the preceding table) do not have a stem change when you use them with *nosotros/as* or *vosotros/as*.

Many of the verbs that are irregular in the present indicative are completely regular in the present subjunctive—in other words, they follow the rules laid out a moment ago. For example, all the irregular verbs in the present indicative that end with -oy (except for ser and ir), -zco, -go, and verbs with an interposed -y- follow the rules for the regular present subjunctive.

◀ SEE ALSO 7.2, "Present Tense: Irregular Verbs" ▶

See the following table for examples of irregular present indicative that are regular in the present subjunctive.

EXAMPLES OF REGULAR PRESENT SUBJUNCTIVE VERBS (IRREGULAR IN THE PRESENT INDICATIVE)

Subject	estar	conocer	hacer	construir
yo	esté	conozca	haga	construya
tú	estés	conozcas	hagas	construyas
él, ella, Ud.	esté	conozca	haga	construya
nosotros/as	estemos	conozcamos	hagamos	construyamos
vosotros/as	estéis	conozcáis	hagáis	construyáis
ellos, ellas, Uds.	estén	conozcan	hagan	construyan

Many Spanish textbooks present the verb dar as being irregular in the present subjunctive, but it is perfectly regular; it follows the rules laid out earlier. When you remove the -oy ending from the yo form of the present indicative, all that's left is the letter d. You then add the "opposite" endings to that d, and you have the following conjugation of dar in the present subjunctive: dé, des, dé, demos, deis, den.

The accent mark in dé distinguishes it from de (of, from).

13.2 FORMATION OF IRREGULAR PRESENT SUBJUNCTIVE

A small but frequently used group of verbs are irregular in the present subjunctive—in other words, they don't follow the rules set forth in Section 13.1. See the following list of verbs in the infinitive, with the *yo* form of the present indicative and the *yo* form of the present subjunctive. You will see that they do not follow the rules set forth in 13.1.

FORMATION OF IRREGULAR PRESENT SUBJUNCTIVE VERBS

Infinitive	Present Indicative *yo*	Present Subjunctive *yo*
ir	voy	vaya
haber	he	haya
saber	sé	sepa
ser	soy	sea

See the full conjugation of the irregular present subjunctive verbs here:

ir: vaya, vayas, vaya, vayamos, vayáis, vayan

haber: haya, hayas, haya, hayamos, hayáis, hayan

saber: sepa, sepas, sepa, sepamos, sepáis, sepan

ser: sea, seas, sea, seamos, seáis, sean

The verb *haber* has two principal uses:

▶ It is the verb used to show existence (*there is, there are,* and so on).

▶ It is the helping verb in the compound tenses.

◀ SEE ALSO 11.5, *"The Verb* haber *to Show Presence/Existence"* ▶

◀ SEE ALSO 11.6, *"Haber Plus Past Participle for Compound Tenses"* ▶

13.2

You will learn about the many uses of the present subjunctive in Sections 13.3 and 13.4.

13.3 USES OF THE PRESENT SUBJUNCTIVE

Sequence of Tenses

Subjunctive in Noun Clauses

The principal task of the *indicative* mood is to report actions or states that happened, happen all the time, are happening, or will happen, even actions that would happen or exist under certain conditions. In any event, it is used to report actions or states.

This is definitely *not* the principal task of the *subjunctive* mood. The main task of a sentence containing the subjunctive mood is to refer to *feelings* concerning an action or state. The feelings are expressed in the indicative mood, but the action or state about which the feeling is expressed is in the subjunctive mood. For example:

Dudo que ella venga.	I doubt she'll come.
Es triste que no puedas hacerlo.	It's sad (that) you can't do it.

Those feelings can be of gladness or sadness about the mentioned actions or states (as in the second example above), or they could be feelings of doubt (as in the first example above) or denial. The feelings might be wishes that these actions or states would happen. Whatever the feeling about the mentioned action or state is, that's what's being reported; therefore, that feeling—not the action or state it refers to—is in the indicative mood. The action or state the feeling refers to is in the subjunctive mood (like *venga* and *puedas* in the previous examples).

There's often the suggestion of the unreal in the subjunctive mood, that the action or state you mention in the subjunctive doesn't actually exist in the real world—or at least you can't be sure of its existence. This is why the main task of a sentence that uses the subjunctive mood is not to report that action or state, but merely to comment on it. For example:

Exijo que salgan.	I demand (that) they leave.

◄ *SEE ALSO 13.7, "Commands"* ►

Just because I demand that they leave doesn't necessarily mean they actually will leave. The main point is my feelings about what they should do. Their obeying my demand cannot be reported as true or untrue. It's in the unreal world of my own desires.

If you doubt or deny that an action takes place or that a state exists, or if you merely wish or demand that an action take place or that a state exist, that action or state is in a kind of never-never-land.

Sequence of Tenses

Spanish has two common subjunctive tenses: the present subjunctive and the imperfect subjunctive. The future subjunctive exists but is no longer commonly used in modern Spanish; it is used only in set phrases and in legal documents.

When you want to use the subjunctive to refer to the present or the future, you use the present subjunctive. This usually means that if the subjunctive follows a verb that is in either the present indicative or the future indicative, you will use the present subjunctive. If the subjunctive follows a verb that is in either one of the past tenses (preterit or imperfect) or even the conditional tense, you will use the imperfect subjunctive. See the following table of the sequence of tenses:

SEQUENCE OF TENSES

Indicative Verb Tense	Subjunctive Verb Tense
Present indicative	Present subjunctive
Future indicative	Present subjunctive
Preterit indicative	Imperfect subjunctive
Imperfect indicative	Imperfect subjunctive
Conditional indicative	Imperfect subjunctive

In this section, you learn how to use the present subjunctive. The imperfect subjunctive is explained in Chapter 14.

All these generalities on the subjunctive probably seem hazy. The ideas will become much clearer when you look into each of the following sections.

13.3

Subjunctive in Noun Clauses

One use of the subjunctive is in noun clauses. A noun clause is a whole clause that performs the function of a noun. For example, a noun might be the object of a verb. See these examples:

> She wants *a drink*.
>
> I deny his *statement*.
>
> We advise *caution*.
>
> I doubt his *willingness*.

The preceding sentences have nouns (drink, statement, caution, willingness) as the object of verbs (wants, deny, advise, doubt). Those verbs could have entire clauses as the object, as in the following sentences:

> She wants that you study.
>
> I deny (that) he was here.
>
> We advise that you be careful.
>
> I doubt (that) he wants to cooperate.

The first of the preceding sentences sounds somewhat forced or overly formal, or perhaps not even modern English. We would ordinarily say, "She wants you to study." The third sentence sounds a bit stiff but not incompatible with modern English. Yet, we would usually say, "We advise you to be careful." But the structure of those four sentences is close to the structure of the parallel Spanish sentences, as you will see.

In the following sections, you will learn which kind of noun clauses in Spanish take the subjunctive mood.

Subjunctive Because of Doubt

If the speaker says that he or she doubts that an action takes, took, or will take place, then it would be impossible to report that this action takes, took, or will take place. The principal task of the *indicative* mood is precisely to report, so you cannot use it. Instead, because you are only providing the speaker's *feeling* about that action, you use the *subjunctive* mood to refer to the action or state. Doubt puts that action or state in never-never-land, the realm of the unreal. See the following examples:

Dudo que Elena venga hoy.	I doubt (that) Elena is coming today.*
Dudan que yo sepa la verdad.	They doubt (that) I know the truth.

Pedro dudará que lo hagas.	Pedro will doubt that you will do it.

* The English could just as well be in the future: "I doubt (that) Elena will come today."

If you do *not* doubt an action or state, you accept it as fact. You then use the indicative rather than the subjunctive. See the following:

No dudo que Elena viene hoy.	I don't doubt that Elena is coming today.
No dudo que Elena vendrá hoy.	I don't doubt that Elena will come today.
No dudarán que yo sé la verdad.	They won't doubt (that) I know the truth.
No dudarán que yo sabré la verdad.	They won't doubt (that) I'll find out the truth.

When no subjunctive is involved, as in the four preceding sentences, the second verb can be in just about any tense, depending on what you want to say:

No dudo que Elena vino ayer.	I don't doubt that Elena came yesterday.
No dudo que Elena vendría si ...	I don't doubt that Elena would come if ...

After the verb *creer* (to believe, to think), you ordinarily use the indicative mood because if one believes something, he or she takes it to be a fact. However, if one does *not* believe something, that is as good as saying he or she doubts it or even denies it. Then, whereas *creer* takes the indicative, *no creer* takes the subjunctive. Contrast the following sentences:

Creo que él trabaja mucho.	I think (believe) (that) he works a great deal.
No creo que él trabaje mucho.	I don't think he works very much.
Creen que yo soy el mejor.	They think (that) I'm the best.
No creen que yo sea el mejor.	They don't think I'm the best.

13.3

It is possible to play with the use or nonuse of the subjunctive with regard to believing or not believing, to convey the *speaker's* feeling. If the person who speaks uses the subjunctive after *creer*, it shows that the speaker has doubts about the action or state, no matter what the subject of the sentence thinks. Conversely, if the speaker uses the indicative with *no creer*, it shows that the speaker considers the action or state to be a fact, no matter what the subject of the sentence thinks. See the following examples:

Creen que yo sea el mejor.	They think I'm the best (but I'm not).
No creen que yo soy el mejor.	They don't think I'm the best (but I think so).

◀ *SEE ALSO 11.3, "Past Participle in the Passive Voice"* ▶

A verb having to do with belief has another peculiarity. If you're asking someone whether that person believes that an action is factual, you can use either the indicative or the subjunctive. If you use the subjunctive in the belief question, you show that you are doubtful that the action is factual. If you use the indicative, this does not necessarily mean that you believe it *is* factual. It can be purely neutral; you're not giving your "hand" away. See the following examples:

¿Crees que él va al club?	Do you think he's going to the club? (neutral)
¿Crees que él vaya al club?	Do you think he's going to the club? (I doubt it.)

A negative belief question is another matter. If you ask somebody, "Don't you think …?" you're expecting the answer to be "Yes." You're almost daring that person to say "No." The same is true in Spanish. Because you expect the answer to be "Yes," you are convinced of the truth of the statement. This means you almost always use the indicative, not the subjunctive, in a negative *creer* question. This is, of course, the opposite of what happens with a negative *creer* affirmation. See the following examples:

No creo que esté allí.	I don't believe (that) he's there.
¿No crees que está allí?	Don't you believe (that) he's there?
No creen que él vaya al club.	They don't think (that) he's going to the club.
¿No creen que él va al club?	Don't they think (that) he's going to the club?

All the details in this section boil down to the fact that if one doubts that an action takes place or that a particular state exists, the verb expressing that action or state is in the subjunctive. Of course, not believing something is equivalent to doubting it. If an action or state is in doubt, it cannot be reported as fact. You then use the subjunctive.

If any noun clause shows certainty, of course, you do not use the subjunctive; you use the indicative. You are (or think you are) stating a fact. You are reporting an action or state. See the following example that uses the indicative:

Sé que está allí.   I know (that) he's here.

Subjunctive Because of Denial

Closely related to doubt is denial. If someone denies the reality of an action or state, that action or state cannot be reported as factual. The main thrust of a sentence that denies the existence of an action or state is to express the subject's *feelings* about that action or state—in this case, the feeling is one of denial. Because someone's feelings are the main point of the sentence, the action or state mentioned must be expressed in the subjunctive. See the following examples:

Niego que ella lo sepa.	I deny that she knows it.
Niegan que tú lo tengas.	They deny that you have it.
Negamos que el mundo sea plano.	We deny that the world is flat.

Of course, *not* denying an action or a state is tantamount to saying that the action or state is factual. Because of this, logically the construction with *no negar* takes the indicative mood. See the following:

No niego que ella lo sabe.	I don't deny that she knows it.
No niegan que tú lo tienes.	They don't deny that you have it.
No negamos que el mundo es plano.	We don't deny that the world is flat.

13.3

If you're not denying an action or state, you do not want to use the subjunctive mood for that action or state. You want to use the indicative.

Subjunctive Because of Emotion

If you use a verb referring to your emotions concerning an action or state, the principal purpose of the sentence is not to report on that action or state; that is secondary. The primary purpose of the sentence is to express emotion about that action or state. This is a central function of the subjunctive. See the following examples:

Me alegro de que vengan.	I'm glad (that) they're coming/will come.
Me entristece que no puedas venir.	It makes me sad that you can't come/won't be able to come.
Lamentan que la situación esté así.	They are sorry ("lament") that the situation is like this/will be like that.
Sentimos que hablen así.	We regret that they speak that way.
¿Te sorprende que yo quiera hacerlo?	Does it surprise you that I want to do it?
No me sorprende que quieras hacerlo.	It doesn't surprise me that you want to do it.

As you can see from these sentences, it doesn't matter whether the emotion is expressed as a statement or a question, affirmatively or negatively. The main point of the sentence is still to express an emotion about an action or state, not to report that action or state. You put that action or state, then, in the subjunctive.

Subjunctive with Wishing, Wanting

If the subject of the sentence expresses a desire for an action to take place or a state to exist, the subject cannot report that the desired action or state actually will take place or exist. The subject merely wants this to happen. He or she is expressing an emotion about the action or state.

If there is no change of subject—in other words, if the subject of the verb of wishing, wanting, or desiring is identical to the subject of the verb that is desired—the infinitive form of the verb is used for the desired action or state. This is just what we do in English as well. See the following examples:

Quieren hablar.	They want to speak.
Deseamos tomar vino.	We wish to drink wine.
¿No quieres hacerlo?	Don't you want to do it?

However, if there is a change of subject—in other words, if the subject of the verb of desire is different from the subject of the verb that expresses the desired action or state—the subjunctive mood is used. See the following examples:

Quieren que tú hables.	They want you to speak.
Deseamos que tomen vino.	We wish (that) you would drink wine.
¿No quieres que lo haga yo?	Don't you want *me* to do it?

The structure of the Spanish sentences that express wishing or wanting—when there is a change of subject between the verb of wishing and the verb expressing the wished-for action or state—is similar to a very formal English usage. Compare the same Spanish sentences with the formal English way of expressing the same thoughts.

Quieren que tú hables.	They want that you speak.
Deseamos que tomen vino.	We want (that) you drink wine.
¿No quieres que lo haga yo?	Don't you want that *I* do it?

Just like the ordinary Spanish way of phrasing it, the formal English sentence is composed of the main clause ("They want") and the dependent clause ("that you speak").

Depending on context, the verb *esperar* can be translated into English either as "to wait (for)," "to hope," or "to expect." If you expect something to happen, you usually treat it as fact that you are reporting and use the indicative mood. If you only hope something will happen, you cannot report that it will or will not happen; you use the subjunctive mood.

See the following examples:

Espero que vendrán.	I expect (that) they'll come.
Espero que vengan.	I hope (that) they'll come.

In English, the different meanings of the two preceding sentences are conveyed by the choice of verb (*expect* or *hope*). In Spanish, the different meanings are conveyed by whether you use the indicative or the subjunctive mood.

13.3

Commanding, Ordering, Advising, and So On

If you command a person to do something or advise him or her to do it, you are not reporting that this person will do it. You are expressing a *desire* for that person to do it. Whether that person will obey your order or take your advice is another matter. For that reason, you use the subjunctive. See the following examples:

¡(Te) Mando que te vayas!	I command you to go away!
(Les) Aconsejo que (ellos) estudien.	I advise them to study.
(Me) Aconsejan que (yo) no lo haga.	They advise me not to do it.
(A ella) Le recomendaré que lo compre.	I'll recommend that she buy it.

In the first sentence, the *te* in parentheses is not really necessary; it is obvious that *you* is the one being commanded to go away because of the reflexive object *te* of the verb *vayas*.

◀ SEE ALSO 12.1, *"Reflexive Object Pronouns"* ▶

In the second and third sentences, everything in parentheses can be used, but most of the time you leave out one of them to avoid overkill.

In the last sentence, if it is clear from context that the *le* refers to *ella* rather than a possible *él* or *usted*, the *a ella* is superfluous.

Notice that the last sentence in English is not like the other English sentences above it. It is more like the Spanish sentence in construction. In English, we wouldn't say "I'll recommend her to buy it," even though we say "I command you to go away." Notice, too, that the last sentence in English uses what is left of the English present subjunctive (*buy* rather then *buys*).

Verbs such as *decir* and *insistir* can deliver a command or simply deliver information (report). When they deliver a command, the verb that follows the command takes the subjunctive. When they simply report data, the following verb takes the indicative. See the following examples:

Me dicen que va a nevar.	They tell me it's going to snow. (report)
Me dicen que me vaya.	They tell me to go away. (command)

Insisto en que están allí.	I insist that they are there. (report)
Insisto en que estén allí.	I insist that they be there. (command)

The *be* in the last English sentence is part of what's left of the English present subjunctive.

Compelling/Forbidding (Use/Nonuse)

When you use verbs that refer to forcing people to do something or, on the contrary, forbidding them to do it, you can either use the subjunctive in a separate clause or, as in English, simply use the infinitive verb. See the following examples:

Hacen que yo salga.	They're making me leave.
Me hacen salir.	They're making me leave.
Prohibo que lo hagas.	I forbid you to do it.
Te lo prohibo hacer.	I forbid you to do it.

For the purposes of compelling or forbidding, the use of the infinitive is more common, no doubt because it is shorter. The use of the separate clause that uses the subjunctive is more formal, more literary.

13.3

13.4 SUBJUNCTIVE WITH IMPERSONAL EXPRESSIONS

Most **impersonal expressions**—but definitely *not all*, as you will see—take the subjunctive mood.

WORDS TO GO . . . WORDS TO GO . . . WORDS TO GO

An **impersonal expression** is an expression that, in English, has the subject *it* plus the verb *to be* plus an adjective.

This isn't because they're impersonal expressions—some of them do *not* take the subjunctive—but simply because the function of most impersonal expressions is not to report an action or state, but to express *feelings* about an action or state. Many of those feelings are of doubt—for example, "It's possible that he's here." The function of this statement isn't to report that he's here or not here, but to tell you that it's a possibility. Besides, if something is only a possibility, there is room for doubt.

Doubt is not the only feeling often expressed by impersonal expressions. Many of the feelings expressed by verbs in the preceding sections (doubt, denial, emotion, wishing, wanting, commanding, ordering, advising, recommending …) are expressed by impersonal expressions. See the following examples:

Es posible que esté aquí.	It's possible (that) he's here. (doubt)
Es imposible que esté aquí.	It's impossible (that) he's here. (denial)
Es dudoso que esté aquí.	It's doubtful (that) he's here. (doubt)
Es aconsejable que esté aquí.	It's advisable for him to be here. (advising)
No es aconsejable que esté aquí.	It's not advisable for him to be here. (advising)
Es probable que ella vaya.	It's probable (that) she'll go. (not certain)

Es improbable que ella vaya.	It's improbable (that) she'll go. (not likely)
Es preferible que ella vaya.	It's preferable that she go. (desire)
Es bueno que ella vaya.	It's good that she's going. (opinion)

As you can see, these sentences—which use impersonal expressions—express the same feelings expressed by verbs of wishing, doubting, denying, advising, and so on. They do not focus on reporting actions or states; they focus on expressing feelings about those actions or states. For that reason, the action or state is in the subjunctive mood.

However, if the impersonal expression demonstrates certainty, the indicative is used instead of the subjunctive. See the following examples:

Es cierto que él está aquí.	It's true (that) he's here.
Es verdad que ella va.	It's true (that) she's going.
Es un hecho que él está aquí.	It's a fact (that) he's here.
No hay duda (de) que ella va.	There's no doubt (that) she's going.

In the preceding four sentences, no doubt or denial is expressed about any of the actions or states mentioned. No one is advising anyone to do anything. No opinions are given on what someone should do. No uncertainty is expressed, nor are desires for certain actions to be taken expressed. In short, none of the reasons for the subjunctive is present in these sentences. The actions or states are presented as fact; they're being reported. And this is exactly what the indicative tenses do.

13.4

13.5 SUBJUNCTIVE IN ADVERBIAL CLAUSES

With Expressions of Time (Use/Nonuse)

Means to an End

Miscellaneous Anticipated Events

"Although," "In Spite Of": Use/Nonuse

In this section, you learn to use the subjunctive mood in adverbial clauses in which there is no obvious doubting, denying, wishing, wanting, or advising. (See Section 13.3, "Uses of the Present Subjunctive.") Yet the underlying feeling is the same in the adverbial clauses that require the subjunctive. The feeling of the unreality of the verb in the subjunctive still exists. The following sections explain the psychological implications of the subjunctive mood. You will learn when to use the subjunctive and when not to use it, in seemingly similar circumstances.

With Expressions of Time (Use/Nonuse)

By "expressions of time," we mean **conjunctions** or **conjunctive adverbs** such as:

al mismo tiempo que	at the same time
antes (de) que	before
cuando	when
cuandoquiera que	whenever
después (de) que	after
en cuanto	as soon as
hasta que	until
mientras	while
tan pronto como	as soon as
una vez que	once

An **adverbial clause** is a clause that performs the same duties as an adverb—to modify a verb, adjective, or another adverb.

A **conjunction** is a word used to connect two words or sentences and to show the relationship between these words or sentences.

A **conjunctive adverb** is an adverb that can be used to connect and coordinate two clauses.

These expressions of time can take either the indicative or the subjunctive mood, but they're not interchangeable; it depends on circumstances.

After an expression of time, use the indicative under either of these situations:

▶ The action/state happens or exists all the time.

▶ The action/state has happened or existed in the past.

See the following examples:

Mi hijo me llama tan pronto como llega.	My son calls me as soon as he arrives.
Mi hijo me llamó tan pronto como llegó.	My son called me as soon as he arrived.

The first sentence reports actions that are customary; they happen all the time. It reports a fact. The second sentence reports something that has already happened. That sentence reports a fact, too.

After an expression of time, use the subjunctive if the action or state takes place in the future. In other words, use the subjunctive after a time expression if the action or state has *not yet* happened.

Mi hijo me llamará tan pronto como llegue.	My son will call me as soon as he arrives.
Llámame tan pronto como llegues.	Call me as soon as you arrive.

The psychology of this Spanish way of thinking is something like, "My son will call me as soon as he arrives. But who knows when that will be? Who knows if he will even get there?" Or (as in the second preceding sentence), "Call me as soon as you arrive, whenever that will be—if you even get there." In other words, when dealing with an expression of time but the action/state hasn't taken place yet, that action/place is in doubt; it is not yet part of the real world. This calls for the subjunctive mood.

Note: unlike all the other expressions of time, *antes (de) que* always requires the subjunctive mood to follow it. This is because, by definition, the expression meaning "before" always refers to an action or state that is in the future with respect to the verb that precedes it. (See "Miscellaneous Anticipated Events" later in this chapter.)

Means to an End

You can introduce an adverbial clause with the expressions *para que*, *a fin de que*, *de modo que*, and *de manera que*. Both *para que* and *a fin de que* are always equivalent to the English expression "so that." The other two *can* also be equivalent to "so that" but might also have another function, as you will see shortly. When we use *so that* in English, the idea is that someone has done something to make something else happen—for example, "He explained it *so that* I would understand." (The purpose of his explaining it was to attempt to have me understand it.) The expression in question explains the *purpose* or *goal* of an action.

The focus in that English sentence is not to report that I understand, or would understand, or will understand—it's possible that, in spite of his explaining it to me, I still will not understand it. It also doesn't necessarily mean that I do *not* understand.

Because of this element of doubt, you cannot report it as true or untrue. The verb *understand* is in the world of unreality. In Spanish, when you can't report that an action or state is factual in an adverbial clause, you do not use the indicative mood. You use the subjunctive mood.

The verb of the adverbial clause following *para que* and *a fin de que* always take the subjunctive. When the expressions *de modo que* and its synonym *de manera que* have the same meaning as the two previous expressions—*and only then*—you use the subjunctive mood in the clause. See the following examples:

Explíquemelo para que lo comprenda.	Explain it to me so (that) I understand it.
Trabajo a fin de que mis hijos coman.	I work so (that) my children may eat.
Lo harán de modo que vengamos.	They will do it so (that) we'll come.
Dígaselo de manera que todo vaya bien.	Tell it to him so (that) all goes well.

Para, which is a preposition, is used by itself before a verb in the **infinitive** form when there is no change of subject. In other words, *para* plus the infinitive is used when the subject of the conjugated verb in the main clause is the same as the subject of the infinitive in the adverbial clause. The same is true of *a fin de* plus the infinitive. See the following examples:

Lo estudiaré para comprenderlo.	I'll study it (in order) to understand it.
Trabajo para comer.	I work (in order) to eat.
Lo estudiaré a fin de comprenderlo.	I'll study it (in order) to understand it.
Trabajo a fin de comer.	I work (in order) to eat.

In these four sentences, the unstated *yo* is the subject of both the conjugated verb and the infinitive. The same person (*yo*) *studies* and intends to *understand*. The same person *works* for the purpose of *eating*. There is no change of subject in either sentence.

WORDS TO GO . . . WORDS TO GO . . . WORDS TO GO

The **infinitive** is the form of the verb that expresses an action or state without showing person, number, or tense.

The other two expressions (*de modo que* and *de manera que*) are always used as the beginning of an adverbial clause, whether there is a change of subject or not. They can be used to introduce a verb in the subjunctive or the indicative mood. See the next paragraph.

The synonymous expressions *de modo que* and *de manera que* can have a function other than explaining the *purpose* or *intent* of an action. Instead, these expressions can show the *result* of an action. The result might be unintentional or even accidental. In this case, do *not* use the subjunctive in the adverbial clause; use the indicative mood. See these examples:

El sol me cegaba, de modo que me caí.	The sun was blinding me, so I fell. (Because of the fact that the sun was blinding me, I fell. The fall was the [unintended] result of the sun's blinding me.)
No sabía hacerlo, de manera que no lo hice.	I didn't know how to do it, so I didn't do it. (Because I didn't know how to do it, I simply did not do it. The not doing it was the result of my not knowing how.)

13.5

In each case, I am actually reporting an action in the adverbial clause. The task of the indicative mood is precisely that: to report an action.

Miscellaneous Anticipated Events

A group of idiomatic expressions imply an action or state that is anticipated as possibility. In other words, they refer to actions or states that have not yet occurred or come into existence and, for all we know, may never do so. See the following list:

en caso (de) que	in case
antes (de) que	before
con tal que	provided that
a menos que	unless
a no ser que	unless
sin que	unless

Because the preceding expressions refer to actions or states that have not yet and may never come into being, you cannot report those events as facts. As usual, this calls for the subjunctive mood. See the following sentences:

Voy en caso de que haya problemas.	I'm going in case there are problems.
Lo haré antes de que me lo prohiban.	I'll do it before they forbid me to do it.
Irá ella con tal que vayamos nosotros.	She'll go, provided we go.
No irá a menos que vayamos nosotros.	She won't go unless we go.

You could just as well use the expressions *a no ser que* and *sin que* in place of *a menos que* in the last preceding sentence.

"Although," "In Spite Of": Use/Nonuse

The Spanish expression *aunque* can be translated either as "although" (or "even though"), or "even if," depending on whether the following clause refers to a fact or to a mere possibility. In English, the use of *although* or *even though* presumes fact, while *even if* does not. In Spanish, you presume reference to a fact when you follow *aunque* with the indicative mood, but not when you follow it with the subjunctive mood. See the following sentences:

Voy aunque llueve.	I'm going even though it's raining.
Voy aunque llueva.	I'm going even if it rains.

The first sentence uses the present indicative of *llover* (ue). It states as a fact that it is raining but that the subject is going anyway. The second sentence uses the present subjunctive of *llover* (ue). The subject is not stating as fact that it is raining. Instead, he is noncommittal, leaving the rain—either present or future—in the world of mere possibility. He is saying that whether it rains or not doesn't matter; he's going in either case.

You would make the same kind of distinction when you use the idiom *a pesar de que* (in spite of). If you follow this expression with a statement you consider to be factual, you use the indicative. If you want to show that you don't know whether the statement is factual, you use the subjunctive. See the following examples:

A pesar de que es inteligente, no tendrá éxito.	In spite of his being intelligent, he won't be successful.
A pesar de que sea inteligente, no tendrá éxito.	In spite of his (possibly) being intelligent, he won't be successful.

The first sentence could have been translated, "In spite of the fact that he is intelligent ...." The speaker considers it a fact that he is intelligent. The second sentence could have been translated "He might be intelligent, but he still won't be successful." The speaker admits that he or she doesn't know whether this person is intelligent, but whether he is or not doesn't really matter. The only thing that the speaker can say with certainty is that this person will not be successful.

13.5

13.6 SUBJUNCTIVE IN ADJECTIVE CLAUSES

Do Not Use in Adjective Clauses

Use in Adjective Clauses

The function of an adjective is to describe or modify a noun. When an entire clause performs this function, it is called an **adjective clause.** This clause, the dependent clause, modifies a noun in the main clause, referred to as the **antecedent.** See the following English sentence:

I know a man who doesn't like chocolate.

Two clauses exist: the main clause, "I know a man," and the dependent clause, "who doesn't like chocolate." The dependent clause is an adjective clause because it modifies the antecedent ("a man") in the main clause.

WORDS TO GO . . .WORDS TO GO . . .WORDS TO GO

An **adjective clause** is a clause that modifies a noun in the main clause.
The **antecedent** is any word that is referred to later in the sentence by another word or words. More specifically, it is a noun that is referred to.

◀ SEE ALSO 5.2, *"Adjectives in Agreement"* ▶

You'll want the verb in the adjective clause to be either in the indicative mood or the subjunctive mood, depending on circumstances. Follow these guidelines:

Do Not Use in Adjective Clauses

If the adjective clause refers to an antecedent that is definite and specific, do *not* use the subjunctive mood. Instead, use the indicative mood. See the following example:

Busco una casa que tiene cuatro dormitorios.	I'm looking for a house that has four bedrooms.
Sí, hay una casa que tiene cuatro dormitorios.	Yes, there is a house that has four bedrooms.

The first sentence uses the present indicative of the verb *tener.* The Spanish sentence provides us with more information than the English one can. Because the speaker used the indicative *tiene,* we know that he or she is referring to a specific house that definitely has four bedrooms. The only problem is that the speaker can't remember where it is.

The second sentence is an answer to a question. You use the indicative mood in this sentence because you are actually reporting the fact that a house exists that has four bedrooms.

Use in Adjective Clauses

You use the subjunctive mood in the adjective clause in two cases: first, if the clause refers to an antecedent that is either indefinite or nonexistent.

Indefinite Antecedent

If the adjective clause refers to an indefinite antecedent, you use the subjunctive mood. See the following example:

Busco una casa que tenga cuatro dormitorios.	I'm looking for a house that has four bedrooms.
¿Hay una casa que tenga cuatro dormitorios?	Is there a house that has four bedrooms?

As you can see, the English translation of the first sentence is identical to the English translation of the first sentence of the previous Spanish set. Once more, the Spanish sentence provides more information than the English one can. Because the speaker used the subjunctive *tenga,* we know that he or she is *not* referring to a specific house. He or she doesn't know whether such a house even exists in this area; therefore, he or she cannot report that it has four bedrooms. He or she may have just come to town and gone to a real estate agency to find out if such a place exists and is available.

The second sentence is a question. If the subject is asking whether such a house exists, he or she obviously doesn't know if it does; that's why he or she is asking the question.

Nonexistent Antecedent

If the adjective clause refers to an antecedent that is nonexistent, you have even more reason to use the subjunctive. If you are referring to something or someone that is nonexistent, you certainly cannot report that it has four bedrooms. See the following example:

En este pueblo no hay ninguna casa que tenga cuatro dormitorios.

The speaker is saying that in this town there isn't any house that has four bedrooms. If this house does not exist, he or she cannot report that it has four bedrooms. For that reason, the subject uses the subjunctive. The four-bedroom house once more is unreal.

13.7 COMMANDS

Commands for *usted* and *ustedes:* Subjunctive

Placement of Object Pronouns

Commands for *tú* and *vosotros*

In this section, you learn how to give an order—or tell someone to do something—in Spanish. In English, the subject of a command is always *you*, the person to whom you are speaking. But you usually don't actually say the word *you*; it's understood, as in "Open the door." In fact, if you *do* use the word *you*, it comes across as extremely rude—for example, "You—open the door."

In Spanish, the subject of a command is also the second person, of course. However, in Spanish, there is more than one kind of *you*: the singular formal (*usted*), the plural formal (*ustedes*), the singular familiar (*tú*), and the plural familiar (*vosotros*).

Each one of the several forms of the second person in Spanish uses a different form of command. In the cases of *tú* and *vosotros*, the affirmative command is very different from the negative command.

◄ *SEE ALSO 4.1, "Subject Pronouns"* ▶

Command for *usted* and *ustedes:* Subjunctive

The command form of the verb for the second-person formal subjects (*usted* and *ustedes*) is actually the present subjunctive form of the verb (see Sections 13.1 and 13.2 for the formation of the regular and irregular present subjunctive). See the following table.

SAMPLE COMMANDS FOR *UD.* AND *UDS,* AFFIRMATIVE AND NEGATIVE

Infinitive Verb	Usted Affirmative	Usted Negative	Ustedes Affirmative	Ustedes Negative
hablar	¡hable!	¡no hable!	¡hablen!	¡no hablen!
comer	¡coma!	¡no coma!	¡coman!	¡no coman!
vivir	¡viva!	¡no viva!	¡vivan!	¡no vivan!
cerrar	¡cierre!	¡no cierre!	¡cierren!	¡no cierren!
ir	¡vaya!	¡no vaya!	¡vayan!	¡no vayan!

13.7

You can see that commands for *usted* and *ustedes* are actually the present subjunctive form of the verb (see sections 13.1 and 13.2). You can also see that the verb forms are identical in the affirmative and negative commands. The difference between the affirmative and the negative is that the negative form follows the word *no*.

You can include the subject of these commands following the verb. Unlike in English (and unlike with the *tú* form of the command), it is more polite to include the subject—for example:

Vaya usted a la oficina, por favor.	Please go to the office.
Por favor, cierre usted la puerta.	Please close the door.

However, if several commands are involved, it is superfluous and awkward to include the subject more than once, with the first command. For example:

Vaya usted a la oficina, luego cierre la puerta y hable con el jefe.	Go to the office, then close the door and speak with the boss.

It would sound clumsy to say *usted* after *cierre* and after *hable*. The subject following the first command in the sentence (*vaya*) is sufficient.

Placement of Object Pronouns

In an affirmative command, attach the object pronoun to the end of the command:

¡Hágalo (Ud.)!	Do it!
¡Hábleme (Ud.)!	Speak to me!
¡Dígamelo! (Ud.)	Tell me about it!

In a negative command, place the object pronoun in front of the command:

¡No lo haga (Ud.)!	Don't do it!
¡No me hable (Ud.)!	Don't speak to me!
¡No me lo diga (Ud.)!	Don't tell me about it!

Commands for *tú* and *vosotros*

The form of the command for the second-person singular and plural depends on whether the command is affirmative or negative.

Negative Familiar Commands: Subjunctive

If the command is negative, you use the present subjunctive mood. See the following table.

NEGATIVE FAMILIAR COMMANDS: SUBJUNCTIVE

Infinitive Verb	tú	vosotros
hablar	¡No hables!	¡No habléis!
comer	¡No comas!	¡No comáis!
vivir	¡No vivas!	¡No viváis!
cerrar	¡No cierres!	¡No cerréis!

Affirmative Singular Familiar Commands: Not Subjunctive

The affirmative familiar commands do *not* use the subjunctive. Almost all the commands for *tú* have exactly the same form as the *él, ella,* and *usted* form of the present tense. For example, "she speaks" is "*ella habla.*" The command form of *hablar* is *habla.* See the following examples of the command form for the subject *tú:*

¡Háblame!	Speak to me!
¡Cómelo!	Eat it!
¡Escríbeles!	Write (to) them!
¡Cántamela!	Sing it for me!

Almost all the command forms of verbs have the same form as the third-person singular form of the present tense. A small group of verbs are different. These irregular commands for *tú* have only one syllable:

decir (to say, tell)	di
hacer (to do, make)	haz
ir (to go)	ve
poner (to put)	pon
salir (to leave, go out)	sal
ser (to be)	sé
tener (to have)	ten
venir	ven

Keep in mind that the negative forms of these forms are subjunctive (see "Negative Familiar Commands," earlier in this section).

See the following sentences that use the *tú* affirmative command:

¡Dímelo!	Tell it to me!
¡Vete!	Go away!
¡Sé bueno!	Be good!

The second sentence uses the reflexive form of the verb: *irse*.

Affirmative Plural Familiar Commands: Not Subjunctive

The affirmative plural commands are very easy to remember because the same rule applies to every verb, no matter what conjugation (*-ar*, *-er* or *-ir*) and no matter how irregular they may be in other tenses. To form the *vosotros* affirmative command, simply do the following:

1. Remove the final *-r* of the infinitive.

2. Replace it with a *-d*.

The following is the process:

1. hablar
2. *habla -r*
3. *habla- + -d*
4. hablad

See the following examples:

Infinitive verb: cerrar, comer, vivir

Affirmative command: cerrad, comed, vivid

No exception exists for this process of forming the affirmative command for *vosotros*. But there is a complication. If you give the *vosotros* command as a reflexive verb—for example, *sentarse*, *vestirse*, and so on—you drop the final *-d* before adding the reflexive object pronoun *-os*. See the following examples:

¡Sentaos!	Sit down!
¡Vestíos!	Get dressed!

The accent mark over the *i* in the last command follows the rules of accentuation set forth in Chapter 1.

The one exception to this rule occurs with the reflexive verb *irse*. The reflexive command of this verb with *vosotros* is *idos*.

◀ *SEE ALSO 12.1, "Reflexive Object Pronouns"* ▶

14

VERBS: THE IMPERFECT SUBJUNCTIVE AND SUBJUNCTIVE COMPOUND

14.1 FORMATION OF THE IMPERFECT SUBJUNCTIVE

Ending in *-ra*

Ending in *-se*

The formation of the imperfect subjunctive is easy to learn; this tense/mood has no irregular verbs. Every single verb follows the rule you are about to learn: However, being able to follow this rule depends on knowing the preterit tense, which has many irregular forms. It's a good idea to review the preterit tense.

◀ *SEE ALSO 8.1, "Preterit Tense: Regular Verbs"* ▶

◀ *SEE ALSO 8.2, "Preterit Tense: Irregular Verbs"* ▶

Ending in *-ra*

You can form the imperfect subjunctive in two ways. In this section, you learn the formation in which the verb ends with *-ra*, and so on.

To form the imperfect subjunctive, follow these steps:

1. Use the *ellos* form of the preterit tense.

2. Remove the *-ron* ending.

3. Add the endings *-ra, -ras, -ra, -ramos, -rais, -ran*.

See the following example for the verb *hablar*:

1. Infinitive verb: *hablar*

2. *Ellos* form of preterit tense: *hablaron*

3. Remove the *-ron* ending: *habla- -ron*

4. Add the ending *-ra*: *habla- + -ra*

5. Imperfect subjunctive for *yo*: *hablara*

Take a look at the verb *decir*. Like all verbs in the imperfect subjunctive, it follows the same rules. However, it is very irregular in the preterit tense (as are so many verbs).

1. Infinitive verb: *decir*

2. *Ellos* form of preterit tense: *dijeron*

3. Remove the *-ron* ending: *dije- -ron*

4. Add the ending *-ra*: *dije- + -ra*

5. Imperfect subjunctive for *yo*: *dijera*

See the following table that shows the full conjugation of several different verbs.

CONJUGATION OF THE *-RA* FORM OF THE IMPERFECT SUBJUNCTIVE

Pronoun	cantar (to sing)	decir (to say)	poner (to put)
yo	cantara	dijera	pusiera
tú	cantaras	dijeras	pusieras
él, ella, Ud.	cantara	dijera	pusiera
nosotros/as	cantáramos	dijéramos	pusiéramos
vosotros/as	cantarais	dijerais	pusierais
ellos, ellos, Uds.	cantaran	dijeran	pusieran

The imperfect subjunctive has no irregular verbs; every verb—whether the first conjugation (*-ar*), the second conjugation (*-er*), or the third conjugation (*-ir*)—obeys exactly the same rules.

Ending in *-se*

You can form the imperfect subjunctive in two ways. The previous section demonstrates the way to form the imperfect subjunctive that ends with *-ra*. In this section, you learn how to form it with the ending *-se*.

Consider this alternate way to form the imperfect subjunctive:

1. Use the *ellos* form of the preterit tense.

2. Remove the *-ron* ending.

3. Add the endings *-se, -ses, -se, -semos, -seis, -sen*.

Take a look at the verb *decir*. It, like all verbs in the imperfect subjunctive, follows the same rules. However, it is very irregular in the preterit tense (as are so many verbs).

14.1

1. Infinitive verb: *decir*

2. *Ellos* form of preterit tense: *dijeron*

3. Remove the *-ron* ending: *dije- -ron*

4. Add the ending *-se: dije- + -se*

5. Imperfect subjunctive for *yo: dijese*

See the following table that shows the full conjugation of several different verbs.

CONJUGATION OF THE *-SE* FORM OF THE IMPERFECT SUBJUNCTIVE

Pronoun	cantar (to sing)	decir (to say)	poner (to put)
yo	cantase	dijese	pusiese
tú	cantases	dijeses	pusieses
él, ella, Ud.	cantase	dijese	pusiese
nosotros/as	cantásemos	dijésemos	pusiésemos
vosotros/as	cantaseis	dijeseis	pusieseis
ellos, ellos, Uds.	cantasen	dijesen	pusiesen

The *-ra* and *-se* are interchangeable, so it doesn't matter which one you use. In Spain, each form is used approximately 50 percent of the time. In Latin American Spanish, the *-ra* is more common, with the *-se* thrown in at times for variety.

14.2 MAJOR USES OF THE IMPERFECT SUBJUNCTIVE

With one exception (see Section 14.3), the imperfect subjunctive is used for precisely the same reasons as the present subjunctive. Chapter 13 covers the situations in which you use the present subjunctive and the reasons for its use.

The principal task of the *indicative* mood is to report actions or states that happened, happen all the time, are happening, or will happen, even on actions that *would* happen or exist under certain conditions. In any event, the function of the indicative mood is to *report* actions or states.

This is definitely *not* the principal task of the *subjunctive* mood. The main task of a sentence in the subjunctive mood is to refer to *feelings* concerning an action or state. The feelings are expressed in the indicative mood, but the action or state about which the feeling is expressed is in the subjunctive mood.

The feelings that give rise to the subjunctive mood can be gladness or sadness, or doubt or denial about the action or state. The feeling can be wanting or wishing for the action or state to take place, or advising, commanding, or insisting that someone do something. There's an air of unreality in the subjunctive. It may refer to something that may happen or may not happen, but in general, the principal task of the subjunctive mood is *not* to report facts. For a detailed explanation of the many uses of the subjunctive mood, see Chapter 13.

When you want to use the subjunctive in reference to the present or to the future, you use the present subjunctive. This usually means that if the subjunctive follows a verb in either the present indicative or the future indicative, you will use the present subjunctive.

You use the *imperfect subjunctive* with reference to the past or to what is conditional. In other words, if the subjunctive follows a verb that is in either one of the past tenses (preterit or imperfect) or even the conditional tense, you use the imperfect subjunctive. See the following table of the sequence of tenses.

14.2

259

SEQUENCE OF TENSES

Indicative Verb Tense	Subjunctive Verb Tense
Present indicative	Present subjunctive
Future indicative	Present subjunctive
Preterit indicative	Imperfect subjunctive
Imperfect indicative	Imperfect subjunctive
Conditional indicative	Imperfect subjunctive

As you can see, the first two situations in the table apply to the present subjunctive, while the last three apply to the imperfect subjunctive. See the following sentences contrasting the use of the present subjunctive and the imperfect subjunctive:

Quiero que estudies.	I want you to study.
Querré que estudies.	I'll want you to study.
Quise que estudiaras.	I wanted you to study.
Quería que estudiaras.	I wanted you to study.
Querría que estudiaras.	I would want you to study.

For the last three sentences—those that contain the imperfect subjunctive—you could just as well use the alternate form *estudiases* as the final word (see Section 14.1, "Ending in -*se*").

14.3 IMPERFECT SUBJUNCTIVE IN *IF* CLAUSES

Do Not Use Subjunctive

Use Subjunctive

"As If ..."

The imperfect subjunctive is used for every one of the reasons to use the present subjunctive, except that, for the present subjunctive, you are talking about either the present or the future, while for the imperfect subjunctive, you are referring to the past or to a conditional situation (see Section 14.2).

However, one use of the imperfect subjunctive has no parallel in the present subjunctive. This involves a **clause** that begins with the word *si* (if). In some situations, you use the indicative mood in an *if* clause; in others, you use the subjunctive here. In this section, you learn when to use each of those moods in an *if* clause.

WORDS TO GO . . . *WORDS TO GO* . . . *WORDS TO GO*

A **clause** is a subdivision of a sentence that has both a subject and a predicate.

Do Not Use Subjunctive

If the *if* clause does not cast doubt and doesn't deny the action or state expressed by the verb in that clause, do *not* use the subjunctive mood; use the indicative in whatever tense you need. See the following examples:

Si Carmen fue a la fiesta, no la vi.	If Carmen went to the party, I didn't see her.
Si vas a Santiago, verás cosas interesantes.	If you go to Santiago, you will see interesting things.
No irán si tú vas.	They won't go if you go.
Está bien si así ocurrió.	It's all right if that's the way it happened.

14.3

In the first sentence, the speaker doesn't imply that Carmen either went or did not go to the party. In the second sentence, the speaker doesn't imply that you will or will not go to Santiago. In the fourth sentence, the speaker doesn't imply either that you are or are not going. In the last sentence, the speaker doesn't imply that it happened or did not happen that way.

The preceding sentences don't imply that the action of the verb in the *if* clause does not/did not take place. They are completely noncommittal, neutral. For that reason, you use only the indicative, never the subjunctive, in those clauses.

Just as in English, it doesn't make any difference whether the *if* clause precedes or follows the **main clause.** The *if* clause is always the **dependent clause,** while the other clause in the same sentence is always the main clause.

WORDS TO GO . . .WORDS TO GO . . .WORDS TO GO

The **main clause** (also called the independent clause and the principal clause) is a clause that forms a complete sentence in itself, as opposed to the subordinate clause.

The **dependent clause** (also called the subordinate clause) is a clause that cannot form a complete sentence in itself but has to be connected to a main clause.

In the first two of the preceding sentences, the *if* clause comes first, while in the last two sentences, the *if* is the second clause. You can reverse the order of the two clauses in each one of the sentences, just as in English, without changing the meaning.

Use Subjunctive

When the *if* clause is contrary to the facts, or when it implies that the action of the verb has not taken and might not take place, you must use the imperfect subjunctive in the *if* clause. See the following examples:

Si Carmen fuera a la fiesta, yo la vería.	If Carmen were to go to the party, I would see her.
Si fueras a Santiago, verías cosas interesantes.	If you were to go to Santiago, you would see interesting things.
No irían si tú fueras.	They wouldn't go if you were to go.

Estaría bien si
así ocurriera.

It would be all right if it
were to happen that way.

Si yo fuera Ud., lo haría.

If I were you, I would do it.

In these sentences—unlike in the sentences of the preceding section—Carmen hasn't gone to the party, and we don't know if she will. You haven't gone to Santiago and we don't know if you will. You haven't gone, and we don't know if you will. It hasn't happened that way, and we don't know if it will. In the last sentence, we know that I am definitely *not* you.

The first four of these sentences refer only to possibilities based on certain conditions. The last one refers to something that is absolutely contrary to the facts. Yet all these examples are usually referred to as "contrary to fact." This is because, in sentences such as the first four, the action of the verb in the *if* clause cannot be reported as a fact. A dependent clause, such as "if you were to go," cannot report that you went, are going, or will go. It all depends. Because you cannot report it as fact, you cannot use the indicative mood.

In this type of sentence, the speaker states that if something *were to happen*, something else *would* take place. This kind of sentence is often expressed in English without using the expression *were to* plus the infinitive form of the verb. See the following sentence:

If Carmen went to the bank, I would see her.

We often use what looks like the preterit tense in English instead of *were to* plus the verb. Be careful—sentences of this type in Spanish would come out as the imperfect subjunctive, not the preterit, because the dependent clause refers to a situation that is contrary to fact. "If Carmen went (were to go) to the bank, I would see her," means "I can't report as fact that Carmen went or goes or will go to the bank, but if she did go or were to go, then I would see her."

If you have difficulty deciding whether an *if* clause is contrary to fact, there is a purely mechanical way to know this: if the verb in the main clause is in the *conditional* tense, the dependent clause, the *if* clause, is contrary to fact and uses the imperfect subjunctive of the verb.

Si Carmen fuera al banco,
yo la vería.

If Carmen went to the
bank, I would see her.

14.3

◄ *SEE ALSO 9.2, "Conditional Tense"* ▶

The word *went* in the preceding sentence doesn't represent the preterit tense, even though it is identical to it. After all, you could add the word *tomorrow* to that sentence, and it would be a normal sentence. That *went* would refer to the possible future because it has the same meaning as *were to go* and is equivalent to the imperfect subjunctive *fuera*.

If the verb in the main clause is in *any other tense*—not the conditional—absolutely no subjunctive should be used in the *if* clause. You use one of the indicative tenses only.

Si Carmen va al banco, la veré.	If Carmen goes to the bank, I'll see her.
Si Carmen fue al banco, la vi.	If Carmen went to the bank, I saw her.

The English word *went* in the last sentence definitely refers to the past and is equivalent to the Spanish preterit indicative *fue*.

See the schematic presentation here:

Si Carmen fuera al banco, la vería.

The *if* clause contains the imperfect subjunctive because the main clause has a verb in the conditional tense. If the main clause uses any other tense than the conditional, the *if* clause will not be in the imperfect subjunctive. Instead, it will be in whichever of the indicative tenses you happen to need.

Never use the present subjunctive in an *if* clause.

"As If ..."

The Spanish expression *como si*, exactly like its English counterparts *as if* and *as though*, refers to an action or state that is contrary to fact. Because of the inherent meaning of the expression, you always use the imperfect subjunctive after *como si*. See the following examples:

Elena se porta como si fuera una reina.	Elena behaves as if she were a queen.
Carlos habla como si supiera la verdad.	Carlos talks as though he knew the truth.
Nos miraron como si hiciéramos un error.	They looked at us as if we were making a mistake.

The first sentence tells us that Elena is not a queen. The second suggests that Carlos does not know the truth. The last sentence indicates that we were not making a mistake. All the clauses that follow *como si* are contrary to fact, so you would use the imperfect subjunctive.

14.4 PRESENT PERFECT SUBJUNCTIVE TENSE

Formation of Present Perfect Subjunctive
Use of Present Perfect Subjunctive

In the following sections, you learn how to form and use the present perfect subjunctive tense.

Formation of Present Perfect Subjunctive

In English, we form the present perfect tense by using the present tense of the helping verb *to have* plus the past participle. Similarly, in Spanish, the present perfect (indicative) tense is formed by combining the present tense of *haber* with the participle.

The present perfect *subjunctive* tense, like all **compound tenses,** combines the helping verb *haber* with the past participle. But to form the present perfect *subjunctive* tense, specifically, you **conjugate** the **auxiliary verb** *haber* in the present subjunctive and place it before the past participle.

◀ SEE ALSO 11.1, *"Forming the Past Participle"* ▶

◀ SEE ALSO 11.6, *"Haber Plus Past Participle for Compound Tenses"* ▶

WORDS TO GO . . .WORDS TO GO . . .WORDS TO GO

A **compound tense** is a tense formed with an auxiliary verb (helping verb).

To **conjugate** a verb is place on it the endings that signal person, number, tense, and mood.

The **auxiliary verb** (also called the helping verb) is a verb combined with another verb to show the mood, tense, or aspect of the main verb.

The present subjunctive of *haber* is formed as follows.

CONJUGATION OF *HABER* IN THE PRESENT SUBJUNCTIVE

Subject Pronoun	Present Subjunctive of *haber*
yo	haya
tú	hayas
él, ella, Ud.	haya
nosotros/as	hayamos
vosotros/as	hayáis
ellos, ellas, Uds.	hayan

You form the present perfect subjunctive by forming the present subjunctive tense of the helping verb *haber* and placing it before the past participle. See the following examples:

Dudan que Pedro lo haya hecho.	They doubt that Pedro has done it.
Es posible que hayan llegado.	It's possible (that) they've arrived.
Ojalá que hayas tenido éxito.	I hope you've been successful.

Use of Present Perfect Subjunctive

You use the present perfect *indicative* to report actions or states that have occurred at some unspecified earlier time. You use the present perfect *subjunctive* for that same time frame, but for all the same reasons you use the present subjunctive—for example, doubt, denial, wishing, wanting, expressing emotion, and so on. It would help to review the uses of the present subjunctive in Chapter 13.

The following examples show the use of the present perfect *indicative* in contrast to the present perfect *subjunctive:*

Han llegado.	They have arrived.
Dudo que hayan llegado.	I doubt (that) they have arrived.
¿Has estudiado?	Have you studied?

14.4

Niego que hayas estudiado.	I deny that you have studied.
Sé que María se ha ido.	I know (that) María has gone away.
Es triste que María se Haya ido.	It's sad that María has gone away.
¿Habrá terminado Ud. para viernes.	Will you have finished by Friday?
Quiero que Ud. haya terminado para viernes.	I want you to have finished by Friday.
Es verdad que la gente ha salido.	It's true (that) the people have left.
Es posible que la gente haya salido.	It's possible (that) the people have left.

The preceding English sentences are in the present perfect indicative because the actions have taken place at some indeterminate time before the present. The Spanish sentences use the present perfect subjunctive because the actions (or nonactions) come after doubt, denial, emotion, and wanting. The Spanish sentences that do *not* employ the subjunctive are reporting or asking about facts.

14.5 PAST PERFECT SUBJUNCTIVE TENSE

Formation of Past Perfect Subjunctive Tense

Use of Past Perfect Subjunctive Tense

In the following sections, you learn how to form the past perfect subjunctive tense and when to make use of it.

Formation of Past Perfect Subjunctive Tense

The past perfect subjunctive tense (also called the imperfect subjunctive compound tense) is formed by placing the imperfect tense of the helping verb *haber* before the past participle.

◀ SEE ALSO 11.1, *"Forming the Past Participle"* ▶

◀ SEE ALSO 11.6, *"Haber Plus Past Participle for Compound Tenses"* ▶

See the conjugation of *haber* in the imperfect subjunctive in the following table.

CONJUGATION OF *HABER* IN THE IMPERFECT SUBJUNCTIVE

Subject Pronoun	Imperfect Subjunctive of *haber*
yo	hubiera
tú	hubieras
él, ella, Ud.	hubiera
nosotros/as	hubiéramos
vosotros/as	hubierais
ellos, ellas, Uds.	hubieran

You form the past perfect subjunctive by forming the imperfect tense of the helping verb *haber* and placing it before the past participle. See the following examples:

Dudaban que Pedro lo hubiera hecho.	They doubted that Pedro had done it.
Era posible que hubieran llegado.	It was possible (that) they had arrived.
¿Lamentaste que lo hubiéramos hecho?	Were you sorry (that) we had done it?

14.5

Use of Past Perfect Subjunctive Tense

You use the past perfect *indicative* to report actions or states that had occurred at some unspecified time before a specific point in the past. You use the past perfect *subjunctive* for that same time frame, but for all the same reasons you use the imperfect subjunctive—for example, doubt, denial, wishing, wanting, expressing emotion, and so on. It would help to review the uses of the imperfect subjunctive in Sections 14.2 and 14.3.

The following examples show the use of the past perfect *indicative* in contrast to the past perfect *subjunctive*:

Habían llegado.	They had arrived.
Dudaba que hubieran llegado.	I doubted (that) they had arrived.
¿Habías estudiado?	Had you studied?
Negué que hubieras estudiado.	I denied that you had studied.
Supe que María se había ido.	I learned (that) María had gone away.
Era triste que María se hubiera ido.	It was sad that María had gone away.
¿Había terminado Ud. para viernes?	Had you finished by Friday?
Quería que Ud. hubiera terminado para viernes.	I wanted you to have finished by Friday.
Era verdad que la gente había salido.	It was true (that) the people had left.
Era posible que la gente hubiera salido.	It was possible (that) the people had left.

The preceding Spanish sentences use the past perfect subjunctive because the actions (or nonactions) come after doubt, denial, emotion, and wanting. The Spanish sentences that do *not* use the subjunctive are reporting or asking about facts.

15

COMMONLY CONFUSED VERBS/ VERBS AS NOUNS

15.1 TWO KINDS OF KNOWING: *SABER* VS. *CONOCER*

Knowing Facts/Having Skills

Acquaintance/Familiarity

Two verbs in Spanish can be translated as "to know." They are not usually inter-changeable because they refer to two kinds of knowledge. In this section, you learn how to use both.

Knowing Facts/Having Skills

The verb *saber* expresses several kinds of knowing:

▶ Having information or data about something or someone

▶ Knowing a subject thoroughly

▶ Knowing how to do something

Review the following sentences:

No sabemos dónde está.	(Data) We don't know where it/he or she is.
María sabe quién viene.	(Data) María knows who's coming.
Ella sabe sus lecciones.	(Thorough) She knows her lessons.
Roberto sabe tocar el piano.	(How to) Roberto knows how to play the piano.
Yo sé bailar*.	(How to) I know how to dance.
Saben cómo funciona.	(Thorough) They know how it works (functions).

* The verb *saber* in the present tense is irregular only in the *yo* form: *sé*.

Notice that in sentences such as four and five, the word *cómo* (how) is not used; you simply use *saber* plus the infinitive verb.

> **WORDS TO GO . . .**WORDS TO GO . . .WORDS TO GO
>
> The **infinitive form** of a verb is the form that expresses action or state without giving information on person or number.

◀ *SEE ALSO 7.2, "Present Tense: Irregular Verbs"* ▶

Acquaintance/Familiarity

The verb *conocer* refers to knowing in the following senses:

▶ Being acquainted with

▶ Being familiar with

▶ Having a slight knowledge of the subject

Review the following sentences:

Conozco al Sr. López.	I know (am acquainted with) Mr. Lopez.
Pedro conoce Chicago.	Pedro knows (is familiar with) Chicago.
Conocen la materia.	They're familiar with the subject (superficially).

Contrast them with the following sentences:

No conocen al Sr. Martínez.	They don't know Mr. Martinez.
Saben dónde vive el Sr. Martínez.	They know where Mr. Martinez lives.
Conozco Chicago.	I know Chicago.
Sé que Chicago está en Illinois.	I know (that) Chicago is in Illinois.

The first of the four preceding sentences refers to (not) having made the acquaintance of Mr. Martínez, of (not) being acquainted with him. The second sentences refers to their having information about Mr. Martínez (his place of residence). The fourth sentence expresses my having some familiarity or experience with Chicago. The last sentence refers to information I have about the location of Chicago.

15.1

15.2 TWO FORMS OF BEING: *SER* VS. *ESTAR*

Showing Existence

Linking Subject to Noun or Pronoun

Connecting Subject to Adjectives

Physical Location vs. Event Location

ser **Combined with** *de*

ser **for Speaking of Time**

ser **for the Passive Voice**

Two verbs in Spanish translate into English as "to be." The two verbs, *ser* and *estar*, are not interchangeable; they have entirely different functions. This section helps you learn how to use these two verbs.

Showing Existence

Just as the English verb *to be* can refer to simple existence, the Spanish verb *ser* can be a synonym for the verb *existir* (to exist).

Pienso, por eso soy.	I think, therefore I am.

The previous sentence is synonymous with:

Pienso, por eso existo.	I think, therefore I exist.

When Shakespeare's Hamlet says, "To be or not to be ...," he is comparing the advantages of existing, remaining alive, with its disadvantages. This sentence is rendered into Spanish as "Ser o no ser ...."

Linking Subject to Noun or Pronoun

Of the two Spanish verbs that mean "to be," only *ser* serves the purpose of linking the subject of the sentence to a noun or pronoun.

See the following examples:

Pedro es un hombre.	Pedro is a man.
(Yo) soy profesor.	I'm a professor.
Uds. son estudiantes.	You are students.

| Es él. | It is he. ("It's him.") |
| Soy yo. | It is I. ("It's me.") |

The first three preceding sentences involve the verb *ser* connecting the subjects with nouns. The last two sentences involve the verb *ser* connecting the subjects with pronouns. The subjects of sentences such as the last two are never expressed; they are implicit.

In the second sentence, *profesor* does not have the indefinite article (*un*) before it. This is because it comes after a form of *ser* and refers to a profession.

◄ SEE ALSO 4.1, *"Subject Pronouns"* ▶

◄ SEE ALSO 3.4, *"Indefinite Articles"* ▶

Connecting Subject to Adjectives

You can use either *ser* or *estar* to connect the subject of a sentence with an adjective. However, particular kinds of adjectives are typically used with *ser*, and other adjectives are customarily used with *estar*. Then again, many adjectives can be used with either verb; however, the meaning or connotation is very different. In this section, you learn exactly when to use *ser* or *estar* with an adjective to obtain the desired effect.

Characteristics

The verb *ser* connects the subject with an adjective to inform about the *characteristics* of a person, animal, or thing, the attributes that are part and parcel of that person or thing. We're talking not about a current condition, but about what is inherent, a part of the person or thing's basic nature. It can also refer to an attribute the speaker *feels* is normal and unchanged for that person or thing.

When we use *ser* to introduce the adjective, we are classifying that person, animal, or thing. See the following examples:

Carlota es alta.	Carlota is tall. (physical characteristic)
Miguel es inteligente.	Miguel is intelligent. (mental characteristic)
Los muchachos son valientes.	The boys are brave. (moral characteristics)
Mi papá es viejo.	My father is old. (age)
María es mexicana.	Maria is Mexican. (nationality)

15.2

Even though age is constantly but imperceptibly changing, and even though one's citizenship can be changed, in Spanish, age and nationality are considered characteristics. Just as you classify a person by physical, mental, and moral characteristics, you do the same using age, nationality, religion, political affiliation, and so on.

Because the verb *ser* plus an adjective refers to characteristics and tells what that person, animal, or thing is like, you must be careful when asking a question about characteristics. You might be tempted to think in English and literally translate the idiom we use to obtain this information. See the following examples of how to elicit this information in Spanish:

¿Cómo es tu amigo?	What's your friend like?
¿Cómo son los argentinos?	What are Argentineans like?

In English, we use an idiom involving the interrogative word *what*, the verb *to be*, and the adjective *like*. In Spanish, the interrogative word *cómo* and the verb *ser* constitute the idiom. When in English we ask what someone or something is like, we are asking for characteristics of that someone or something. We want that someone or something to be classified.

Be careful: if you hear or see the question in Spanish, resist the temptation to think in English terms. Do not translate literally "How is …" or "How are …." But these English idioms do not ask about conditions; they refer to characteristics only. For conditions, see the following section.

Closely related to the idea of using *ser* with an adjective to characterize or classify the subject is the use of *ser* plus an adjective when the speaker believes he or she is making a statement of *objective fact*, referring to a quality considered normal or expected for the subject. Saying "María es bonita" indicates that the speaker is not only classifying María among the people considered pretty, but also assumes that this is an obvious, objective fact. It is normal for her to be pretty. This is how she is; there has been no change. It is expected, by anyone who has seen her, for her to be pretty.

Conditions

The verb *estar* connects the subject of a sentence to adjectives to inform concerning the subject's *condition*. It is *never* used to characterize or classify the subject. See the following examples:

Miguel está ocupado.	Miguel is busy.
Carlota está preocupada.	Carlota is worried.
Los chicos están enfermos.	The boys are ill.
Mi papá está muy bien.	My dad is very well.

Being busy, worried, ill, or in good health are all conditions that people happen to be in. These can fluctuate. The boys will probably recover from their illness.

Be careful, though. Do not confuse *condition* with the idea of *temporary*, nor the idea of *characteristics* with the idea of *permanent*. This is a misapprehension. There are such things as permanent conditions—for example, "El hombre está muerto" ("The man is dead"). But being dead is a condition; previously, the man was in the condition of being alive. If you were asked what someone was like (characteristics), you would never say, "He's tall, thin, and *dead*." In Spanish, you would need two different verbs to express those two characteristics (tall, thin) and one condition (dead): "Es alto y flaco. Está muerto."

Because there are such things as permanent conditions, it is always possible to use a word such as *siempre* with reference to a condition: "Siempre está ocupada" ("She's always busy").

It is also possible, and very common, to say such things as "Roberto es una persona muy ocupada" ("Roberto is a very busy person"). But this is *not* a case of having to think whether you're speaking of a characteristic or a condition to choose between *ser* and *estar*. Here, the case is very clear cut: you're connecting the *subject* with a *noun*. This always requires the verb *ser*. It matters not at all that the noun is question is modified by an adjective. (See "Linking Subject to Noun or Pronoun," previously.)

Closely related to the idea of using *estar* with an adjective to describe the subject's condition is the use of *estar* plus an adjective—*not* to make an objective statement of fact, but, on the contrary, to give a *subjective* idea of the *impression* the subject is making on the speaker at the moment. For example, by saying "María está bonita," the speaker isn't characterizing or classifying María, but simply giving his impression of her. Depending on the situation, the suggestion could be—but does not have to be—that María's being pretty is unexpected, even a departure from the norm. It could suggest that she has changed her appearance in some way. The statement simply makes no attempt at objectivity; it merely provides a fleeting personal impression. As we say colloquially, she just "strikes" him as being pretty at that moment.

15.2

Same Adjective, Different Meaning

Many adjectives can be used with either *ser* or *estar*. However, the resulting statements will be different. The **connotation** or even the **denotation** will be entirely different, depending on which verb is employed. Using the adjective for "pretty" (*bonito/a*), for example, it is possible to say, "María es bonita," yet it is also possible to say, "María está bonita." The implications are very different (see the preceding paragraph).

WORDS TO GO . . .WORDS TO GO . . .WORDS TO GO

Connotation is the ideas and associations that a word suggests.
Denotation is the actual meaning of a word.

Contrast the following sentences:

María es bonita.	María is pretty. (She is a pretty girl.)
María está bonita.	María is looking pretty.
La sopa es buena.	Soup is good. (Soup is a good thing.)
La sopa está buena.	This soup tastes good.
Carlos es flaco.	Carlos is thin. (He's a skinny guy.)
Carlos está flaco.	Carlos is thin. (He's gotten thin.)

Don't be misled by the use of the definite article in the two sentences about soup. In English, we don't use the definite article with a noun in the general sense, but in Spanish, we do.

◀ **SEE ALSO 3.3,** *"Definite Articles"* ▶

In some cases, the difference between using *ser* with the adjective is so different in meaning from using *estar* with the same adjective that the English adjective is different in translation. See the following:

La mujer es lista.	The woman is clever (mentally alert).
La mujer está lista.	The woman is ready (prepared).
Esteban es cansado.	Esteban is tiresome (annoying).
Esteban está cansado.	Esteban is tired.

Tu amigo es aburrido.	Your friend is boring.
Tu amigo está aburrido.	Your friend is bored.

When you use *ser* with an adjective, you are classifying the subject and speaking of inherent features. When you use *estar* with an adjective, you are referring to the condition the subject is in or the way the subject "strikes" you at the moment.

Physical Location vs. Event Location

To speak of where something or someone is located, you can use either *estar* or *ser*. But they are not interchangeable. The choice depends on various factors.

If you are speaking about the physical location of a person, animal, vegetable, or inanimate object, the verb to use is invariably *estar*. See the following examples:

El libro estuvo en la mesa.	The book was on the table.
Elena estaba en su cuarto, cuando ...	Elena was in her room, when ...
El Empire State Building está en Nueva York.	The Empire State Building is in New York.

If you are speaking of the location of an event or any place where things are happening, people are interacting, and so on, the verb to use is *ser*. See the following examples:

El concierto fue en el teatro.	The concert was (took place) in the theater.
La fiesta es en el parque.	The party is (taking place) in the park.

The situations presented in the preceding five sentences are pretty cut and dried. However, in some situations the choice of *estar* or *ser* depends on the point of view of the speaker. In those cases, the differences are more subtle. See the following examples:

Mi casa está aquí.	My house (the structure) is (located) here.
Mi casa es aquí.	My home (where my family and I live and interact) is here.
¿Dónde está la clase?	Where is the class (room located)?

15.2

¿Dónde es la clase?	Where is the class (the teacher and students interacting) going on?

If you can substitute the English expression "to take place" for the verb *to be*, you're talking about an event. You're focusing on the activities and interactions of people, and you should use the verb *ser*.

ser Combined with *de*

The verb *ser* is used in combination with the preposition *de* in three specific situations.

◀ SEE ALSO 6.1, "Prepositions" ▷

Origin (to Be From)

The verb *ser* used in conjunction with the preposition *de* refers to the origin of someone or something; it refers to where this person, animal, or inanimate thing is from *originally*. A *question* concerning origin always starts with the expression "¿de dónde?" See the following sentences:

¿De dónde es Ud.?	Where are you from?
Soy de Madrid.	I'm from Madrid.
¿De dónde son las camisas?	Where are the shirts from?
Son de (la) China.	They're from China.

Certain countries traditionally take the definite article before the name (la China, el Perú, la India, la Argentina, el Uruguay, los Estados Unidos, and so on). However, nowadays there is a tendency to drop the definite articles from the name of those countries. Either way is correct: *Estados Unidos* = (the) United States.

Material (to Be Made of)

The verb *ser* used in conjunction with the preposition *de* refers to the material of which an item is composed. A *question* concerning material always starts with the expression "¿de queias[]?" See the following sentences:

¿De qué son las camisas?	What are the shirts made of?
Son de algodón.	They're made of cotton.

¿De qué es la casa?	What's the house made of?
Es de madera.	It's made of wood.

Possession (to Belong to)

The verb *ser* used in conjunction with the preposition *de* refers to possession. That is, it informs about whom the item in question belongs to. A *question* concerning possession always starts with the expression "¿de quién?" See the following sentences:

¿De quién son las camisas?	Whose shirts are they?
Son de Roberto.	They're Robert's.
Sí, son suyas; son de él.	Yes, they're his.

The last sentence uses the possibly ambiguous third-person possessive pronoun (*suyas*), and then, to make certain the meaning is clear, adds the more specific *de él*.

De quiénes es la casa?	Whose house is it?
La casa es de los López.	The house belongs to the Lopezes.

Because the last question makes use of the plural *¿quiénes?* rather than the singular *¿quién?*, the questioner assumes that the house belongs to more than one person.

◀ *SEE ALSO 5.5, "Possessives"* ▷

◀ *SEE ALSO 7.3, "Asking Questions"* ▷

The construction using *ser* + *de* + a noun has the function of the apostrophe -s (*'s*) in English.

ser for Speaking of Time

The verb *ser* is used to speak of time, whether the day, month, year, or hour. See these examples:

¿Qué hora es?	What time (hour) is it?
Son las ocho.	It's eight o'clock.
¿Qué día es hoy?	What day is today?
Hoy es miércoles.	Today is Wednesday.
¿Cuál es la fecha?	What's the date?
Hoy es el cinco de junio de 2008.	Today is June 5, 2008.

◀ *SEE ALSO 2.3, "Dates"* ▶

◀ *SEE ALSO 2.4, "Time"* ▶

Even though ordinarily the Spanish word *¿qué?* is the equivalent of the English question "what?" when the Spanish equivalent of "what?" comes directly in front of any form of the verb *ser*, you use the interrogative word *¿cuál?*, as in the fifth example. The only time *¿qué?* is used before *ser* is when you are asking for a definition, when you don't know the meaning of a word or expression. Compare these sentences:

¿Cuál es la capital del Perú?	What's the capital of Peru?
¿Cuál es tu nombre?	What's your name?
¿Cuál es su problema?	What is his/her/your problem?
¿Qué es "silla"?	What is "silla"? (What does "silla" mean?)
¿Qué es un guajalote?	What is a guajalote?
¿Qué es esto?	What is this?

Only the last three sentences ask for a definition and therefore use *¿qué?* in front of the verb *ser*.

ser for the Passive Voice

The **passive voice** in English is formed by combining the verb *to be* with the past participle. In Spanish, the passive voice is formed by combining the verb *ser* with the past participle.

WORDS TO GO . . . WORDS TO GO . . . WORDS TO GO

A sentence in the **passive voice** is one in which the subject receives the action of the verb.

A sentence in the **active voice** is one in which the grammatical subject performs the action of the verb, and the object receives the action of the verb.

◀ *SEE ALSO 11.1, "Forming the Past Participle"* ▶

◀ *SEE ALSO 11.3, "Past Participle in the Passive Voice"* ▶

You will find a full and complete explanation of the passive voice and how to form it in Chapter 11.

15.3 VERBS AS NOUNS

In both English and Spanish, you can use verbs as though they are nouns. Just as you can use nouns as the subject or the object of a verb, you can use verbs in the same way. See the following examples:

(El) Comer es un placer.	Eating is a pleasure.
Noto el ir y venir de la gente.	I notice the goings and comings of people.
(El) Salir no es una opción.	Leaving is not an option.
Les gusta cantar.	They like singing.

(The last preceding sentence could just as well be translated as "They like to sing.")

It is important to notice several things:

▶ In Spanish, unlike English, the only form of the verb when used as a noun is the infinitive.

▶ The second example sentence uses the verbal nouns (*ir* and *venir*) as the *objects* of the conjugated verb *noto*.

▶ The other three sentences have the **verbal nouns** as the *subject* of the verb. *Comer* is the subject of the conjugated verb *es* in the first sentence. *Salir* is the subject of the conjugated verb *es* in the third sentence. *cantar* is the subject of the conjugated verb *gusta* in the fourth sentence. (See Section 15.4, "Liking: *gustar*.")

▶ When the verbal noun is the subject, you can use the definite article *el* or not, as you please. If you choose to use the definite article in this way, it must always be the masculine singular one.

◄ SEE ALSO 3.3, *"Definite Articles"* ▷

Just as nouns can be used as subjects or objects of a verb, a noun can be the object of a preposition. The same is true of verbs used as nouns. See the following examples:

Antes de contestar ...	Before answering ...
Para hablar así ...	To speak that way ...
Salió sin decir adios.	He left without saying goodbye.
Además de llegar tarde ...	Besides arriving late ...

15.3

The only form of a verb that you can use after a preposition is the infinitive.

WORDS TO GO . . .WORDS TO GO . . .WORDS TO GO

A **verbal noun** is a verb that is used as one would use a noun.

15.4 REVERSE ENGLISH: LIKING, LOVING, INTEREST, CARING ...

Liking: *gustar*

Loving Things: *fascinar, encantar*

Interested In ...

I Care, Don't Care ...

Both English and Spanish have many ways of expressing liking or loving things, and having an interest in and caring about things. Some of the ways these feelings are expressed in Spanish clash with the structure we use in English. In this section, you learn how to express these ideas in Spanish.

Liking: *gustar*

The first thing to understand is that Spanish has no verb that means "to like." This is worth repeating: No verb in Spanish means "to like."

To express the idea of liking, you use the verb *gustar*, which means "to please" or "to be pleasing" or "to give pleasure." This means that the thing you like in English will be the thing that pleases you in Spanish. The subject and object are reversed going from English to Spanish. See the following examples:

Me gusta leer.	I like to read. (Reading pleases me.)
Me gustan leer y jugar al fútbol.	I like to read and to play soccer. (Reading and playing soccer please me.)
Me gusta el helado.	I like ice cream. (Ice cream pleases me.)
Me gustan los deportes.	I like sports. (Sports please me.)

In the preceding sentences, the object is *me*, as it would be in an English sentence that uses the verb *to please*. But our usual way of expressing this concept is to use the verb *to like*; in those cases, the same person becomes the subject *I*.

In the first and third example sentences, the subjects are singular (*leer* and *el helado*). For that reason, the verb is the singular *gusta*.

In sentences two and four, the subjects are plural (*leer y jugar* and *los deportes*). For that reason, the verb is in the plural *gustan*.

15.4

285

In English sentences that use the verb *to like*, when we change the identity of the one who experiences pleasure, we change the subject. In Spanish, you change the object. See the following examples:

Me gusta leer.	I like to read. (Reading pleases me.)
Te gusta leer.	You like to read. (Reading pleases you.)
Le gusta leer.	He or she likes to read. (Reading pleases him/her.)
Nos gusta leer.	We like to read. (Reading pleases us.)

◀ SEE ALSO 7.1, *"Present Tense: Regular Verbs"* ▶

◀ SEE ALSO 4.2, *"Object Pronouns"* ▶

In Spanish, the subject does not have to go before the verb; it can come after the verb. Sentences that use *gustar* usually place the subject after the verb, as in the preceding sentences, but it would not be incorrect to place it before the verb—for example, "(El) Leer nos gusta."

The important matter in the preceding Spanish sentences is that reading is pleasing. To tell who is being pleased by reading, you just change the object pronoun (*me, te, le, nos, os, les*).

Loving Things: *fascinar, encantar*

In Spanish, you do not use the verbs *amar* or *querer* (ie) to speak about loving inanimate objects or activities. You use those verbs only with people or animals—with someone or something that can love you back.

When inanimate objects or an activity is the object of your affection, you use the verb *encantar* or the verb *fascinar*. These verbs work the same way as *gustar* (see the preceding section). See the following examples:

Me fascina el álgebra.	I love algebra. (Algebra fascinates me.)
Nos encanta patinar.	We love to skate. (Skating enchants us.)
¿Te fascinan los deportes?	Do you love sports? (Do sports fascinate you?)

Interested In ...

The verb *interesar* functions in the same manner as the verbs *gustar*, *fascinar*, and *encantar* (see the preceding sections). See the following examples:

Me interesa la novela.	I'm interested in the novel. (The novel interests me.)
¿Te interesan los deportes?	Are you interested in sports? (Do sports interest you?)

As you now know, both types of English sentences, are common. The two English sentences in parentheses have the same construction as the Spanish equivalents.

I Care, Don't Care ...

The English verb *to care* really has at least two different meanings. In Spanish, then, those meanings are expressed with completely different verbs and different structures. When *to care* for someone means "to take care of" that person, the verb to use is *cuidar*. See the following example:

Rosa cuida a su madre.	Rosa cares for (takes care of) her mother.

The structure is basically the same in both languages. However, if the English *to care (about)* is another way to say that someone or something *matters* or *is important* to someone, you use the verb *importar* (to matter, to be important). In this case, the Spanish structure is like that of *gustar*. See the following examples:

¿Te importa si me voy?	Do you care if I go away? (Does it matter to you if I go away?)
Me importa mucho.	I care a great deal. (It matters a great deal to me.)
Nos importa la verdad.	We care about the truth. (The truth matters to us.)
¡No me importa!	I don't care! (It doesn't matter to me!)
Las apariencias importan.	Appearances matter.

The first four sentences can come out in English in two ways. The ones in parentheses (with the verb *to matter*) have the same structure as the Spanish equivalents. But we often use the verb *to care* in this type of sentence; the structure of the *to care* sentences is the reverse of the Spanish structure with respect to the

15.4

287

subject and object. The last sentence has no object in Spanish; in this type of sentence, the English uses only the *to matter* structure.

16

COMPARISON AND URGES/OBLIGATIONS

16.1 MAKING COMPARISONS

Comparison of Equals

Comparison of Unequals

Superlatives

This section shows you how to make comparisons—of both equals and unequals—in Spanish.

Comparison of Equals

This section shows you how to compare equals in both quality and quantity.

Equal in Quality

In English, we use the expression *as ... as* before and after the adjective to modify that adjective to demonstrate equal quality. In Spanish, you accomplish the same task by using the adverbs *tan ... como* to surround the adjective you want to modify.

The formula is: *tan* + adjective + *como* = equality. See the following examples:

Carlos es tan inteligente como tú.	Carlos is as intelligent as you.
Elena es tan bonita como Mercedes.	Elena is as pretty as Mercedes.
Son tan jóvenes como ustedes.	They are as young as you.

(If you drop *como* and whatever follows it in the three preceding sentences, the adverb *tan* is the equivalent of the English *so*. It refers to the degree to which the person or thing has the quality described by the adjective. For example, "Carlos es tan inteligente" means "Carlos is so intelligent.")

◀ *SEE ALSO 5.6, "Adverbs and Adverbial Phrases"* ▶

The structure described here conveys the meaning that one person or thing possesses the qualities described in the adjective to the same extent as the other person or thing.

The same combination of *tan ... como* used previously with adjectives is used with adverbs in English as well as in Spanish to show equality in the way one person or thing performs the action of the verb compared to the way another person or thing does.

The formula is: *tan* + adverb + *como* = equality. See the following examples:

Pedro corre tan rápidamente como Carlos.	Pedro runs as fast as Carlos.
María escribe tan bien como yo.	María writes as well as I do.
Ella habla tan francamente como su papá.	She speaks as frankly as her father.

The structure described here conveys the meaning that one person or thing performs the action of the verb in the same manner as the other person or thing.

Equals in Quantity

In English, we use the expression *as much … as* or *as many … as* before and after the noun to modify that noun for the purpose of demonstrating equal quantity. In Spanish, you accomplish the same task by using *tanto/a/os/as … como* to surround the noun you want to modify. Keep in mind that *tanto* is an adjective and, as such, must agree in **number** and **gender** with the noun it modifies.

WORDS TO GO . . .WORDS TO GO . . .WORDS TO GO

Number, as used in grammar, refers to singular and plural.
Gender refers to whether a noun is feminine or masculine.

◄ SEE ALSO 5.2, *"Adjectives in Agreement"* ►

The formula is: *tanto/a/os/as* + noun + *como* = equality of amount. See the following examples:

López gana tanto dinero como su jefe.	López earns as much money as his boss.
Esta casa tiene tantas ventanas como la mía.	This house has as many windows as mine.
¿Puedes tomar tanta cerveza como yo?	Can you drink as much beer as I?

Keep in mind that the adjective *tanto* can take four possible forms, as do all Spanish adjectives whose masculine form ends in *-o*.

16.1

Notice that English uses *as much* to modify a singular noun and *so many* to modify a plural noun. In Spanish, you use *tanto* or *tanta* to signify *so much*, and *tantos* or *tantas* to signify *so many*.

(If you drop *como* and everything that follows it in the preceding sentences, you are not making a comparison. You are merely commenting on the amount: "López gana tanto dinero" means "López earns so much money.")

You can also use *tanto* as an adverb to modify a verb. In that case, *tanto* is the equivalent of the English *so much*.

The formula is: verb + *tanto* = the extent to which someone or something performs the action of the verb. See the following examples:

José estudia tanto.	José studies so much.
Ella trabajó tanto.	She worked so much. (She worked so hard.)
Han comido tanto.	They've eaten so much.

When you use *tanto* to modify a verb, you are using it as an adverb. Like all adverbs, the form remains unchanged. This adverb always ends in *-o*.

Comparison of Unequals

In this section, you learn how to compare persons, things, actions, or states that are not equal. Some are more; some are less.

Unequal in Quality

To express that one person or thing possesses a quality to a greater extent than another person or thing, the formula is: *más* + adjective + *que*. See the following examples:

Este curso es más difícil que el otro.	This course is harder (more difficult) than the other one.
Carlos es más alto que Roberto.	Carlos is taller than Roberto.
Elena no es más bonita que María.	Elena is not prettier than María.

To indicate that one person or thing possesses a quality to a lesser extent than another person or thing, the formula is *menos* + adjective + *que*. See the following examples:

El otro curso es menos difícil que éste.	The other course is less difficult than this one.
Roberto es menos alto que Carlos.	Roberto is less tall than Carlos.
María es menos bonita que Elena.	María is less pretty than Elena.

In sentences two and three, we would be more apt to say this in English:

The other course isn't as hard as this one.

Roberto isn't as tall as Carlos.

These last two sentences feel more "comfortable" in English, but the meaning is the same as in the Spanish sentences that use *menos*.

Unequal in Quantity

To express the idea that the action of the verb involves a greater number of the noun in question, the formula is: *más* + noun + *que*. See the following examples:

Escribes más cartas que ella.	You write more letters than she (does).
Papá gana más dinero que mi tío.	Dad earns more money than my uncle.
Pepe puede tomar más cerveza que tú.	Pepe can drink more beer than you.

To express the idea that the action of the verb involves a lesser number of the noun in question, the formula is: *menos* + noun + *que*. See the following examples:

Ella escribe menos cartas que tú.	She writes fewer letters than you (do).
Mi tío gana menos dinero que papá.	My uncle earns less money than Dad.
Tú puedes tomar menos cerveza que Pepe.	You can drink less beer than Pepe.

We would probably be more likely to express the last sentence as "You can't drink as much beer as Pepe" in English. The meaning is the same as in the Spanish sentence.

16.1

Unequal in Action

To indicate that someone or something engages in an activity to a greater extent than someone or something else, the formula is: verb + *más que* + person/thing. See the following examples:

Borges escribió más que Sábato.	Borges wrote more than Sábato.
Carlota sabe más que tú.	Carlota knows more than you (do).
José habla más que Roberto.	José talks more than Roberto.

To indicate that someone or something engages in an activity to a lesser extent than someone or something else, the formula is: verb + *menos que* + person/thing. See the following examples:

Sábato escribió menos que Borges.	Sábato wrote less than Borges.
Tú sabes menos que Carlota.	You know less than Carlota (does).
Roberto habla menos que José.	Roberto speaks less than José.

Naturally, if the person(s) with whom you are having a conversation already know(s) what or whom is being compared, then just as English uses *less*, all you need to use in Spanish is *menos*. See the following examples:

Mi tío gana menos.	My uncle earns less.
Tú puedes tomar menos.	You can drink less.
Tú sabes menos.	You know less.
Roberto habla menos.	Roberto talks less.

We would probably state the second sentence as "You can't drink as much" in English. The meaning is the same as in the Spanish sentence.

Irregular Comparisons of Unequals

Both English and Spanish have irregular methods of making comparisons of unequals. The Spanish irregular forms do not use *más* + adjective + *que* for inequality of quality, or a verb + *más que* + person/thing. Instead, one word is used. See the following very brief table of irregular comparative adjectives.

IRREGULAR UNEQUAL COMPARATIVES

Adjective	Comparative	English Adjective	English Comparative
bueno/a	mejor	good	better
malo/a	peor	bad	worse
grande	mayor	big	bigger/greater/older
pequeño	small	menor	small/lesser/younger

You can see by this table that the same adjectives that have an irregular comparative form in English also have an irregular form in Spanish.

Some explanation of the **semantics** of the last two entries in the preceding table is necessary. Actually, two methods exist for comparing unequals with respect to *grande* and *pequeño*. In addition to the irregular *mayor* and *menor*, there is the regular *más grande* and *más pequeño*. These are not interchangeable, because they have different meanings.

WORDS TO GO . . .WORDS TO GO . . .WORDS TO GO

Semantics refers to meaning.

The regular *más grande* and *más pequeño* refer to physical size—literally, "bigger" and "smaller." The irregular *mayor* and *menor* have a figurative meaning, such as "older" and "younger," or "greater" and "lesser," or "major" and "minor." See the following examples:

Pedro es mi hermano menor.	Pedro is my "kid" brother. (younger)
Carlos es mi hermano mayor.	Carlos is my "big" brother. (older)
Mi casa es más pequeña que la tuya.	My house is smaller than yours.
Esta botella es más grande que ésa.	This bottle is bigger than that one.

Superlatives

In English, we construct the **superlative form** of an adjective by placing the words *the most* in front of the adjective ("She is the most beautiful one"), or we add *-est* to the adjective ("Mary is the smartest girl in the class"). We also have irregular superlatives (good/best, bad/worst).

16.1

In Spanish, the superlative does not have a form different from the comparative (see Section 16.1, "Comparison of Unequals"). The only difference between the comparative and superlative adjectives in Spanish is that you use the **definite article** in front of what otherwise would be the comparative. See the following examples.

WORDS TO GO . . .WORDS TO GO . . .WORDS TO GO

The **superlative form** of an adjective is the form that indicates that something or someone has a particular quality more than anything or anyone else. The **definite article** in English is the word *the.*

Carlos es el estudiante más inteligente de la clase.	Carlos is the most intelligent student in the class. (Carlos is the smartest student in the class.)
Carlos es el más inteligente.	Carlos is the most intelligent (the smartest).
Elena es la chica más bonita de la clase.	Elena is the prettiest girl in the class.
Elena es la más bonita.	Elena is the prettiest.
Son los mejores jugadores.	They are the best players.
Tú eres el peor.	You are the worst.
Esas casas son las menos costosas.	Those houses are the least costly.

◄ SEE ALSO 5.2, *"Adjectives in Agreement"* ►

As you can see in the preceding sentences, you can exclude the noun—in both English and Spanish—if the listener(s) know(s) what that noun is. However, even if you leave out the noun, the Spanish definite article must agree in number and gender with that noun.

Note below the progression from the simple description to the comparative form to the superlative form:

Elena es simpática.	Elena is nice (likeable, agreeable).
Carmen es más simpática que Elena.	Carmen is nicer than Elena.

Pero María es la más simpática.	But María is the nicest.
Carlos es un trabajador bueno.	Carlos is a good worker.
Pedro es un mejor trabajador que Carlos.	Pedro is a better worker than Carlos.
Ernesto es el mejor trabajador de todos.	Ernesto is the best worker of all.

16.1

16.2 URGES AND OBLIGATIONS

Necessary to Do ...

"Feel Like" Doing ...

Have to Do

Must, Ought to, Should

Necessary to Do ...

In this section, you learn how to use idioms that refer to urges and obligations. You learn how to state idiomatically what you "feel like" doing, what you have to do, what you must do, what is necessary for anyone to do, and so on.

As a non-native speaker of Spanish, you would probably have difficulty understanding a Spanish **idiom** if it were not explained to you. This is because the individual words used in the expression do not necessarily add up to the meaning of the expression. The native speaker understands the idiom without needing to have it explained because he or she has heard the idiom used over and over in context. In this section, you learn how to use idioms that refer to your urges and obligations.

> **WORDS TO GO . . .WORDS TO GO . . .WORDS TO GO**
>
> An **idiom** is an expression that is peculiar to a language and contains a meaning that might not be logically understood by the usual rules of grammar or by the meaning of the individual words in the expression. The idiom might even go against those rules or the logic of the individual words used in it.
>
> **Idiomatically** is the adverb that refers to the use of idioms.

"Feel Like" Doing

The English idiom *to feel like* plus the **present participle** of a verb is a **colloquial** way of saying that you have an urge, a desire, or an impulse to perform the action expressed in the present participle. If you "feel like" eating, you really have the urge, desire, or impulse to eat.

The Spanish idiom expressing the same idea is *tener ganas de* plus the infinitive form of the verb. See the following example.

The **present participle** in English the verb form that ends in -*ing*.
Colloquial refers to an informal or familiar level of speech or writing.

Tengo ganas de comer.	I feel like eating.
¿Tienes ganas de ir al cine?	Do you feel like going to the movies?
No teníamos ganas de ver la televisión.	We didn't feel like watching television.

Another even more idiomatic expression also means *to feel like* doing something.
It is comprised of the verb *dar*, always in the third person plural, plus the noun
ganas plus *de* plus the infinitive form of the verb. If you use this idiom, you need
to indicate who feels like doing something by placing the **object pronoun** in
front of *dar*. See the following examples.

Object pronouns are pronouns that take the place of object nouns.

Me dan ganas de comer.	I feel like eating.
¿Te dan ganas de ir al cine?	Do you feel like going to the movies?
No nos daban ganas de ver televisión.	We didn't feel like watching television.

You can also use the singular *dar la gana*, but this is usually (though not necessarily) used as the answer to a *why* question. See the following examples:

¿Por qué comiste?	Why did you eat?
Porque me dio la gana.	Because I felt like it.
¿Por qué vas al cine?	Why are you going to the movies?
Porque me da la gana.	Because I feel like it.

16.2

Sometimes the adjective *real* is used in *dar la gana* in front of *gana*. You should avoid using this form of the idiom because it sounds very arrogant and rude. See the following examples:

¿Por qué comiste?	Why did you eat?
Porque me dio la real gana.	Because I felt like it.

The English translation doesn't do this *real gana* idiom justice; it doesn't capture the rudeness and arrogance that it conveys. The feeling underlying this idiom is something like "... and it's none of your business, anyway" or "... and if you don't like it, tough." The adjective *real* has two meanings: "real" and "royal," depending on context. In the idiom under discussion, the meaning is *royal*. In other words, if you use this expression, it's as though you are a king, and whatever you feel like doing is your business and no one else's.

Have to Do

One of the ways you can express an obligation in Spanish is by using *tener* + *que* + an infinitive verb. This idiom is very much like the English *to have* plus an infinitive verb. See the following examples:

Tengo que trabajar.	I have to work.
Tendrán que estudiar.	They'll have to study.
¿Tuviste que irte?	Did you have to go away?

Because the verb *tener* in this expression can be conjugated to fit any subject, you can point out the specific person who is under the obligation to perform the action of the infinitive verb. This is identical to what happens in the English expression *to have to*, but very different from the expression *haber* + *que* (see "Necessary to Do ...").

Must, Ought to, Should

The verb *deber* plus an infinitive shows obligation, very often of the moral, ethical type. It can be translated as "must" but often has the feeling of "should" or "ought to." See the following examples:

Debes pensar en el futuro.	You must (should, ought to) think of the future.
Deben salir ahora.	They ought to leave now.
No debías decirlo.	You shouldn't have said it.

Like the verb *tener* used with *que* plus the infinitive verb (see the previous section), the verb *deber* in this expression can be conjugated to fit any subject. You can point out the specific person who ought to perform the action of the infinitive verb. This is very different from the expression *haber + que* (see "Necessary to Do …").

If you want to seem less blunt, more like you're merely suggesting a course of action, you can use the conditional tense of *deber*. The English translations basically are the same as in the previous sentences, but the tone is more polite. See the following examples:

Deberías pensar en el futuro.	You ought to think of the future.
Deberían salir ahora.	They ought to leave now.

We can't use this conditional tense for the meaning of the third sentence in the previous group of sentences because it would not refer to the past.

You can establish a tone that is even more polite, more diplomatic, more diffident by using the imperfect subjunctive (but only the form that ends with *-ra*, not the one that ends in *-se*) of the verb *deber*. See the following examples:

Debieras pensar en el futuro.	You ought to think of the future.
Debieran salir ahora.	They ought to leave now.
No debieras decirlo.	You shouldn't have said it.

The last sentence is ambiguous; it is not really clear that it refers to the past, as the English translation seems to indicate. It could also be translated as "You shouldn't say it." To make it absolutely clear that you are referring to a past action, you could use the imperfect subjunctive *debieras* plus the infinitive compound tense of *decir*. See the following example:

No debieras haberlo dicho.	You shouldn't have said it.

This sentence makes it absolutely clear that you are referring to a past action that you politely suggest should not have taken place.

◄ *SEE ALSO 9.2, "Conditional Tense"* ▶

◄ *SEE ALSO 14.1, "Formation of the Imperfect Subjunctive"* ▶

◄ *SEE ALSO 11.6, "Haber Plus Past Participle for Compound Tenses"* ▶

16.2

The formula *deber* + *de* + infinitive verb can also translate as the equivalent of the English *must*, but it's *must* in the sense of probability rather than obligation. See the following examples:

Yo debía de estar comiendo.	I must have been eating. (I probably was eating.)
Elena debe de estar en casa.	Elena must be home. (Elena probably is home.)
Deben de ser argentinos.	They must be Argentines. (They probably are Argentines.)

The idea of probability can be shown in other ways, of course. One way is to use the future tense to show probability in the present, and to use the conditional tense to show probability in the past.

◀ *SEE ALSO 9.3, "Wondering and Probability"* ▶

The verb *deber* also means "to owe":

Me deben cien dólares.	They owe me a hundred dollars.
Te debo la vida.	I owe you my life.

As a noun, of course, *un deber* means "a duty, an obligation":

Fue mi deber luchar.	It was my duty to fight.
La lealtad es un deber.	Loyalty is a duty.

Of course, you can see the conceptual connection between verbs such as *must*, *ought to*, and *should*, on one hand, and the noun *duty*, on the other. And, of course, when you *owe* something to somebody, it is your *duty* to pay that debt.

Necessary to Do

You can use the verb *haber* to show what must be done, what it is necessary to do. Unlike the idioms that show obligation by using the verbs *tener* or *deber*, you cannot show that the obligation falls on a specific person. When you use *haber* to show the necessity of doing something, you never indicate for whom it is necessary; it's just necessary, in general. Because of this, you always want to use it in the third-person singular form (*él, ella, usted*), in any tense you need to use.

When you use the verb *haber* for this idiom, the present **tense** is irregular; it comes out *hay*. This is the same form of the verb used to show existence, but not the form you use when it is the helping verb for the present perfect tense. See the following examples:

Hay que hacerlo.	It is necessary to do it. (It has to be done.)
Hubo que huir.	It was necessary to flee.
Habrá que trabajar.	It will be necessary to work.

◀ *SEE ALSO 11.5, "The Verb haber to Show Presence/Existence"* ▷

◀ *SEE ALSO 11.6, "Haber Plus Past Participle for Compound Tenses"* ▷

Unlike the idioms of obligation using *tener* and *deber* (covered earlier), the idiom using *haber* doesn't state for whom it is necessary to carry out the action of the infinitive verb. It is impersonal and not directed at anyone in particular. This is why when you use *haber* to show obligation or necessity, it always is conjugated in the third person singular.

16.2

16.3 BEGINNINGS

Several verbs refer to the beginning of an action in English and in Spanish (*to start, to begin, to commence*, and so on; *empezar* [ie], *comenzar* [ie], and so on). However, several idioms in Spanish have the same meaning, although, because they are idioms, you wouldn't understand them by the literal meaning of the individual words in the idioms.

One idiom that means "to begin" has this formula: *echar* + *a* + infinitive verb.

The verb *echar*, when not used in this formula, means "to throw, to toss." But when you use it as part of the formula you see in the previous sentence, it means "to start." See the following examples:

Echó a correr.	He or she began to run.
Echamos a reír.	We began to laugh.

Another idiom that means "to begin" has this formula: *ponerse* + *a* + infinitive verb.

The verb *poner* has many meanings, depending on the context and the prepositions you use with it. The most common meaning is "to put, to place." When you use it as a reflexive verb with an article of clothing, it means "to put on" that article of clothing. The idiom having to do with beginnings is also reflexive, but it has nothing to do with either placing something somewhere or with putting on an article of clothing. See the following examples:

Se puso a correr.	He or she began to run.
Nos pusimos a reír.	We began to laugh.

◁ **SEE ALSO 6.1, "Prepositions"** ▷

◁ **SEE ALSO 12.2, "The True Reflexive"** ▷

Of course, you can always use the nonidiomatic verbs *empezar* (ie) and *comenzar* (ie) to express the idea of beginning. But you will want to recognize and understand the idiomatic expressions shown here.

Other verbs could be translated as "to start." But the verbs we are about to mention cannot be used to introduce another **verb.** Instead, you would use them to introduce a noun.

For example, we commonly talk about *starting* a business. In Spanish, the verb to use is *inaugurar* plus a noun, which you can modify or not, as you wish. See the following example:

| El Sr. López ha inaugurado su nueva empresa. | Mr. López has started his new business. |

Of course, you can also use this verb to mean "to inaugurate." It also has the meaning of "to unveil" (a statue, a painting, and so on). The **noun** that is related to this verb is *la inauguración*.

If you are talking about starting some kind of process, you can use the verb *iniciar* plus the noun that stands for the process. You can modify this noun or not, as you please. See the following example:

| Ella inició la conversación conmigo. | She started the conversation with me. |
| Yo inicié la discusión con ellos. | I started the discussion with them. |

This last sentence could also have a connotation more like "I started the argument with them."

The verb *iniciar* has the same meaning as the English "to initiate." When reflexive (*iniciarse*), it means "to be initiated." In an ecclesiastical context, the reflexive form of this verb means to receive first orders as a nun.

You never use the last two verbs, *inaugurar* and *iniciar*, before a verb.

16.3

17

ADVERBS INDICATING LOCATION/ DEMONSTRATIVES

17.1 POSITION ADVERBS

Adverbs Indicating Location

Demonstrative adjectives and **demonstrative pronouns** have their own section because the demonstrative adjective and the demonstrative pronoun are basically the same word. The demonstrative adjective is really the demonstrative pronoun used as though it were an adjective. It's used with the noun it modifies. The demonstrative pronoun, which is used in place of the noun it represents, points to the location of that noun. The demonstrative adjective points to the location of the noun and is used with that noun.

When you understand the position adverbs, it is easier to understand the demonstratives.

WORDS TO GO . . .WORDS TO GO . . .WORDS TO GO

A **demonstrative adjective** points out the location of the noun it modifies and accompanies.

A **demonstrative pronoun** points out the location of the noun whose place it takes.

In this section, you learn the adverbs that refer to position (here/there), as well as how to use the demonstrative adjectives and demonstrative pronouns.

A strong link exists between the Spanish adverbs of position *aquí/acá, ahí,* and *allí/allá,* and the demonstrative adjectives. You will want to understand the use of these position adverbs as a background for understanding the use of the demonstrative adjectives.

Adverbs Indicating Location

Modern English has only two position adverbs: *here* and *there*. This means that in modern English we think in terms of only two positions: near the speaker and away from the speaker. Spanish has three positions: near the speaker, near the listener, and far from both. English once had the third position as well.

Aquí refers to an area close to the one who is speaking. This is equivalent to the English "here." *Acá* refers to the same area; it, too, basically means "here."

Officially, *aquí* is more precise than *acá*, so *aquí* is somewhat like "right here," whereas *acá* is somewhat like "around here." In addition, *acá* is the one preferred after verbs of motion.

In some Spanish-speaking countries this is more or less the actual situation, but in many others, it is not. In many regions, *aquí* is almost always preferred, while in other regions, *acá* is almost always used. Some areas use them interchangeably. No matter which one is used, it refers to an area close to the speaker and is equivalent to English "here."

Ahí refers to an area close to the person who is listening. If you are the speaker, it is the area near the person you are talking to. This comes out as "there" in English.

Allí refers to somewhere far removed from both the speaker and the listener. In modern English, this is expressed by the word "there." The form *allá* basically means the same as *allí*, but the difference between *aquí* and *acá* is the same as the difference (or lack of it) between *allí* and *allá*.

The fact that modern English has only two positions (*here* and *there*) clashes with the fact that Spanish has three positions. Shakespeare's English had three positions; the third position (far from speaker and listener) was *yonder*.

These three Spanish positions are closely linked to the demonstrative adjectives and demonstrative pronouns.

17.2 DEMONSTRATIVE ADJECTIVES

Near the Speaker

Near the Listener

Far Removed

Partly because modern English has only two positions (*here* and *there*), the English demonstrative system is simpler than the Spanish one. In English, we have only four demonstrative adjectives: two of them are the singular *this* and the plural *these*. Both of these refer to an item (or items) close to the one who is speaking. They refer to the same position as the adverb of position *here*.

The other two are the singular *that* and the plural *those*. These latter two indicate an item (or items) anywhere that is not close to the one who is speaking. They correspond to the position indicated by the adverb of position *there*.

Spanish has 12 demonstrative adjectives because there are three positions and, in each position, four adjectives: masculine singular, masculine plural, feminine singular, and feminine plural.

Near the Speaker

If the item is near the person who is speaking, that person will use either *este*, *estos*, *esta*, or *estas*. See the following examples:

(masculine singular) este libro	this book
(masculine plural) estos libros	these books
(feminine singular) esta mesa	this table
(feminine plural) estas mesas	these tables

It is important to note that the masculine singular form of the demonstrative adjective ends with the letter *-e*. The masculine plural ends with *-os*. The feminine forms are *-a* for the singular and *-as* for the feminine for the plural. The only one that is tricky is the change from masculine singular to masculine plural: from *-e* to *-os*. This is a departure from the normal way adjectives and nouns are pluralized in Spanish.

◀ SEE ALSO 5.2, *"Adjectives in Agreement"* ▶

◀ SEE ALSO 3.2, *"Singular and Plural Nouns"* ▶

The position involved for *este* and the three others corresponds to the adverb of position *aquí/acá*. (See the section "Position Adverbs.")

Near the Listener

If the item is near the person you are speaking to (the listener), the speaker will use either *ese, esos, esa,* or *esas.* See the following examples:

(masculine singular) ese libro	that book
(masculine plural) esos libros	those books
(feminine singular) esa mesa	that table
(feminine plural) esas mesas	those tables

In these demonstrative adjectives, the same peculiarity arises that you see in the previous set: the change from the masculine singular, which ends with -*e*, to the masculine plural, which ends with -*os*.

The position involved for *ese* and the three others corresponds to the adverb of position *ahí*. (See the previous section on position adverbs.)

It might be helpful to think of this group of demonstrative adjectives as meaning "that book near you," and so on, when you are the speaker. The *you* in "near you," of course, stands for the person you are addressing.

Far Removed

If the item is far removed from both the speaker and the listener (the one you are speaking to), the speaker will use either *aquel, aquellos, aquella,* or *aquellas.* See the following examples:

(masculine singular) aquel libro	that book
(masculine plural) aquellos libros	those books
(feminine singular) aquella mesa	that table
(feminine plural) aquellas mesas	those tables

This batch is somewhat tricky, too. You should notice that the masculine singular form of this group of demonstrative adjectives ends with *-l*, yet the masculine plural form first doubles the *-l* so that it becomes *-ll* and then ends the adjective with *-os*.

You can see that mere translation does not help; the English translations of this group are exactly the same as those for the preceding group (that/those). Yet Spanish-speakers use different demonstrative adjectives because they think in terms of three positions, not two, as we do in standard English. (In an older form of English, one that still survives in some isolated dialect pockets of the Southern Appalachians, this last group would be *yon[der]* as the demonstrative adjective for the position that is far from the speaker and the listener.)

Because translation alone does not help you distinguish between *ese*, *aquel*, and so on, it is important to remember the positions they represent. The position involved for *aquel* and the three others corresponds to the adverb of position *allí/allá*. (See the section on position adverbs.) Think of this group of demonstrative adjectives as meaning "that book way out there," and so on.

17.3 DEMONSTRATIVE PRONOUNS

The demonstrative pronouns in Spanish are identical in spelling and, therefore, pronunciation to the corresponding demonstrative adjectives. Because they are pronouns, they do not accompany a noun; they replace the noun. They must agree in **number** and **gender** with the noun they replace.

> ### WORDS TO GO . . . WORDS TO GO . . . WORDS TO GO
>
> **Number** refers to the grammatical difference between singular (one person, animal, or thing) and plural (more than one person, animal, or thing).
> **Gender** refers to the grammatical difference between masculine and feminine.

However, a rule provides for differentiating, in the written language, between the demonstrative adjective and the demonstrative pronoun. You saw in Section 17.2, "Demonstrative Adjectives," that the demonstrative adjectives have no accent marks. This is because they follow the rules of accentuation, and the stress automatically falls according to those rules.

◀ *SEE ALSO 1.4, "Accentuation (Stress) and Capitalization"* ▶

For no reason other than to differentiate between the demonstratives (the adjective and the pronoun), you must place an accent mark over the vowel that is automatically stressed. In other words, the accent mark is not needed to show where the word is stressed, but only to indicate in writing that you are dealing with a demonstrative pronoun instead of the demonstrative adjective.

You can use the demonstrative pronoun, of course, only when the person you are addressing already knows the noun that you are deleting. In the same way, in English you wouldn't say "This one is mine" unless the people you're speaking with already know what "this one" is, either because you've been talking about it or because they see what you're pointing at.

If you're discussing books and someone says, "Which one do you want?" you don't have to say, "I want that book," using the demonstrative adjective (that) plus the noun (book). You would simply say, "I want that one," omitting the word *book*.

The same thing happens in Spanish, except that you don't use the word meaning *one* to fill in for *book*. In Spanish, if people know you are discussing *libros* and ask which you prefer, you wouldn't need to say, "Prefiero este libro." Instead, you would simply say, "Prefiero éste." Notice the accent mark over the first e, which is where the stress automatically would fall.

See the following examples that contrast the use of the demonstrative adjective with the use of the demonstrative pronoun, plus the English translation of the pronoun.

DEMONSTRATIVE ADJECTIVES COMPARED WITH DEMONSTRATIVE PRONOUNS

(Number/Gender) Pronoun	Adjective & Noun	
Near the Speaker		
(masc. sing.) este libro	éste	this one
(masc. plural) estos libros	éstos	these
(fem. sing.) esta mesa	ésta	this one
(fem. plural) estas mesas	éstas	these
Near the Listener		
(masc. sing.) ese libro	ése	that one
(masc. plural) esos libros	ésos	those
(fem. sing.) esa mesa	ésa	that one
(fem. plural) esas mesas	ésas	those
Far Removed		
(masc. sing.) aquel libro	aquél	that one (out there)
(masc. plural) aquellos libros	aquéllos	those (out there)
(fem. sing.) aquella mesa	aquélla	that one (out there)
fem. plural) aquellas mesas	aquéllas	those (out there)

Compare the preceding table with the information on demonstrative adjectives in Section 17.2, "Demonstrative Adjectives."

Notice the accent marks in the demonstrative pronouns in the second column, and the lack of them in the demonstrative adjectives in the first column.

17.4 NEUTER DEMONSTRATIVE PRONOUNS

Spanish has 12 demonstrative adjectives because there are three locations, *aquí/ acá, ahí,* and *allí/allá.* (See 17.1, "Position Adverbs.") In each location, there are four demonstrative adjectives (masculine singular, masculine plural, feminine singular, and feminine plural).

There are also 12 demonstrative pronouns because they must agree in number and gender with the nouns they replace and represent. They are spelled and pronounced exactly the same as their corresponding demonstrative adjectives, except that they contain an accent mark.

In Spanish, every noun is either masculine or feminine. Absolutely *no* neuter nouns exist in Spanish. Yet there are three more demonstrative pronouns that are not covered in the preceding section; these are the neuter demonstrative pronouns.

The natural question is, if all Spanish nouns are either masculine or feminine, what nouns could the neuter demonstrative pronouns replace, represent, or agree with? The answer is none. You use the neuter demonstrative pronouns when you cannot pin it to any specific noun. You would want to do this in two kinds of situations:

1. You don't know the name of the item.
2. You can't pin a complex idea to a specific noun.

In English, you could say, "What is this?" The fact that you are asking for this item to be identified means ...

1. You don't know its name.
2. In Spanish, if you don't know its name, you don't know whether it's masculine or feminine.
3. If you don't know whether it's masculine or feminine, you cannot use any one of the masculine or feminine demonstrative pronouns to represent it.

Because you cannot use any of the masculine or feminine demonstrative pronouns to represent this unknown object, you use one of the neuter demonstrative pronouns: *esto, eso,* or *aquello.*

The masculine form of the demonstrative pronoun ends with -e, while the feminine form ends with -a. The three neuter demonstrative pronouns end with -o. Being neuter, these three demonstrative pronouns have no parallel among the demonstrative adjectives because adjectives must agree in number and gender with the noun they modify. But these three pronouns do not represent a specific Spanish noun.

None of the demonstrative adjectives is parallel to these three pronouns—none of them is spelled the same—there is no need for accent marks to distinguish them from any other word. This is why they have no accent marks.

The speaker will use *esto* if the unknown object is located near him or her or if the entire, complicated idea is somehow more associated with him or her than with the listener. The same speaker will use *eso* if the unknown object is located closer to the listener or if the entire idea is mentally associated with the listener. The speaker will use *aquello* if the unknown object is in the distance or the entire idea seems remote to both the speaker and the listener. When referring to ideas, the borders around these three pronouns can be hazy.

See the following examples of the use of the three neuter demonstrative pronouns when used to ask the identity of unknown objects:

¿Qué es esto?	What is this? (the object is near the speaker)
¿Qué es eso?	What is that? (the object is near the listener)
¿Qué es aquello?	What is that? (the object is far from speaker and listener)

See the following examples of the use of the three neuter demonstrative pronouns when referring to an entire idea that cannot be pinned to a specific noun:

Alberto: *Oye, la semana que viene voy a levantarme a las seis, ducharme inmediatamente después, desayunarme, vestirme y después ir al trabajo.*

(Alberto: Listen, next week I'm going to get up at six, take a shower right after that, have breakfast, get dressed, and then go to work.)

Roberto: Eso me parece bien.

(Roberto: That sounds good.)

Alberto has just provided a list of all the activities he plans to engage in next week. Roberto listens and sums up all those activities with the English word *that*.

In English, we don't have to think about whether the demonstrative pronoun is masculine, feminine, or neuter. But in Spanish, we do. Because there is no single noun that the pronoun *that* can refer to, when speaking Spanish, we can't use the masculine *ése* or the feminine *ésa*. Instead, we use the neuter *eso*.

Roberto uses *eso* (near the listener) because he associates the ideas expressed by Alberto with Alberto. Those ideas are "near" Alberto.

If Alberto had expressed those ideas and then commented on his own ideas in English, he would have used the pronoun *this*; because he associates his own ideas with himself, they are "near" him. In Spanish, he would say, "Esto es lo que voy a hacer" ("This is what I'm going to do").

If either one of them was referring to events in a far-off country, such as China, he would say something like, "Aquello de la China me interesa" ("That business about China interests me").

You now know how to use Spanish demonstratives, both the adjectives and the pronouns.

A
GLOSSARY

abstract   Refers to an idea or concept, as opposed to a concrete thing.

abstract noun   One that cannot be seen, felt, tasted, heard or perceived by any of our five senses. For example, love, hate, freedom, slavery, intelligence, and so on, are abstractions.

active voice   A sentence in which the grammatical subject performs the action of the verb, and the object receives the action of the verb. See *passive voice*.

adjective   A word that modifies or describes a noun.

adjective clause   A subordinate clause that modifies a noun in the main clause.

adverb   A word that is used to modify either a verb, an adjective, or another adverb.

adverbial clause   An entire clause that is used for the same purpose as an adverb: to modify a verb, an adjective, or an adverb.

adverbial phrase   A phrase that performs the same duties as an adverb.

affirmative command   Orders a person to do something.

agreement   In the context of the relationship between nouns and adjectives, refers to the adjective having to reflect both the gender and number of the noun it modifies.

alveolar ridge   The hard ridge of gum right behind and above the upper teeth.

antecedent   In grammatical terms, the noun in the main clause that is modified in the dependent clause by another word or words.

articles   See *definite article* and *indefinite article*.

aspect   With regard to verbs, refers to whether the action or state indicated by the verb is viewed as being completed or ongoing, or as having happened at a particular moment or as being a repeated habitual matter.

augmentative suffix   An ending added to a noun or adjective to suggest the idea of bigness, of large size.

auxiliary verb   Also called the helping verb, a verb combined with another verb to show the mood, tense, or aspect of the main verb.

cardinal numbers   The numbers we usually use for counting—for example one, two, three ....

circumlocution   A roundabout way of making a statement.

clause   A subdivision of a sentence that contains a subject and a predicate.

colloquial   Refers to an informal or familiar level of speech or writing.

common noun   Designates an entire category, type, or group, or any members of them—for example, *boy, book, school, soldier, forest,* and so on.

compound tense   A tense formed with an auxiliary verb (helping verb).

concrete   Refers to a person, an animal, or any object that has physical substance and can be perceived by the five senses.

conjugate   To give the verb its various forms to show number, person, tense, and mood.

conjugated verb   A verb whose endings signal person, number, tense, and mood.

conjunction   A word used to connect two words or sentences and to show the relationship between these words or sentences.

conjunctive adverb   An adverb that can be used to connect and coordinate two clauses.

connotations   The ideas and associations suggested or implied by a word or term.

defective verb   A verb that lacks certain forms of conjugation that most verbs have.

definite article   A word placed in front of a noun to show that the noun refers to a specific member of the class named by the noun. In English, the definite article is *the*. In Spanish, the definite articles are *el, la, los,* and *las*.

demonstrative adjective   An adjective that points out the location of the noun it modifies and accompanies.

demonstrative pronoun   A pronoun that points out the location of the noun whose place it takes.

denotation   The actual meaning of a word or phrase, as opposed to the connotation.

dependent clause   Also called the subordinate clause, a clause that cannot form a complete sentence in itself, but must be connected to a main clause.

diphthong   The combination of two vowels in a single syllable.

direct object   Receives the action of the verb directly.

gender   Refers to the opposition of feminine vs. masculine.

generic noun   Refers in general to all the members of a group classified by as a noun.

Iberian Peninsula   The two nations of Portugal and Spain. "Iberian" or "Peninsular" Spanish refers to the Spanish spoken in Spain as opposed to that of Latin America.

idiom   An expression that is peculiar to a language and that contains a meaning that might not be logically understood by the usual rules of grammar or by the meaning of the individual words in the expression. The idiom might even go against those rules or the logic of the individual words used in it.

idiomatically   The adverb that refers to the use of idioms.

impersonal expression   An expression that, in English, has the subject *it* plus the verb *to be* plus an adjective.

indefinite article   In English, the word *a* (a book) or *an* (an apple).

indicative   The verbal mood that indicates that the action or state of the verb is considered to be a fact.

indirect object   The noun that receives the action of the verb indirectly.

infinitive ending   In Spanish, either *-ar*, *-er*, or *-ir*. All infinitive verbs in Spanish end with one of those combinations.

infinitive verb   Indicates only the action or state, but does not indicate person, number, tense, or mood.

interpose   To insert something between one item and another.

interrogative words   The words that ask questions—for example, *why*, *what*, *when*, *who*, and so on.

intonation   Refers to the rise and fall of voice pitch to convey various types of meaning.

intransitive verb   A verb that cannot take an object—for example *to shudder*.

main clause   Also called an independent clause and a principal clause, a clause that forms a complete sentence in itself, as opposed to the subordinate clause.

metaphorical   Pertaining to *metaphor*, the use of one word to represent a different word. A method of likening one thing to another by calling it by the other's name.

mood   A variation in the conjugation of a verb that shows the way in which the action or state of the verb is carried out or exists.

morpheme   The smallest unit of meaning. For example, the word *boyishness*, while being one word, contains three morphemes: *boy* + *ish* + *ness*.

negative command   Orders a person *not* to do something.

noun   The name of a person, place, or thing.

number   Refers to the distinction between singular and plural.

object   The person or thing that receives the action of the verb in an active sentence.

object pronouns   Pronouns that take the place of object nouns.

ordinal numbers   Refer to the order in which an item is placed—for example, first, second, third ....

orthographical   Relates to orthography, the spelling system.

orthography   Refers to the spelling system of a language.

parenthetical expression   An expression that is not the main idea of the sentence and is not necessary for the sentence to be complete. This type of expression is usually found between commas, dashes, or parenthesis marks.

passive voice   A sentence in which the grammatical subject receives the action of the verb. See *active voice*.

penultimate   Next to last.

person   Refers to the grammatical difference between the one who is speaking (first person), the one(s) being addressed (second person), and the one(s) being spoken about (third person).

phrase   A group of words that do not have either a subject or a predicate.

plural   More than one.

possessive adjective   An adjective that shows possession (*my*, *your*, *his*, and so on.)

predicate   The word or words that describe a property or condition (or lack of them) of the subject of the sentence.

preposition   A word placed in front of another word to show the grammatical relationship of the second word to the sentence as a whole—for example, *to*, *for*, *from*, *in*, *on*, *off*, *with*, *without*, and so on.

prepositional phrase   A noun or pronoun preceded by a preposition that indicates the function of the noun or pronoun within the sentence or phrase.

present participle   A verbal form like the English verb form that ends in *-ing*, except that it is never used as a noun. The Spanish present participle always ends in *-ndo*.

preterit tense   Refers to an action, event, or state that was completed at some point in the past. The Spanish word for this tense is *pretérito*.

pronoun   A word that takes the place of a noun.

proper noun   The name of one very specific person, place, or thing—for example, *Mary, Boston, Mexico, Robert,* and so on.

reciprocal verb   A verb used to represent mutual action by two or more subjects.

redundancy   With reference to grammar or sentence structure, this is the inclusion of superfluous or unnecessary words, especially those that constitute repetition.

reflexive verbs   Verbs in which the subject of the verb is identical to the object of that same verb. The subject is doing something that *reflects* back on him/her/itself.

regular verbs   Verbs that are conjugated the way most verbs are conjugated. They follow the usual pattern.

relative pronoun   A pronoun that connects the main clause to a dependent clause and refers to a noun in that dependent clause.

root   Synonymous, grammatically speaking, with the stem. Consequently, one term for a verb that undergoes changes in the root is *radical-changing verb*.

semantic   Refers to meaning.

sentence structure   Refers to the position of elements of the sentence, such as the subject, the verb, the object, and so on.

stem   Refers to the part of the verb that remains after the infinitive ending is removed. One term for a verb that undergoes changes in the stem is *stem-changing verb*.

strong vowel   Refers to the vowels *a, e,* and *o*.

subject   The person or thing that performs the action of the verb in an active sentence but is the recipient of the action of that verb in a passive sentence.

subject pronoun   A word that takes the place of a noun when that noun performs the action of the verb.

subjunctive   The verbal mood that indicates that the action or state of the verb is considered to be hypothetical.

subordinate clause   Also called the dependent clause, a clause that cannot form a complete sentence in itself but has to be connected to a main clause.

superlative   A form of an adjective that indicates that something or someone has a particular quality more than anything or anyone else.

temporal clause   An adverbial clause that indicates the time a particular action or state occurs. It is introduced by an adverb of time (*when, while, before, after, as soon as*, and so on).

tense   Refers to the action of the verb taking place in the past, present, or future, and so on.

transitive verb   A verb that can take an object—for example *to hear*.

tuteo   The Spanish term for the practice of using the subject pronoun *tú* as the second-person familiar pronoun.

verb   A word that expresses an action, a state of being, or a condition.

verbal noun   A verb that is used as one would use a noun.

voseo   The Spanish term for the practice of using the subject pronoun *vos* for the second-person familiar instead of *tú*.

vowel   A sound produced by an unobstructed flow of air through the throat and mouth, with vibration of the vocal cords.

weak vowel   Refers to the vowels *i* and *u*.

B

REFERENCE MATERIAL

This section contains reference material for further study of Spanish.

Bilingual Dictionaries

Below are listed Spanish/English dictionaries. Some are general Spanish/English dictionaries, while others refer to specialized fields.

1001 Most Useful Spanish Words. Seymour Resnick. Dover Publications, 1996.

The American Heritage Larousse Spanish Dictionary: English/Spanish-Español/ Inglés. Berkley Publication Group, 1989.

The American Heritage Spanish Dictionary: Spanish/English-English/Spanish, Second Edition. Houghton Mifflin, 2001.

Easy Spanish Phrase Book: Over 770 Basic Phrases for Everyday Use. Dover Publications, 1994

Harper Collins Spanish Dictionary: Spanish to English/English to Spanish. Harper Collins, 2006.

Larousse Unabridged Dictionary: Spanish-English/English-Spanish. Editors of Larousse, 2004.

Larousse Concise Spanish-English/English-Spanish Dictionary. Editors of Larousse, 2006.

Oxford Spanish Dictionary (book and CD ROM). Beatriz Galimberti-Jarman, et al., 2003. (This is a Spanish-English/English-Spanish dictionary.)

Twenty-First-Century Spanish-English/English-Spanish. Philip Lief. Princeton Language Institute, 1996.

The University of Chicago Spanish Dictionary: Spanish-English/English-Spanish. Universidad de Chicago Diccionario Español-Inglés, Inglés-Español, Fifth Edition. David Pharies (editor) et al., 2002.

Medical, Psychiatric, and Health

Kaplan, Steven M. *Wiley's English-Spanish/Spanish-English Dictionary of Psychology and Psychiatry/Diccionario de Psicología y Psiquiatría Inglés-Español/Español-Inglés*. John Wiley & Sons, 2004.

Kelz, Rochelle K. *Delmar's English-Spanish Pocket Dictionary for Health Professionals*. Delmar Publishing, 1997.

Rogers, Glenn T. (ed.). *English-Spanish/Spanish-English Medical Dictionary = Diccionario Médico Inglés-Español/Español-Inglés*. McGraw-Hill, 2006.

Stedman, Thomas Lathrop. *Stedman's Medical Dictionary, English to Spanish and Spanish to English: Diccionario de Ciencias Médicas Stedman Bilingüe.* Editorial Médica Panamericana, 1999.

Legal and Commercial

Alcaraz Varo, E. and Brian Hughes. *Spanish-English, English-Spanish Legal Dictionary/Diccionario de Términos Jurídicos Español-Inglés, Inglés-Español.* Planeta Publishing Corp., 2004.

Collin, P. H. (Editor). *Business Spanish Dictionary: Spanish-English/English-Spanish, Español-Inglés/Inglés-Español.* Peter Collins Publishing, 2001.

————. *Pocket Business Spanish Dictionary.* A&C Black Publishers, Ltd., 2004.

Jacobus, Charles J., et al. *English-Spanish Real Estate Dictionary (Diccionario de Bienes Raíces Español-Inglés).* The Thomson Corp., 2004.

Williams, Martha R., Wellington J. Allaway, et al. *Bienes Raíces: An English-Spanish Real Estate Dictionary.* Kaplan Publishing, 1995.

Science and Engineering

Headworth, Howard, and Sarah Steines. *English-Spanish Dictionary of Environmental Science and Engineering.* John Wiley & Sons, 1997.

Kaplan, Steven M. *Wiley's English-Spanish/Spanish-English Chemistry Dictionary = Diccionario de Química Inglés-Español/Español-Inglés.* John Wiley & Sons, Wiley-Interscience, 1998.

————. *English-Spanish/Spanish-English Electrical and Computer Engineering Dictionary = Diccionario de Ingeniería Eléctrica y de Computadoras Inglés-Español/Español-Inglés.* John Wiley & Sons, 1998.

Idiom and School-Related Bilingual Dictionaries

Thuro, Barbara. *A Bilingual Dictionary of School Terminology.* Ammie Enterprises, 1985.

————. *A Bilingual Dictionary of School Terminology.* (Audiocassette.) Hampton-Brown Books, 1985.

Vox. *Vox Gran Diccionario de Frases Hechas: Vox Dictionary of Spanish Idioms.* Vox. McGraw-Hill, 2003.

Spanish-Only Dictionaries

Alboukrek, Aaron, et al. *Diccionario de Sinónimos, Antónimos e Ideas Afines.* Larousse Kingfisher Chambers, 2002.

Fitch, Roxana. *Jergas de Habla Hispana (Slang of Various Spanish-American Countries).* BookSurge, LLC., 2006.

García Pelayo y Gross, Ramón. *Diccionario Larousse del Español Moderno.* Larousse Publications, 1983.

Real Academia Española. *Diccionario de la Lengua.* Planeta Publishing Corporation, 2001.

Santillana Rae and Real Academia Española. *Diccionario Panhispánico de Dudas.* Santillana USA Publishing Company, 2005.

Vine, William E. *Diccionario Expositivo de Palabras del Nuevo y Antiguo Testamento de Vine.* Thomas Nelson, 1998. Deals with explanations of words found in the Old and New Testaments.

For technological, computer-related, and Internet terminology, go to http://spanish.about.com/od/technologoydictionaries/.

Verb Books

Devney, Dorothy M. *Practice Makes Perfect: Spanish Verb Tenses.* NTC Publishing Group, 1996.

Kendris, Christopher, *501 Spanish Verbs: Fully Conjugated in All the Tenses.* Barron's Educational Series, 2003.

Textbooks

A great number of Spanish textbooks for beginners and intermediate students are available. You can find lists of them online at Amazon.com and Barnes & Noble.

Self-Teaching Spanish Books

This category is for people who do not have time to attend formal classes yet want to learn Spanish on their own time, in the privacy of their homes. It takes the place of a professor by explaining step by step how the Spanish language works and by providing useful vocabulary for various situations and circumstances.

Stokes, Jeffery D. *¡Qué Bien Suena!: Mastering Spanish Phonetics and Phonology.* Houghton Mifflin, 2004.

Zlotchew, Clark M. *Alpha Teach Yourself Spanish in 24 Hours, Second Edition.* Alpha Books, 2004.

————. *Estilo Literario: Análisis y Creación.* Dumont, Snyder & Kocin, 1990. A course designed for the advanced student or native speaker who wants to improve abilities in literary analysis and/or writing literary Spanish.

Self-Teaching Media

Pimsleur, Dr. *Conversational Spanish.* On CD-ROM. Simon & Schuster, 2005.

Rosetta Stone. *Rosetta Stone Spanish* (Latin America), Levels 1, 2, and 3. On CD-ROM or online. Fairfield Language Technologies, 2006–2007.

Rosetta Stone. *Rosetta Stone Spanish* (Spain), Levels 1, 2, and 3. On CD-ROM or online, 2006–2007.

Websites

Amazon.com   Look under "Spanish Grammar" and "Spanish Dictionaries."

Google.com   Look under "Spanish Grammar" and "Spanish Dictionaries."

BarnesandNoble.com   Look under "Spanish Grammar" and "Spanish Dictionaries."

www.columbia.edu/~fms5/   Spanish Language Drill; interactive drilling in Spanish grammar)

www.studyspanish.com/   Learn Spanish: A Free Online Tutorial

www.activa.arrakis.es/ind~en.htm   General English-Spanish dictionaries

Journals

Alba de América, published by the Instituto Literario y Cultural Hispánico

For journals and news magazines from all over the Spanish-speaking world, go to http://libraries.mit.edu/guides/types/flnews/spanish.html

Hispania, published by the American Association of Teachers of Spanish and Portuguese, Inc.

PMLA (Publication of the Modern Language Association)

INDEX

augmentative suffix, 73
aunque, 244
auxiliary verbs, 266

B

B pronunciation, 7-8
in back (of), 91
badly, 87
bañar, 217
to bathe, 217
to be. *See estar; ser*
to be able. *See poder*
beber
   present tense, 112
   preterit tense, 134
to be born, 118
before, 244
to begin, 115, 304
beginning action idioms, 304-305
behind, 91
being verbs
   connecting subjects to adjectives,
     275
     characteristics, 275-276
     conditions, 276-277
     connotations/denotations,
      278-279
   connecting subjects to nouns/
     pronouns, 274-275
   passive voice, 282
   physical location versus event
     location, 279-280
   ser + de
     to be from/origin, 280
     to be made of/materials, 280
     to belong to/possession, 281
   showing existence, 274
   time, 281-282
to be in the habit of, 116
to believe. *See creer*
belonging, 281
below, 90
beneath, 91
beside, 90

better comparisons, 295
between, 91
bigger comparisons, 295
to bless, 139
blond, 69
book, 40
boy, 46
to break, 190
to bring. *See traer*
to bring again, 120
to bring back, 120
to build. *See construir*
buscar
   present tense, 111
   preterit tense, 133
by. *See por, para*

C

C pronunciation, 11
caber
   present tense, 121
   preterit tense, 137
caer
   present participle, 172
   present tense, 120
calendar. *See dates*
to call, 143
cantar
   imperfect subjunctive, 257-258
   present tense, 111
   preterit tense, 133
capitalization, 16-17
   months, 34
   proper nouns, 16
cardinal numbers, 20
   1–100, 20-22
   100–999, 22-23
   1000 and higher, 23-24
   accentuation, 21
   dates, 27
   modifying nouns, 24-25
   punctuation, 23
caring, 287-288
cause and effect present participles, 175

N

Because time is the scarcest commodity of all

The brand-new series, *At Your Fingertips*, lets readers pinpoint the exact information they need without wasting time on unrelated material. Each book covers the gamut of information in concise but complete bites that are easy to find and easy to understand. Based on the notion that time is the scarcest commodity of all, *At Your Fingertips* offers readers the shortest path to the answers they need.

GRAMMAR & STYLE
AT YOUR FINGERTIPS

Nouns
Verbs
Adjectives
Adverbs
Pronouns
Interjections
Verb Tenses
Subject and Verb Agreement
Dangling Modifiers
Metaphors
Split Infinitives
Prepositions
Clauses
Sentence Structure
Compound Sentences
Punctuation
Numbers and Symbols
Capitalization
Abbreviation
Spelling
Exposition
Proofreading
Citations
Footnotes and Endnotes

Lara M. Robbins

978-1-59257-657-9

SPANISH
AT YOUR FINGERTIPS

Nouns
Verbs
Adjectives
Adverbs
Pronouns
Conjunctions
Verb Tenses
Subject and Verb Agreement
Gender
Subjunctive
Articles
Prepositions
Questions
Sentence Structure
Compound Sentences
Punctuation
Numbers and Measures
Capitalization
Forms of Address
Verb Tables
Idioms
Common Phrases
Pronunciation
Spelling

Clark M. Zlotchew, PhD.

978-1-59257-638-8

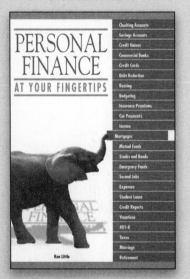

PERSONAL FINANCE
AT YOUR FINGERTIPS

Checking Accounts
Savings Accounts
Credit Unions
Commercial Banks
Credit Cards
Debt Reduction
Renting
Budgeting
Insurance Premiums
Car Payments
Income
Mortgages
Mutual Funds
Stocks and Bonds
Emergency Funds
Second Jobs
Expenses
Student Loans
Credit Reports
Vacations
401-K
Taxes
Marriage
Retirement

Ken Little

978-1-592 57-644-9

ACCOUNTING
AT YOUR FINGERTIPS

Assets
Liabilities
Income
Sales Costs
Expenses
Debits and Credits
Depreciating Assets
Prepaid Expenses
Cash Operating Procedures
Cash and Credit Transactions
Accounts Receivable
Purchases
Inventory Costing
Discounts and Allowances
Accounts Payable
Cash Disbursements
Salary and Wages
Payroll Taxes
State and Federal Regulations
Cash Receipts Journal
Cash Disbursements Journal
Posting to the General Ledger
Producing Balance Sheets
Producing P&L Statements

George R. Murray, CPA, and Kathleen Murray, CPA

978-1-59257-649-4

ALPHA
Penguin.com